Being There Together

Oxford Series in Human-Technology Interaction

Series Editor
Alex Kirlik, University of Illinois at Urbana-Champaign and the
Beckman Institute

Being There Together

Social Interaction in Virtual Environments

RALPH SCHROEDER
Oxford Internet Institute
University of Oxford

UNIVERSITY PRESS

2011

OXFORD
UNIVERSITY PRESS

Oxford University Press, Inc., publishes works that further
Oxford University's objective of excellence
in research, scholarship, and education.

Oxford   New York
Auckland   Cape Town   Dar es Salaam   Hong Kong   Karachi
Kuala Lumpur   Madrid   Melbourne   Mexico City   Nairobi
New Delhi   Shanghai   Taipei   Toronto

With offices in
Argentina   Austria   Brazil   Chile   Czech Republic   France   Greece
Guatemala   Hungary   Italy   Japan   Poland   Portugal   Singapore
South Korea   Switzerland   Thailand   Turkey   Ukraine   Vietnam

Copyright © 2011 by Ralph Schroeder

Published by Oxford University Press, Inc.
198 Madison Avenue, New York, New York 10016
www.oup.com

Oxford is a registered trademark of Oxford University Press

Library of Congress Cataloging-in-Publication Data
Schroeder, Ralph.
Being there together: social interaction in virtual environments/
Ralph Schroeder.
p. cm. — (Oxford series in human-technology interaction)
ISBN 978-0-19-537128-4 (pbk.: alk. paper) 1. Social interaction.
2. Shared virtual environments. I. Title.
HM1111.S37 2010
302.23'1—dc22
2010031435

9 8 7 6 5 4 3 2 1
Printed in the United States of America
on acid-free paper

Preface

This book is the product of many years of work on virtual reality and virtual environments, much of it done in collaboration with others. My first efforts began at Brunel University and resulted in a book on what was then still a very new technology (Schroeder 1996). During that time I met Mel Slater and Anthony Steed and their colleagues at University College London, and my research association with these two leading computer scientists in the field has been a long and productive one. Anthony was also very helpful with comments on the whole book and with help with images, as was Amela Sadagic, an alumna of the University College group. When I moved to Chalmers University in Sweden, I was fortunate to supervise the Ph.D. theses of Ann-Sofie Axelsson (2004), Ilona Heldal (2004), and Maria Spante (2009). Many of the findings reported here are a result of several years of great teamwork that was also good fun. There are many others with whom I've collaborated on individual studies, and it is a pleasure to acknowledge Asa Abelin, Jeremy Bailenson, Andy Hudson-Smith, Ray Lee, Alexander Nilsson, Dave Roberts, Jolanda Tromp, Josef Widestrom, and Nick Yee. At the Oxford Internet Institute, I've been able to step back again somewhat and see virtual environments in the larger context of how we use networked computers, and I've enjoyed the help and collaboration of Eric Meyer and Malte Ziewitz. Many thanks to Eric also for help in picture and diagram preparation.

The research for the studies reported here has been supported in Sweden by KFB (subsequently Vinnova), the James Martin 21st Century School at Oxford, and the Peach project of the European Commission. The final draft of the book was written while I was a visiting research fellow at the University of Sydney, where Albert Zomaya was a generous host. While in Sydney and away from home and colleagues, my "being there together" with others for ten weeks was purely electronic— and this presented an interesting means to reflect on the limits and possibilities of mediated communication. As ever, my greatest thanks go to my family.

Contents

Figures and Tables

Abbreviations Used

AW – ActiveWorlds
CMC – computer-mediated communication
CVE – collaborative virtual environment
F2F – face-to-face
HMD – head-mounted display
ICTs – information and communication technologies
IPT – immersive projection technology
MUVE – multiuser virtual environment
OT – OnLive Traveler
PC – personal computer
RL – real life
SL – Second Life
VE – virtual environment
VR – virtual reality
VW – virtual world

Being There Together

I

Virtual Environments and the Changing Landscape of Information and Communication Technologies

Definitions and Overview

This book is about how people interact in multiuser virtual environments (MUVEs), and it has three aims. The first is to provide an overview of research findings in this area, including studies of "presence," collaboration, avatar appearance, and social patterns in large-scale online virtual worlds. A second aim is to put this research into a larger context: how does MUVE technology compare with other information and communication technologies (ICTs), such as videoconferencing, instant messaging, and social networking sites? The third aim is to make an argument about the social implications of the technology, for which large claims have often been made. As we shall see, virtual environments (VEs) technology on its own is a rather small niche among new media, yet I shall argue that, combined with what we know about the uses of other ICTs, MUVEs can tell us quite a lot about the future of mediated forms of "being there together."

The book covers a wide range of topics and will be of interest to several different audiences. Parts of the book deal mainly with research in human–computer interaction and the social psychology of computer-mediated communication. Other parts address the sociology of new technologies and how this technology can be a tool to carry out social research. Still other parts draw on and engage with research about new media. A key argument will be made that while all these disciplinary perspectives are useful, it essential to have a synthetic picture to put the social implications of MUVEs and other new technologies into an overall context. One reason for this is that claims for MUVEs and other new media are often exaggerated without this context. This introductory chapter will make a start on this synthetic argument, but the task of cementing it will fall to the main substantive chapters.

Before we proceed any further, it will be useful to provide a definition of MUVEs, especially because the word "virtual" has come to mean different things in different contexts. The VEs discussed here relate to virtual reality (VR) technologies. In a previous book, I defined *virtual reality technology* as "a computer-generated display that allows or compels the user (or users) to have a feeling of being present in an environment other than the one that they are actually in and to interact with that environment" (Schroeder 1996: 25; see also Ellis 1995)—in short, "being there."[1] In the context of a book about *multiuser* VEs (MUVEs)—or *shared* or *collaborative* VR systems, as they are sometimes known—we can therefore define these environments or systems as those in which users experience other participants as being present in the same environment and interacting with them—or as "being there together." This definition of MUVEs fits closely with what researchers in a particular research community have been working on for some years, and it is also grounded in a particular understanding of the social implications of new technologies (we will return to this). Nevertheless, because the question of defining MUVEs and setting them apart from other technologies and new media raises some tricky questions, we will need to revisit this definition on a number of occasions in this book.

VR and VE technology has undergone rapid changes in recent years.[2] In the early 1990s, the dominant image of VR, and what most laboratories and developers focused on, was single-user head-mounted display (HMD) systems (Ellis 1995; Kalawsky 1993). Currently, on the hardware side, there is a range of single-user systems, including immersive projection technology (IPT) or CAVE-type[3] VR systems (Cruz-Neira, Sandin, and deFanti 1993) in which the environment is projected onto several walls. The main change apart from display and interaction technology, however, is that VEs have become networked; that is, they provide the means whereby people in different locations can share the same space. This applies to high-end immersive HMD or IPT systems, which can be networked such that a few users can share the VE (the restriction to a few users is partly because these systems are expensive and partly because it is technically difficult to network them). But it also applies on a much larger scale at the inexpensive end, when people use (often) free software that runs on personal desktop computers (PCs) and allows thousands of users to share virtual worlds, even if they do not have the experience of an "immersive" VE in the same way. In the future, we will no doubt see an even greater variety of technologies that enable people to interact in and with VEs.

The attentive reader may have noticed that in the previous paragraph the ground shifted from immersive "environments" to online "worlds," and treating these jointly may seem odd. As fields of research and types of technology, the highly immersive environments and the simple avatars on desktop virtual worlds are not normally dealt with in the same place. But as we shall see, there is much to be gained from making connections between them. For the moment, we can use "environments" and "worlds" interchangeably and will return to the differences between them at various points—one difference is that the former typically consist of spaces for brief and specific uses such as visualization and experimental work, whereas the latter provide large-scale persistent places that many users can inhabit together. In any event, online multiuser worlds have become the most well-known use of MUVE technology.

The feasibility of linking many users simultaneously in shared VEs or MUVEs only took off in the mid-1990s, when Internet use became widespread. Today, with broadband connectivity, there are dozens of Internet-based VEs such as Second Life where participants spend a lot of time in very large online spaces containing virtual shopping malls, churches, museums, and classrooms—many built by the users themselves. These online worlds can also include highly elaborate, massively multi-player games like World of Warcraft, which in some cases have hundreds of thousands of simultaneous players. Immersive MUVEs are less well-known, but many systems and applications are in development at computer science laboratories and in companies around the world (Brooks 1999). The technologies in development include different display systems and types of input/output devices, and applications include conferencing, scientific co-visualization, virtual therapy, and personnel training.

Even though these technologies and applications comprise a wide variety, I will argue that it is necessary to develop a systematic and comprehensive understanding of how people interact in MUVEs. Such a systematic account—a theory, if you like—will be important for understanding and developing the technology and its uses. An equally important argument, however, will be that VEs point the way toward a better understanding of online relationships in new media in general. This is because they allow us to think about a future in which people spend their time together in a range of more and less immersive virtual worlds. MUVEs therefore provide important clues—among other things—about the kinds of "richness" or "poverty" of different communications modalities, about the kinds of online relationships that people have, and about how they collaborate together online.

Although the book is mainly about VEs, it is also about the changes that are taking place in how we communicate and spend time online with each other. To anticipate, I will argue that MUVEs are one of a few technological options (in fact, there are only two, with the other being videoconferencing systems) that allow people at a distance to *be there together* in the same environment. Moreover, it is possible to foresee how these two options will develop technically, and thus to speculate in a useful way about the future of communications technologies or technologies for online togetherness. The book will thus present insights from virtual worlds to reflect on other new media—and vice versa—in order to explore the wider implications of computer-mediated communication.

This point—or preview—leads to another, which is that there is a tension in this book between these future uses of MUVEs and present-day ones, and this tension can foregrounded immediately: today's major large-scale uses of virtual worlds are for online socializing and gaming. The remaining uses, especially of expensive high-end "immersive" systems, are mainly in specialized niches and for demonstration or research purposes. This book is premised on the idea that MUVEs will become widely used, and used for purposes outside of leisure. This premise is speculative; there is no way to know for certain how and to what extent MUVEs and virtual worlds will be used—or indeed if the leisure or gaming uses will continue.

My personal view is that such a popularization or diffusion beyond leisure uses will take place, for the following reasons (more detailed and grounded reasons will be given in Chapters 9 and 10):

• Although video conferencing has not taken off despite being technologically available for decades and many predictions to the contrary (later chapters will analyze why), the various pressures for developing an effective and enjoyable technology for distributed meetings and socializing at a distance are now enormous.

- As has often been argued, there are certain specialized niches that are likely to involve regular uses of MUVEs because they are cheaper and more effective than the alternatives—for example, training for dangerous situations, therapy, co-visualizing complex three-dimensional models, social research that cannot be done face-to-face, and the like. These uses, too, will proliferate.

- The technology or, more accurately, the technologies involved (large screens, high bandwidth networks, intuitive input/output devices, graphics software, voice communication over the Internet) are developing rapidly and becoming cheaper.

But again, although I will argue that it is possible to foresee ("predict" is perhaps too strong) certain technological and—to a lesser extent—social developments, it is impossible to know for certain what the future of MUVEs will bring. There are many examples of technologies that have developed in unanticipated ways—the telephone and mobile phone are just two examples: The telephone was initially foreseen as being mainly used for important instrumental communication, but it turned out to be used primarily for social calls during the first decades (Fischer 1992). And the mobile phone was forecast to have at most a few thousand users as late as the 1980s, whereas it has in fact become the most rapidly diffusing consumer technology ever, faster than television and the Internet (Ling 2004). No doubt MUVEs will also have unanticipated uses, but even if it impossible to predict these, it can safely be anticipated that various forms of virtual togetherness will become increasingly popular in the future.

Before delving further into details, it will be useful to present how interaction in VEs has been subdivided as a topic and thus provide a map of the book. The remainder of Chapter 1 will set the stage: How did the technology develop? What makes shared VEs technology unique? What are the main research questions surrounding the uses of this technology? As already mentioned, research on MUVEs has been undertaken in several social science and computer science disciplines, and there are a number of core issues that can be identified. The first chapter will introduce these and finish by presenting one of the key arguments of the book—namely, that the future of VE technology (and of videoconferencing) are in a certain sense predestined to provide the two main alternatives for "being there together," with lessons for technology developers and for analyses of computer-mediated interaction.

Chapter 2 will start with two core concepts that have been central to MUVEs: "presence" and "copresence." This is the area to which most of the research has so far been devoted, although there is much more research on "presence" than on "co-presence." Whenever there is more than one user in the VE, the focus is on the experience of "copresence," or on the experience of the other user rather than on the experience of another place or space. But with social interaction, the issues become much more complex than with presence, because the experience of another person has many dimensions. At the same time, interaction in MUVEs is far less complex than face-to-face interaction, even if it is a more novel and still underresearched phenomenon. By identifying the most widespread uses of MUVE technology and types of interaction, it will be possible to develop an inventory of technological constellations and experiences in MUVEs, which will provide a useful basis for the in-depth analyses of individual aspects of interaction in MUVEs that follow.

Chapter 3 looks specifically at the appearance of avatars and of virtual spaces and worlds. How does the sense of being there together with another person or persons depend on the appearance of the avatar or the other users of the MUVE? To what extent does the experience of being there together depend not only on the behavioral and representational realism of the avatar, a topic on which there is a considerable amount of research, but also on what it is possible to do with them, such as gesturing to them or manipulating objects together? And in view of the fact that MUVEs are most often visual, how does the appearance of spaces or places afford different possibilities for having a sense of being in a place other than the one that one is in physically, and again how does this experience vary with what one can do in these places—for example, building things or owning them? Finally, how do users interact with virtual worlds and adapt to being together in a mediated environment?

Chapter 4 examines interaction at a detailed level, mainly for collaboration and mainly in immersive spaces. One of the key questions here is, what kinds of things can people do better together in immersive spaces than in nonimmersive, PC-based ones? As we shall see, the advantages relate mainly to navigation, manipulation of objects, and mutual awareness in highly spatial tasks. Here it also possible to compare various types of tasks and to compare short tasks and longer collaborations over time. This chapter will also look at other dimensions of small group interaction: Are there differences between how people collaborate who know each other well compared with strangers? How do avatars position themselves in relation to each other? How do their capabilities vary with the systems they use and the input/output devices? Finally, how do the issues of small group encounters between avatars in immersive systems relate to interaction in larger groups, as well as to interaction in related new technologies with small group meetings such as videoconferences and text-based environments?

Chapter 5 analyzes interpersonal activities and relations in online worlds with large populations. How are social groups created and sustained in MUVEs? How should we understand the relation between online and offline relations? Interpersonal relations in MUVEs are in some ways more difficult to establish than in face-to-face ones because of the absence of many social cues and conventions. Yet at the same time, they can be experienced as all the more personal and patterned because users can (over)compensate for this. Hence we can ask: What kind of norms obtain in online worlds? Online spaces with larger populations have developed complex social relations, including forms of governance and economic exchange, and this applies to worlds for gaming and for socializing. This chapter will examine a number of such worlds, including Active Worlds and Second Life.

Chapter 6 is focused on communication. It compares MUVEs with text and voice communication and compares both with face-to-face communication: How does the absence of certain social cues in MUVEs affect communication? How does communication in small groups differ between text, voice, and face-to-face? One section of the chapter will concentrate on text-based communication—in particular, the question of how different languages and cultures encounter each other. Online worlds typically use text, and this is one reason for focusing on text, even if worlds with voice are a better fit with the definition of MUVEs here. But even in MUVEs with voice communication, collaboration is often difficult because participants struggle to establish common ground and rapport. A number of studies will be presented that have tackled these issues, and this will pave the way for comparisons with other digital media.

Chapter 7 describes the possibilities of using MUVEs to study different kinds of social behavior. MUVEs can be used to study phenomena that would be difficult or impossible in face-to-face situations or in offline social interactions.[4] They can also be used as experimental laboratories to study different types of mediated interaction. The chapter will survey these possibilities and present some of the methods and disciplinary perspectives that are used in the study of interaction in MUVEs. One advantage of MUVEs is that it is possible to record and analyze the interaction in detail, and this can be done with quantitative tools for identifying and measuring the most common types of interaction as well as qualitative approaches that highlight particularly revealing aspects of interaction. Examples of both will be given. This chapter, in short, will discuss the techniques for using MUVEs in social science research and present examples of how this has been done.

Chapter 8 addresses the social issues in MUVEs, an area where there has been much speculation in the media but little analysis. Some of these social issues relate to research ethics: since it is possible to capture online interaction and to manipulate, for example, people's avatar appearance in experiments, are there any limitations that need to be imposed on research in—and using—MUVEs? Other questions relate to the uses of MUVEs and include legal questions about the ownership and control of property in online worlds, such as the objects that people have built and avatars they have designed. Still others concern the ethics of online interaction: how should avatars behave toward each other in that their encounters are "only" virtual? These questions will raise more general issues to do with the longer-term uses and social implications of the technology.

In Chapter 9, findings about interaction in MUVEs will be related to other new media. The field of virtual reality technologies, in both research and development, has become specialized into a number of subfields, with areas such as projection technology displays, mixed and augmented reality technology, brain–computer interfaces, and various application areas developing communities of their own. Other technologies, such as mobile telephony, instant messaging, and social networking sites, partly overlap in their research agendas but also raise the question of whether a convergence of various forms of computer-mediated communication is taking place. And finally, videoconferencing is the technology that is in some ways closest to MUVEs while also being quite different—so again, we can ask about possible convergences and divergences. This chapter will relate the findings of various digital media to the different aspects of "being there together" discussed in previous chapters.

To conclude, Chapter 10 puts MUVEs into a larger context. Where do they fit into the landscape of emerging electronic media? Will they develop separately from, or merge with, ongoing developments in graphical interfaces on desktop computers or in larger immersive and interactive displays? Do they provide unique and useful tools for meeting or collaborating at-a-distance, or are their main uses confined to online gaming? What kinds of suggestions can social science provide for the design and implementation of MUVEs? This will bring us back to the overall argument of the book and the different future options for "being there together" in a variety of contexts. The final chapter presents the outlook for MUVEs and for how we interact with each other via computers and other media.

The Development of Shared Virtual Environments Technology

Before we turn to current technologies, some brief background on the development of MUVEs will be helpful: The history of MUVE technology has various strands. Networked interactive computer graphics were first demonstrated in 1972 on ARPANET, the computer network developed by the U.S. Advanced Research Projects Agency (Norberg and O'Neill, 1996: 119–152). One of the main purposes of this project was to allow for time-sharing of what were then costly and scarce computer processing resources. Battlefield simulations were one application of these networked environments, which were developed in the United States from the mid-1980s on and are still an important part of MUVE development. One driving force behind developing these networks were lower training costs: it is much cheaper to bring together personnel and blow up virtual vehicles on a computer network than in real-life training exercises. Recently the military has even turned to online gaming for training and recruitment purposes (see, for example, the game America's Army, http://www.americasarmy.com/). Yet the rationale that some things are cheaper and easier to do in MUVEs has also driven VR and MUVE research in nonmilitary areas. To say, therefore, that MUVEs were primarily driven by the needs of the military (Lenoir 1999), as in the case of the Internet as such, is an exaggeration (as Hughes [1998: 255–300] also argues for the Internet).

The second important driver of multiuser VR were networked computer games. But an important distinction immediately needs to be made between online gaming and online social spaces or worlds: The use of networked social spaces can be traced to text-based multiuser dungeons or MUDs (which sometimes had fantasy elements), also known as multiuser dimensions (Bartle 1990; Curtis 1992; Cawson, Haddon, and Miles 1995: 135–174; Pargman 2000). From the mid-1980s until the mid-1990s, the only networked online space for socializing with interactive computer graphics was Habitat (Morningstar and Farmer 1991), first piloted in the United States, where it failed, and subsequently in Japan, where it was very successful. Nowadays, there are many such online social spaces. Yet social spaces have been vastly eclipsed in popularity by online games—or massively multiplayer role-playing games (MMRPGs), as they are also known (Taylor 2006; Vorderer and Bryant 2006). As we shall see, there are many issues in online gaming and socializing that overlap and that also overlap with the workaday applications of MUVEs. Yet there are also separate social issues and forms of social interaction that apply differently to the various technologies and formats of these recreational uses of MUVEs (and the distinction between social spaces and games will be elaborated in Chapter 5).

VR technology itself is a third strand in the development of MUVEs. The possibility of putting two or more users within the same virtual world in the form of local networks was part of the development of VR systems from the start. When Jaron Lanier's company VPL introduced the first commercial VR systems in the late 1980s and early 1990s, one configuration was a system for two users, VPL's RB2, or "Reality Built for Two." Similarly, early immersive VR games like those produced by the firm Virtuality were designed to allow up to four users using HMDs to share the same space from the time when they were first introduced in the early 1990s. The history of (single-user) VR technology and the early stages of MUVEs has been charted elsewhere (Schroeder 1996), and various display systems and interaction devices will be encountered later. In any event, when the perspective shifts from single-user VR systems to networked or online MUVEs, the issues, as we will see, become much more complex. To what extent the various systems and devices are proliferating and diverging—and to what extent there are overlaps between the various technologies for being there together—are core questions of this book.

Finally, it can be mentioned that despite many changes in technology and uses, there has been constant speculation about its potential implications from the early 1990s onwards. Addiction, virtual sex, the possibility of multiple identities, identity deception, and many other futuristic possibilities have been widely discussed (Rheingold 1991, Turkle 1995, Schroeder 1996: 123–136). More recently, much of this speculation, especially concerning online deviance, has reemerged with the rising popularity of Second Life and other online worlds. Much of this discussion, I will argue, has missed the mark because these questions have not been closely tied to the actual possibilities and constraints of existing systems (or indeed conceivable ones). Still, some of the actual and foreseeable social issues around MUVE uses will be addressed in the conclusion.

This book focuses on MUVEs rather than on single-user VR systems and on online spaces for socializing rather than on online gaming. This is because MUVEs have become the most dynamic area of technical development in VR, and networked worlds pose the most interesting questions in terms of their implications for the future of digital media. The same goes for the focus on online social spaces, which raise more interesting issues about social interaction than online games (although the distinction is sometimes hard to draw, and online games can of course also be spaces for online socializing). In any event, although an argument will be made about the future of technologies for MUVEs, the emphasis is not on the technology[5] but on how people interact in MUVEs.

Two Technological End-States

From the past, we can go straight to the future: There are two types of systems for being there together with different technologies and environments: videoconferencing and immersive (and nonimmersive) VEs. Online worlds, MUVEs with large populations in vast spaces, could be seen as a third, but since they are analytically indistinguishable from VEs, we will treat them together—although online worlds will get a chapter of their own (Chapter 5) because they are by far the most common type of MUVE and they have different dynamics in the sense that much depends, for example, on the social rules and conventions governing different online worlds.

At this point it will be useful to preview an argument that will inform the rest of the book, and that will play a major role in synthesizing the findings in the final chapter. This argument takes us from how MUVEs have developed up until now and into the future of technological developments. The argument, as mentioned earlier, is that we can foresee the endpoint of the development of technologies for being there together, though it comes in two forms: immersive VEs and immersive video-environments.[6] Much of the technology for both forms of being there together is already available—here we can think of CAVE-type VEs, but also of the less well-known technology for capturing people's real full bodies and putting them into a holographic three-dimensional (3D) video image of a real scene (see Figures 1.1 and 1.2; these technologies will be described further in Chapter 2).

These two technological end-points can be foreseen because it can be envisioned (at least in terms of visual and auditory displays and devices for interacting with the environment) that fully immersive and well-functioning VEs and video environments will become available.[7] The endpoints of technological development can therefore also be foreseen to produce a particular experience for the users: a purely mediated relationship in which the user experiences "being there together" (copresence) with others in a fully immersive environment. But again, the technologies for this endpoint, whereby users and environments are represented to each other in fully immersive displays, come in two quite different forms: *either* in the form of computer-generated embodiments and scenes *or* in the form of the 3D video capture of people and scenes.

FIGURE 1.1   Avatars solving a Rubik's Cube-type puzzle in an IPT system. (Image courtesy of Will Steptoe and Anthony Steed at University College London and Dave Roberts of Salford University.)

FIGURE 1.2   Person in the blue-C system. (Photograph courtesy of Markus Gross, Swiss Federal Institute of Technology Zurich.)

Although there are current technical limitations to both scenarios (again, we will come to them later), these immersive displays represent two end-states in the sense that—barring direct sensory input into the brain (in the manner of science fiction novels such as William Gibson's *Neuromancer* and Neal Stephenson's *Snow Crash*)—synthetic environments for "being there together" that are displayed to the users' senses cannot in the future be developed further than perfectly and fully immersive VEs or video-environments.

The difference between video 3D environments (essentially holographic videoconferencing systems) versus computer-generated 3D environments will be important for the discussion that follows, so it is important to spell it out clearly. Both are end-states of non—co-located people completely immersed in mediated communication environments and interacting with each other, but they have quite different capabilities: video environments *capture* the appearance of real users and real places, while VEs *generate* user representations (avatars) and virtual places or spaces. The two technologies therefore also allow the user to *do* different things: video environments are realistic and are constrained by this realism, while VEs allow manipulation that is not limited by realism. VEs, on the other hand, do not capture real scenes.

To appreciate this difference, picture yourself—your body and those of others with whom you may be sitting, as well as the real place around you—captured by 3D cameras and reproduced in full. Now add the fact that, although this capturing has been done digitally, the digital environment of 3D video images is such that objects (including people) can only behave according to the laws of the physical world—in other words, the realistic representation cannot be altered. A simple example: if the camera has captured an image of a table, you will not be able to throw it in air unless it is a very light table.[8] In other words, this is a 3D videoconferencing scenario in which the space around the users is included.

Now picture, by contrast, your body controlling a computer-generated avatar along with other such avatars in a computer-generated environment. In this scenario, the second end-state, the appearance and behaviors of the person and the environment may be programmed so as to be unconstrained by real-world laws—or constrained by them. For example, you may be able to throw the table or walk through it—or not—depending on the whims of the software. Note that the difference between the two scenarios is not just "realism" but also what control is exercised over one's body—is it captured or tracked?—and over the environment—are the objects captured and realistic or fantastical, and how can they be manipulated? In the computer-generated environment, you will be able pass through others and throw the table around—or not, if the system is programmed to make the table immoveable. In any event, throwing the table will not cause damage to the person behind the avatar at whom you may have thrown the table and may have bounced off of or smashed the avatar—again, depending on the whim of the software. In contrast, in the 3D videoconferencing scenario, the table will have caused damage to the other person if the scene has been captured realistically and, for example, the impact of the table can be conveyed via force feedback (otherwise, "transporting" the realistic table from one realistic place to another will require that the table is computer-generated and weightless, and thus we are back to a VE instead of a video-captured one).

In fact, these two end-state scenarios may be mixed in practice. For example, capturing the user on video but putting them into a computer-generated environment, or putting a computer-generated avatar into a video-captured environment. Another example is to combine 3D videoconferencing with working to together on computer-generated objects, as in Figure 1.3 (from the National Teleimmersion Initiative; see Sadagic et al. 2001 and Towles et al. 2002). This figure shows how two people can collaborate as if they were sitting across from each other at the same table, and they are also working on a synthetic object together and seeing each other and the objects in 3D because they are wearing stereoscopic displays. Indeed, while this way of working together is intuitive, Towles et al. (2002: section 7) say that "almost all users react to the system as if they are working with a person sitting across the table." One of the main problems is that it is difficult to have eye contact while wearing 3D glasses and to have a natural interaction wearing a head-tracking device. Note finally that this is quite a realistic workaday scenario: working together with objects that can easily be moved about and reconfigured is a common task, and so this kind of mixed end-state may be a useful one (we shall return to these scenarios in Chapters 9 and 10).

Many other combinations are possible. In their pure forms, however, they are quite different in terms of their affordances (or the way the environment is perceived and how it can be acted on; we shall return to "affordances"). It is important to add here that the experience of being there or presence is a sensory one in both cases—primarily visual and also audio (and sometimes haptic). This is important because there are

FIGURE 1.3   Two people collaborating remotely on virtual objects as if they are sitting across the table from each other, from the National Tele-immersion Initiative. (Photograph courtesy of Amela Sadagic, Henry Fuchs, and Herman Towles.)

debates about whether media that do not afford sensory experiences of another place or person—a book, say, or a text-based MUD—can be discussed in the same context as VEs (Klimmt and Vorderer 2003). This has been ruled out by the definition that was given earlier: unless the experience is a sensory one, one based on the perception of a place or person via our sensory apparatus, experiences such as those "mediated" by books or television and the like are excluded.[9]

The two environments, computer-generated versus video, therefore represent two quite *different* end-states—even though they *both* represent an experience of being there together in a place other than the one that users are physically in. If they are fully realized in the way described here, they are also, as mentioned earlier, the furthest possible extensions of technologies for being there together or of shared synthetic environments, because no conceivable system could go beyond providing a more fully immersive experience of being there together.[10] Now one reason for previewing the idea of these two end-states is that it allows us to understand the various approximations toward these end-states in the light of what the full development of this technology will eventually look like. That is, if we have these two end-states in mind as we discuss other currently available technologies, we can crystallize the difference between them: as mentioned, they may be mixed in practice, but in their pure form, they allow users to do quite different things.

A second reason for distinguishing the two end-states is that these two end-states will also allow us, in the conclusion, to analyze many other new and old media—telephones and letters but also social networking sites and Internet-enabled mobile phones—as approximating the end-states and affording the experience of "being there together" in different ways. This will enable us to put MUVEs into the changing landscape of information and communication technologies. Before we do this, in the chapters to come, we shall have to examine the social patterns we find in the actual uses of MUVEs. Once we have done this, we will be able to compare how these patterns differ from videoconferencing and from face-to-face interaction.

NOTES

1. The idea of "presence" or "being there" will be discussed at greater length in the next chapter. Ijsselstjein points out that there are two aspects to interaction: "the essential characteristic of any interactive system is that it will allow the user some measure of control over the media form and/or content ... it is useful to distinguish between two different types of user-system interaction: navigation and manipulation. *Navigation* will allow the user to explore a given computer-generated or distant real environment .... *Manipulation* on the other hand, allows the user to affect a meaningful change in the real or virtual environment itself" (2003: 31–32). The use of "interaction" in the definition of VEs presented here is intended to include both—and for shared VEs, there is a third: interaction with others in the VE.

2. For a brief history of the technology, see Schroeder 1996: 17–25.

3. CAVE stands for Cave Automatic Virtual Environment, and the term is a registered trademark of the University of Illinois Board of Regents. Nowadays, there are a number of systems which use similar technology, and Immersive Projection Technology (or IPT) is commonly used.

4. I will use "physical world" or "real world" when the contrast is with the virtual place or space and "offline world" when the contrast is with what people do in online worlds. But in view of the definition, the pairs of terms could be used interchangeably. Face-to-face interaction will be contrasted with interaction inside the VE or online interaction or interaction between avatars.

5. See Singhal and Zyda (1999) for how the technology of networked VEs works; Bowman, Kruijff, LaViola, and Poupyrev (2004) for interaction technologies; Slater, Chrysanthou, and Steed (2001) for 3D graphics. A state-of-the-art overview of the technology is Steed and Oliveira (2010).

6. It can be mentioned that "video environments" may be a somewhat misleading term: video is normally associated with two-dimensional (2D) video screen technology. It would be technically more accurate to use "3D real-time acquisition of data" or "real-time 3D scan" here. However, I have used 3D video here in the sense of videoconferencing and 3D capture of real scenes as a shorthand and also as a term that can be readily grasped in nontechnical terms. It may also be useful to note in relation to display technology that videoconferencing technology typically uses 2D displays without head-tracking equipment (but see Figure 1.3, which does use head-tracking), and this technology is therefore not really "immersive." Again, however, the emphasis here is on the experience of the user rather than on the technology, and in this "relaxed" sense of the term "immersive," even a high-end videoconferencing system, for example, can seem immersive and provide a sense of "being there together." In any event, the main contrast for the two end-states is between a computer *generating* an environment, and a camera (or set of cameras) *capturing* a real environment, whatever technology is used.

7. A related technology are brain–computer interfaces. This technology is currently still quite far from providing the experience of "being there," and very far from "being there together," although this may change in the longer-term future.

8. This kind of realism does not always work "realistically"—in the video-captured environment, you may be able to walk through the table, but in that case you will not be able to push it, as you would a table in the physical world. This highlights the fact that in this case, it is necessary to distinguish between the real world that is being captured, and how it is displayed in the environment: you can only capture real-world phenomena, but you can display "fantastical" things in the environment, such as a table that you can walk through (but it is not possible to display a photo-realistic purple cow, for example).

9. Thus, a complete end-state will provide an environment for being there together for *all* the senses. But since sensory inputs and outputs apart from vision, sound, and position tracking and limited haptics are rather remote, we can concentrate on those that are currently available. Mixed or augmented reality devices, where the user is partly inside a VE and partly engages with the physical world, will constitute approximations to these two ideal immersive end-states.

10. Note that there will be lots of other forms of online togetherness in the future, which will be discussed in the final chapter. But again, these will be approximations toward two end-states. Further, there will be convergence in the sense that all these forms of "being there together"—whether VE or video, generated, or captured—will be digital, and they will converge in this sense. Still there will be no convergence in the sense that there will be one device—there will be several.

2

The Varieties of Experiences of
Being There Together

The first chapter has introduced the idea that the future of multiuser virtual environment (MUVE) technology can be foreseen. This may seem a rather speculative approach to understanding MUVEs, but the main purpose of thinking about two end-states is to inform how we can think about the uses of MUVE technologies among other communication technologies and new media. The aim of Chapter 2 is to bring the discussion back to present-day realities: What do we know about how MUVE technologies are being used so far? What types of experiences do people have when they interact in VEs? Once we have a general sense of how people interact in MUVEs, we will be able to look in more detail in subsequent chapters at particular aspects of interaction in MUVEs. This chapter will discuss some of the main concepts in the field, such as presence and copresence, media richness and social cues, and the affordances of different technologies.

One reason for surveying actual experiences is that discussion of MUVEs can often take rather undisciplined forms: some claim that anything is possible in virtual worlds (VWs)—you can be anyone, do anything, virtual spaces are without limits, and the technology therefore brings about fundamental changes. Equally vocal, it seems, are the skeptics, who argue that VEs and online worlds are not so different from other technologies and that virtual spaces are invariably much like real-world spaces. These ideas, often with both points of view represented within the same text, pervade popular accounts of MUVEs (Au 2008), but they are also common in academic discussions (Turkle 1995). There is a further view that MUVE technologies, like others, can be used in many different ways or that they cannot be analytically distinguished from other technologies in a clear manner, so that it is impossible to generalize about them.[1] And finally, some argue that online and offline relations between people cannot be separated (Taylor 2006) and that it is therefore not useful to deploy concepts and theories that apply specifically to VEs or to online interaction.

These ideas, I will argue, prevent a coherent approach to understanding interaction in MUVEs. Briefly put, MUVEs do not allow any type of behavior in online spaces, but they are also not the same as offline or face-to-face interactions. To make this argument, however, it is important to examine actual uses of technologies, the range of settings they are used in, and what kind of experiences people have when they are used. As we shall see, the concepts used in the study of MUVEs are still in flux. However, that does not mean that we cannot synthesize the findings that we have about MUVEs and develop an overall framework for how people interact in VEs.

The Range of MUVE Settings

Current MUVE systems and uses can be put into two broad categories:

- Instrumental uses with research or prototype systems
- Leisure uses for gaming and socializing, using PCs and widely available and commercially developed software

In the first category of instrumental uses of research or prototype systems, we can put experimental or early-stage uses; immersive, high-end, or expensive devices; specially developed software; dedicated networks; small numbers of users; specialized uses in industry or engineering or other settings such as medicine; and short periods of use.[2] Into the second category of leisure uses for gaming or socializing, we can put commercially available software and VWs, routine or everyday uses, nonimmersive desktop PC systems, inexpensive software or free downloads, Internet-based large populations of users, and extensive or regular periods of use.

The reason for making this distinction is that, as we shall see, different kinds of research and different issues arise for these two types of systems and uses. Even if, in the future, the two may converge—and one of the points of this book is to argue that many issues overlap between the two—it will be useful to bear the distinction in mind in order to highlight that they cover the two quite different types of uses of MUVEs. The main reason for identifying these two types of *current* uses is that this will allow us to develop an inventory of the types of experiences that users have of being there together.

Clearly, there are many features of the two major uses that fall into *both* types. To give an example, immersive systems have been used for leisure purposes, as when head-mounted displays (HMD) were used in networked mode to allow two people to play together in arcade games in the mid-1990s (Schroeder 1996: 45–68) or when leisure uses have been explored experimentally in immersive systems (Persky and Blascovich 2006). And desktop PC-based systems have been used for instrumental purposes, such as for conferencing in shared spaces for collaboration or in educational applications (for examples, see Churchill, Snowdon and Munro 2001). Nevertheless, the features of the two types currently cluster together, and making this distinction in the first instance will make it easier to think about the overlaps between them later. Finally, one feature that the two types share is that they consist overwhelmingly of graphical and auditory environments and allow visual interaction with other users and with the environment. This leaves out haptic systems with force feedback, and these systems occupy quite specialized niches.

A key difference between instrumental and leisure uses is that the former are typically used for short periods. This means that many of the issues relating to the longer-term leisure uses do not apply to short-term uses—for example, the persistence of the avatar and of the environment or world. Conversely, many of the issues that pertain to short periods of instrumental uses do not apply for longer-term leisure uses—for example, the health and safety issues that need to be considered even for short periods of using immersive systems, or the accuracy and lag of position-tracking devices that may impair the performance of brief tasks.

The MUVEs that fall into the category of instrumental uses are diverse in terms of devices and applications. The devices include highly immersive displays such as immersive projection technology (IPTs, also known as CAVE-type systems) and HMD systems. Applications include architectural walkthroughs, training, therapy, scientific visualization, and the like, all of which have been developed for shared or multiuser use. Nevertheless, the vast majority are not used on a regular or routine basis, and this is so even though there has been more than a decade of exploration into how they might be used. This is partly to do with the cost and resource requirements of the equipment, including that a technician typically needs to be present when immersive systems are used—which is especially costly with systems at two or more different sites. (We can already think ahead here to the uses of high-end videoconferencing equipment, which often have the same problem.) Another reason for the lack of large-scale or routine use is that on the user side, it is necessary to go to a dedicated facility.

It can be mentioned here in passing (we will return to it later) that on the side of these research and prototype uses, the research and development community has become very specialized. So, for example, on the side of the technology, there are communities focusing on computer graphics, augmented and mixed reality, IPT systems, collaborative VEs, artificial agents in MUVEs, and other areas. On the applications side, there has also been a proliferation of research communities, such as VEs for disabilities and medicine, for heritage and museums, and for education. An Internet search for keywords of these technologies and applications will reveal a plethora of conferences and journals, as will a perusal of the list of references in this book. Again, one reason for mentioning these fields is to point out to the reader who may not be familiar with this research that this account will try to go beyond these special fields to offer a synthetic account—and also link to broader studies of mediated communication and mediated social interaction.[3]

This brings us back to MUVEs that fall into the category of leisure, for both gaming and socializing. In this domain, too, there are various communities of researchers: computer game studies, studies of new media and online communities, and research on desktop online VWs for uses other than gaming such as work-related VWs. These, by contrast with research and prototype uses, have become widely and regularly used. It can be noted in passing that some would not regard nonimmersive desktop MUVEs as virtual reality (VR) systems, but the distinction is hard to maintain in light of the definition used here: these MUVEs offer a first-person perspective and thus a sense of being there in the environment—and of direct interaction with it. As we shall also see, however, there are major differences between immersive and nonimmersive experiences of being there together. In these leisure uses of MUVEs, the largest number of users can now be found in massively multiplayer role-playing games (MMRPGs) such as World of Warcraft or "first-person shooters" such as Quake and the like. These online games mainly follow the fantasy role-playing and shoot-'em-up formats. Online games typically meet the requirement of the definition of MUVEs even less than do online worlds for socializing—because players are constrained by predefined actions and roles (more on this point shortly).

MUVEs for socializing, such as ActiveWorlds, OnLive Traveler, and Second Life, constitute a separate subcategory within the category of leisure uses. The main activity in these MUVEs is just to spend time together in relatively open-ended activities. MUVEs for socializing have been in existence for longer, but they have attracted smaller numbers of users than have online "games." They are, however, closer to the definition of VR/MUVEs given here than are MMRPGs or gaming MUVEs because the avatars are intended to represent real users and the aim is to socialize with other such user representations—as opposed to representing a "character" in the game and concentrating on the activities that the rules of the game prescribe. Still, the line between the social spaces and games may be hard to draw in practice. Both types of MUVEs, for gaming and for socializing, have become highly popular—while nonleisure routine uses of VWs such as for education[4] and work are still quite rare.

The social aspects of MUVEs are interesting partly because they will influence how the technology will develop. This is because when technologies are new, there is much uncertainty about their future shape and appropriate uses. A good example (mentioned briefly in Chapter 1) is the early history of the telephone. When this technology was still new in America, it was unclear what kind of system would emerge and prevail. Issues of technical standards, ownership of the network, and the functionality of devices were still fluid. This also applies to the emergence of "correct" telephone behavior: How should people answer the telephone—should the caller or the receiver of the call speak first? How should they identify themselves—by their name, location, or telephone number? (See Fischer 1992: esp. 183–187.) Similarly, the uses to which telephones should be put were quite uncertain in the early days and took decades to emerge. For a contemporary example, we can think of the mobile phone where the nature of the device (is it primarily for voice or other functions?) and behaviors (for example, use in public places) have only partly settled and are still partly fluid (see Ling 2004).

It will be the same with MUVEs. Many of the issues that will be discussed relate to the fact that established or routine ways of using the technology have not yet emerged. This applies both to leisure and instrumental uses. The technology and its uses are still fluid, even if they have also become congealed in certain forms for the moment. As for users finding the "correct" or appropriate ways to behave in using these systems, various conventions will emerge over time, with some transferred from real-world contexts into MUVEs and others emerging to suit this novel context.

Nevertheless, bearing in mind the fluidity of the technology and its uses, we can now begin to look more closely at some of the main current experiences and aspects of people's interaction in MUVEs. First, however, it will be useful to be clearer about what makes MUVEs unique as a technology and a new medium. The definition of MUVEs that was presented in the first Chapter distinguishes this technology from other new technologies and new media: unlike other tools, MUVEs provide users with a direct experience of engaging with the environment and with others. So, for example, VR systems are different from simulators; they are aimed at putting the user in a space other than the one they are physically in, rather than putting the user into a simulated vehicle or other simulated situation. And unlike teleoperator systems, MUVEs are aimed at putting the user in a computer-generated place, not transporting them to a remote physical location.

One problem in pinning down the experience of users in MUVEs is that "presence" (a term we will return to frequently), the sense of being in another place or space, depends partly on the context or the task. *Presence* has been defined as the "illusion of non-mediation" (Lombard and Ditton 1997) and it is one of the most intensely researched areas in VE technology (copresence much less so). But there is also an important problem in this research area: It is not clear how significant the level of immersiveness is in fostering presence—compared with the level of interactivity or the manipulability of the environment. Put differently, does presence depend on being there, or what you can do there?

For shared VEs or MUVEs, there is the added complication of weighing the extent to which presence is affected by the "copresence," the sense of being there with other users—and vice versa. And again, how much does copresence depend on the sense of being there with people, compared with doing things with them? Furthermore, there are only a few studies that have made a start in investigating the relation between presence and copresence. And the studies that have investigated presence and copresence have typically consisted of a single short task in a laboratory setting, while there are few studies in naturalistic settings over longer periods or that compare different tasks and situations.

At this point, we can step back for a moment and look at the larger context of people inside VEs. In the lab or in experimental settings, "presence" has been a major research topic among researchers who, for example, ask subjects in experiments to rate their sense of presence in trials (Scheumie, van der Straaten, Krijn, and van der Mast 2001) or measure their heart rate or take other physiological measures as they interact with the environment (Meehan, Insko, Whitton, and Brooks 2002). We will return to these measures on a number of occasions. Yet it may also be that, in these experimental settings, it is the unfamiliar physical setting and technology, rather than the immersiveness of the technology as such, that influence the sense of presence. For example: How does the experience of entering into an IPT or CAVE-type system, or talking to others outside this system, or leaving the system, affect the user's experience (Steed, Spante, Heldal, Axelsson, and Schroeder 2003)? The same applies to measures of copresence when users interact with life-size avatars for the first time: How is the sense of copresence affected by the novelty of interacting with an avatar? Put another way, Is it the case that users might have a different experience if these settings were to become regular or everyday uses of MUVEs rather than being in an experimental setting? For MUVEs used for gaming and socializing, on the other hand, we may also want to measure a sense of "presence" of users in a virtual environment that has become relatively familiar. Yet the intense involvement in a game on the user's part may, for example, be related to the task and to the impression made by the environment rather than to having the experience of being in another place.

The research on MUVEs can put in an even wider context: What are researchers "getting at" when they study "presence"? How does "presence" or "copresence" relate to our experience of using computers or other media in our homes and offices (as we shall see later, especially in Chapter 9, researchers have begun to use "presence" and "copresence" in describing other new media experiences, such as the experience of using mobile phones)? Researchers working on VEs study presence by exposing subjects to different conditions in the laboratory and asking them to fill out a questionnaire or taking various physiological measures. Yet we could equally ask how the experience of an immersive MUVE experience fits into people's lives. Or, to turn the example around, we could also undertake measurements of "presence" in a desktop MUVE in an everyday setting and ask whether we would expect results that are different from those in the laboratory. The point is that media research about "presence" is about building up our knowledge of certain conditions—to get a better understanding of cognitive or sensory processes, for example—but there could also be different research agendas such as those aimed at improving devices in terms of screen size and the like. These are key topics that contribute to our understanding of the psychology of interacting with computers and new media. The study of using MUVEs and other new media might thus examine how the experience of *immersion* (to use a different word instead of *presence* for a moment) is shaped by, or has ramifications beyond, the laboratory setting.

Another broader way to understand MUVEs might be in the context of online relations in general and how they affect offline relations and vice versa (see Baym 2002 for this issue in relation to computer-mediated communication). For example, even in an everyday setting such as gaming or socializing with desktop MUVEs, where the technology is routine and familiar, this activity is also distinct from other online and offline everyday activities. Similarly, when the technologies in labs and research settings become integrated within everyday settings and other media uses, this, too, will have an effect on the experience and on the social implications of the technology. This wider context of VR technologies has not been extensively studied—and of course it cannot be studied insofar as technologies and experiences have not yet become routine. Still, in the concluding chapter we will need to return to these limitations in current research.

It has been argued that it is difficult to measure presence in a scientific way and that questionnaires (which are often used) on their own are inadequate (Slater 2004).[5] It is indeed worrisome that there has been a lack of agreement on the subjective as well as objective measures of presence in a way that we might like. Still, the body of research that has accumulated in relation to "presence" has proved to be useful for improving different systems and applications and gaining insights into the users' experience. Some key findings will be summarized in different places later, but the focus of the book is not on the physiological or experimental measures of presence and copresence. Instead, the focus is on the interaction between users. Even if this interaction depends on the setting and the familiarity of the user with the technology, this should not prevent researchers from attempting generalizations across these settings. Laboratory settings yield such generalizations, but as we shall see, they can also be obtained from "naturalistic settings." Furthermore, as I shall now go on to argue, the range of settings and experiences in MUVEs is not, in fact, very large.

The Range of Experiences in MUVEs

As mentioned earlier, VR and VWs have led to much speculation about the possibilities different kinds of experiences in shared VWs. But if we take as our starting point what people actually *do* in MUVEs, and what they do *together*, then it becomes apparent that this consists of a much narrower range of phenomena than is often supposed. One way to describe this range is to identify the main technological systems and uses that have just been presented. A different approach is to give an account of the range of experiences of users.

Sensory Experiences

Of the five senses, we can leave out smell and taste, because these input/ output devices are not yet widespread, and even if they are feasible, they are unlikely to be implemented except in very confined niches. Thus, we will only need to bear in mind that the *absence* of these two senses contributes to the lack of "media richness" or an absence of "social cues" in interpersonal interaction.[6]

Haptics (touch) is more common, and apart from many studies with single-user systems, there is now a growing number of studies of, for example, how haptics affect copresence and task performance (Durlach and Slater 2000; Sallnas 2002). Haptic systems will, for the foreseeable future, be used for specialized collaborative tasks and therefore will feed into our knowledge of interaction in MUVEs to a limited extent (although we will return to them).[7] Unlike interaction in the physical world, most VE experiences consist of a kind of "pseudo-touch," which works by means of visual collision detection or visual manipulation of objects. Because the user is represented by an avatar (see Chapter 3), and sometimes the motion of the user's body is tracked, this body will be the means whereby this "pseudo-touch" and interaction with the visual environment take place. (Note that so far, the focus is mainly on the sensory experience of single users—how they navigate and interact with the environment and with others is to be discussed soon).[8]

As for audio, "ambient" sounds in the environment may or not be powerful shapers of the experience—as far as I am aware, this has not been examined systematically. However, sound is often used in VEs, mainly to create an atmosphere and to present different objects aurally. Apart from this, in most MUVEs what we are left with is that people can communicate via voice (or text, if the definitions of VEs and presence are relaxed; see Chapter 6), and they can see each other and interact with others and with the environment visually. In short, we are left with a visual and auditory experience and setting for the interaction, with audio mainly used for communication. (At this point the reader may wonder, what happened to virtual *reality*? And in a sense I would agree with the criticism that has often been voiced that the term is misleading. Still, the definition *is* based on experiencing another place, and it is important to focus on what existing and foreseeable systems *actually* do.) It can also be noted here in passing—we will return to it in Chapter 6, Communication—that even if it may seem that the visual part of the environment is of overwhelming importance in the MUVE, the voice of another person can act as an important sensory "reality check" in MUVEs. The real voice of another person may provide a more realistic sense of the person than their avatar, but this will depend on avatar appearance. Still, against the backdrop of this initial "narrowing" to a visual and aural experience, we can now turn to joint experiences.

Experience with Others

If we turn to social experiences, we find that here, too, people do a remarkably small range of things together in MUVEs: they perform simple tasks and socialize. Putting it the other way around, if we were to compare social experiences in MUVEs with our face-to-face experiences in the real world, the range of experiences in MUVEs would be a very small subset of our real-world experiences. The findings about these joint experiences in VEs relate mainly to how small groups experience doing limited short-term tasks with each other and how larger groups of people establish relations with each other in Internet-based desktop MUVEs for gaming and socializing. Again, this is not a wide swath of activities compared with our face-to-face social activities. It entails a limited range of experiences whereby participants are focusing on certain things together or are aware of doing things together.

This point about the narrowness of interaction in MUVEs should not be misinterpreted to imply that this cannot be a "rich" form of interaction. As Walther (1996) argues by means of his concept of "hyperpersonal" relations, people may have highly expressive relations vis-à-vis each other despite—or perhaps because of—the absence of multiple channels in computer-mediated communication. This absence allows us, for example, to "put more into" (in my words, not Walther's) how we present ourselves to each other in mediated interactions. Moreover, the interactions with others in Internet-based desktop MUVEs for socializing and gaming can become very complex, such as building up extensive systems of social norms, just as short-term tasks in immersive systems have many complexities. Yet even if these relationships or forms of interaction are acknowledged to be "rich" and complex, they are not as multifaceted as face-to-face relations. Summing up this section so far: a common auditory and visual experience and the experience of doing a limited range of things together constitute the bulk of phenomena that will be analyzed in this book.

Experiences of Being There Together with Different VR Technologies

If we now examine the factors among the range of systems and how they affect presence, copresence, and interaction, clearly, despite what was said earlier about the fact that the experience depends on the "task" or the "setting," technology is a key variable with important effects on collaboration and performance—and on socializing. One result that is consistent across various studies is that, other things being equal, the more immersive VR system creates a greater sense of presence and copresence.

An early study that supports this point was a study in which the participant using an immersive HMD system was identified as the leader in a group of three participants where the two others were using a desktop system to solve a word puzzle task (see Slater, Sadagic, Usoh, and Schroeder, 2000). This is an important finding because the participants in the study were not aware of what kind of system the other persons were using and no participant was identified as the leader in the equivalent real setting.

These findings were extended in the Rubik's Cube trial (which will be referred to on a number of occasions), in which 128 pairs of participants worked on a Rubik's Cube–type puzzle—a very spatial task—using different VR systems: IPT, desktop, and HMD, with pairs using either the same system or different systems—and in the equivalent real setting with cardboard box cubes (see Schroeder et al. 2001 and Chapter 4 for more details). This trial built on the findings of the Slater, Sadagic, Usoh, and Schroeder (2000) study and found that presence and copresence covary; that is, if users have a stronger sense of copresence, they also have a stronger sense of presence. Similarly, it found that the more immersed participant was regarded as the leader in the task. And again, participants in all cases—apart from the real-world setting—were not aware of the technology or system that their partner was using.

Apart from presence and copresence, there were important effects of the technology and the VE in this trial on what each participant *does*: for example, there are differences in what participants focus on when they use different systems—the person using the desktop system typically focuses more on communication, whereas the immersed person focuses more on navigating and manipulating the objects. This means that a division of labor occurs when two people work on different systems—with one person, for example, taking a more "supervisory" role of communicating about the task and the other taking a more active role with regard to the object-oriented part of the task of manipulating the cubes (again, without being aware of what system the other used, and without necessarily being aware that the labor was being divided between them).

Overall, then, we know that, for small groups of two or three persons who are doing short collaborative tasks, certain technological factors play a strong role, and that in this case (as mentioned earlier) highly immersive HMD or IPT-type systems can provide a more powerful experience of "being there together" than do desktop systems. What is still missing in the study of interaction in MUVEs is that not much is known about how the experience of being there together varies across *different* activities or environments within the *same* system; in other words, how does *what* people do, or the type of environment they are in, affect copresence? Systematic studies of this topic are still missing, although later we shall encounter some findings that are germane to this question.

It could therefore be useful to study not, as hitherto, how people use different systems to do the same task but rather how persons carry out different tasks with the same system. Ellis (1996), for example, has advocated measuring "equivalence classes"—performance measures for using the same system but for different tasks in the same environment. To advance this research area, it might be useful to test the following hypotheses, with the system held constant and varying the environment and the activities:

- The more involved in the task, the less presence and copresence. This is counterintuitive: if users are intensely involved in the MUVE, they should experience more presence and copresence. But it could equally be argued that if users are very intensely involved in an activity or task, they might "forget" that they are in a VE, which may take away from presence or copresence (as with the notion of being engrossed in the "flow" of a task, which can entail that you lose a sense of where you are; see Csikszentmihalyi 1990).
- The more visually rich and complex the VE, the more presence and copresence. Again, this seems obvious, but it is not: rich VEs may "overwhelm" and thus "alienate" the user, whereas simple ones may make the users more "at home." Of course, the offline real world can also be "overwhelming" in this sense, but the experience can be compounded in a VE, which may be a novel environment and/or where many offline cues or means of orientation are absent.
- The more realistic (in the sense of true-to-the-real-world) the VE, the more presence and copresence. Again, this has often been assumed by VR researchers, and there are some studies to support it.[9] Yet anecdotal observations suggest that people also regard "fantastic" or abstract scenes as highly engrossing, and they find environments that

just slightly depart from being realistic as unbelievable (the "uncanny valley" effect, a term coined by Masahiro Mori [1970], which also applies to avatar appearance). Further, it will be difficult to separate realism in the sense of "detail" (for example, a highly detailed architectural model) from realism in the sense of "true-to-the-real-world" (a building recognized as true-to-life).

- Similarly for the realism of avatars, it is often assumed that the more realistic the avatar, the greater the presence/copresence (it is important to distinguish between behavioral and appearance realism; see Garau 2006), and some results support this. In relation to the realism of the other person, it has been shown that in certain settings, for example, the more realistic the appearance of the other person, the higher the copresence or "social presence," in Blascovich's (2002) terminology. But again, it may turn out that people are more at ease, and thus experience more copresence, with each other in the case of "simpler" avatars in simple VE settings.

These hypotheses are partly presented to indicate possible future research directions but also partly to give an idea of the state of knowledge (or lack of knowledge) in the field at this stage.

We will see later that it is possible to draw together findings that point to partial answers related to these hypotheses, but much systematic research is still needed. Another problem that these hypotheses illustrate, however, is how interrelated the various aspects of MUVE experiences are (this may account for the difficulty of generalizability: too many dimensions vary). It may, for example, be difficult to disaggregate the influence of the realism of the environment and the "intensity" of the activity (or interactivity) in MUVEs: highly "unrealistic" scenes like the Rubik's Cube, for example, can be very engaging because of the high level of interaction, but this is hardly a visually rich or realistic environment (a simple Rubik's Cube floating in the middle of the three-dimensional [3D] space, with no other features). On the other hand, a highly realistic scene with highly realistic avatars may yield a powerful experience of presence and copresence—even if there is little or no interactivity with the avatars or with the environment. In experimental studies, two or more factors will interact with each other (realism and level of interactivity, for example), or one may override the other. Even if these conditions can be experimentally disaggregated, the next problem is that laboratory studies and findings may or may not travel well outside of the laboratory or apply to naturalistic settings. However, again, having said all this—this does not mean that it is not worth trying to pull what we know together.

Online Relations in Internet-Based VEs

Going from one extreme to the other (skipping over the interaction and types of tasks, which will be discussed later): What about the social experiences in MUVEs? Before going on to describe what these consist of, it is worth reiterating that experiences in online worlds are not all alike. First, not all Internet-based or online MUVEs are for leisure, MUVEs where the main purpose is to socialize or play games. Some are used in education or for work (for examples, see Churchill, Snowdon, and Munro 2002). It can also be mentioned that it is not only the experiences in these MUVEs—but also the methods used to study them—that are varied: the study of desktop online MUVEs often takes the form of participant observation or ethnographic research (although it is not confined to these)—but these methods could equally be used to study experiments in immersive VE settings. And online MUVEs can also be studied with experimental methods, such as setting up a social world with certain parameters or using quantitative methods based on capturing data in MUVEs (Smith, Farnham, and Drucker 2002; Penumarthy and Boerner 2004). Finally, we can note that the effects of the technological system are not limited to high-end systems but also apply to desktop MUVEs. Examples of how the technology or the system affects interaction in online worlds include bandwidth, communication capabilities, and ease of navigation (Axelsson 2002; Becker and Mark 2002; Nilsson, Heldal, Schroeder, and Axelsson 2002; Pausch, Proffitt, and Williams 1997).

That said, for the moment, and despite the fact that Internet-based MUVEs are quite varied, we can concentrate on some of the findings for online desktop MUVEs with larger populations for leisure purposes. Presence and copresence have not often been studied for online desktop VEs, although there are exceptions (see Schubert, Friedmann, and Regenbrecht 2002) and some studies compare desktop and immersive systems. Clearly, however, presence and copresence in desktop systems should be researched because these experiences are central to the inter-action among users. And although "presence" in desktop systems may not generally be experienced as powerfully as in an immersive system, it is not easy to say the same for copresence. At the same time, there may be a "novelty" effect to copresence in PC-based MUVEs (and, as mentioned earlier, even more so for immersive systems), which may make it difficult to rely on a short study. Copresence may be something "one gets used to," and thereafter one can perhaps concentrate more on communicating and engaging with others.

One limitation of research in this area that has already been hinted at is that there are few links between short experimental trials and longer-term interaction in MUVEs. A topic that could tie the two together, for example, might be: What is the impact of a short and delimited task/activity, as opposed to an unstructured and longer one, on presence and copresence? From the experimental side, this could be formulated as a hypothesis to be tested: The longer the task or time spent in the MUVE, the greater the sense of presence or copresence. Again, it may turn out that the opposite is true: that with adaptation, the sense of being in a VE and being there with others will "fade." Still, it is clear that it will be difficult to study longer periods experimentally (but see Williams, Caplan, and Xiong 2007 for a quasi-experimental study). But the larger question—how we can apply the insights from longer-term and non–task-centered interpersonal relationships in VEs to short-term tasks/activities in shared VEs, and vice versa—is a topic, again, that we will need to return to.

Be that as it may, the main issue for online MUVEs is interpersonal relationships. Some of the rules governing online relationships in desktop MUVEs are different from those governing offline relationships and from the zero-history relationships that are typical in experimental studies. Among the findings here—again, we will go into more detail later—are that long-term relationships can be meaningful and rewarding for users (for example, Cheng, Farnham, and Stone 2002), that long-term users trust each other (Schroeder and Axelsson 2001), that they tend to adopt stable identities in terms of appearance and name (Smith, Farnham, and Drucker 2002; Schroeder and Axelsson 2001), that they use nonverbal communication less the longer they inhabit the VE (Smith, Farnham, and Drucker 2002), that they take an active interest in the choice of their appearance and in shaping the MUVE (Cheng, Farnham, and Stone 2002; Anderson, Ashraf, Douther, and Jack 2001), and that they develop a "stake" in the social environment (Axelsson and Regan 2006; Schroeder, Huxor, and Smith 2001).

On the other hand, some offline rules or conventions of interpersonal interaction apply to or can be seen to hold in online social VEs, such as following the conventions of interpersonal distance (Becker and Mark 2002; Smith, Farnham, and Drucker 2002; see also Blascovich 2002 and Slater, Sadagic, Usoh, and Schroeder 2000 for immersive systems); greeting, addressing, and taking leave of others (Becker and Mark 2002); and preferring avatar representations that are not too unrealistic (Cheng, Farnham, and Stone 2002). Other findings with echoes of offline social relations are concerned with hierarchy and stratification—how insider versus outsider relations are established and how other forms of stratification emerge inside the MUVE (Axelsson 2002; Schroeder 1997). There can also be stratification based on the fact that users may use systems with different capabilities (graphics quality, connection speed) or stratification that is "imported" from the real world into the MUVE—such as being able to afford being online in the first place or being able to type faster than others when you communicate with them in a text-based system.

These findings and others will be discussed in greater detail in later chapters. The main reason for listing them here is to highlight that online relations in MUVEs are very complex. We find, for example, that many norms are imported from offline settings into MUVEs, albeit in a form that is adapted to the virtual setting, yet we also find that various kinds of interaction have developed within the environment itself. A key starting point will therefore be that MUVEs are highly structured on all levels, from micro-interactions among a few participants—to macro-relationships among a large population of users. The sense that one often gets when one initially enters these MUVEs, of the "anything goes" atmosphere of the environment and of the playful interaction, diminishes over time—or at least, one quickly adapts to this new setting and obtains a sense of the social conventions as one would with a foreign place that one visits for the first time.

Apart from the findings about interpersonal relations that have been mentioned so far, many of the remaining studies of interaction in MUVEs (other than online gaming) have been studies of specific aspects: navigation (Munro, Höök, and Benyon 1999), collaboration (Churchill, Snowdon, and Munro 2001), and adaptation (Anderson, Ashraf, Douther, and Jack 2001; Spante 2009). These more specific topics can be related to one another, and some of the areas to be discussed later therefore include topics like how navigation supports avatars exploring an environment together and how collaboration affects online relationships.

Some of the most interesting findings related to copresence and interaction are those that are not limited to a short task or studies of "everyday" behavior in MUVEs for online socializing but rather combine day-to-day and experimental behavior: for example, a series of virtual meetings involving an acting rehearsal (Slater and Steed 2002) or a series of virtual meetings involving building and other activities (Nilsson, Heldal, Schroeder, and Axelsson 2002). In these cases, we can see how small groups (two and four participants, respectively) interact over a number of sessions (five half-hour sessions and ten one-hour sessions, respectively) and collaborate in situations where they are directly copresent with each other—with their interpersonal relations clearly affected by the environment. In the acting rehearsal study, for example, Slater and Steed found that participants had a better sense of each other and that collaboration improved over the course of the five meetings. Similarly, the Nilsson, Heldal, Schroeder, and Axelsson (2002) study suggests that the offline personality of the participants (who knew each other well) increasingly "shines through" over the course of the meetings. What we see, in other words, is how interaction in small groups changes over the course of time, and although these groups engaged in specific tasks (acting rehearsals, meetings with different tasks), the interactions have a different dynamic than short experimental tasks but also differ from longer-term interaction among larger populations.

Here it may also be useful to mention again that behavior in MUVEs is different from behavior in real settings, but that some "real" behaviors are also imported into virtual settings. One example is the finding that avatars are more inclined to maintain interpersonal distance in OnLive Traveler, an online desktop MUVE with audio, than in a MUVE like Active Worlds with text-only communication (Becker and

Mark 2002). In this case, it makes sense that avatars communicating via voice should keep more interpersonal distance than those who communicate via text (in face-to-face settings, one might also keep more distance from someone who is speaking rather than writing), but it is not clear why conventions should be maintained this way in *virtual* environments in which avatars can go up to and through each other just as easily in both systems. Equally, it is possible to get used to doing some things that are not possible in the "real" world, such as flying or moving rapidly or being able to manipulate virtual objects. Yet in this case we could equally ask: why should people walk at all in situations when flying is more convenient? Going through objects or through other people is an interesting case here: in some cases it is easy, but in others it is awkward (this will be described further in Chapter 4).

There are similarly mixed findings in relation to avatar appearance compared with offline interactions: on the one hand, people want to be able to influence their avatar's appearance (Cheng, Farnham, and Stone 2002; Vasalou, Joinson, Banziger, Goldie, and Pitt 2008); on the other hand, some users seem to pay little attention to it—as one long-term user put it (Schroeder and Axelsson 2001), "it's just graphics." Finally, one question that has not been addressed so far at all in research, and where short-term experimental trials and studies of long-term interaction in online MUVEs for socializing could complement each other, would be: Which is more important for presence—realism of the other participants—or that of the scene? Both might have an important bearing on presence and copresence, but it would be interesting to know which is more powerful when—also for the design of VEs.

As can be seen, much remains to be done to extend and integrate the various findings about interaction in MUVEs. One point to note is that the two types of findings (small groups in immersive settings versus large populations in online worlds) have developed mostly in isolation from each other. Yet it be can envisaged that the features of long-term social behavior within VEs will affect the types of technologies currently used for short-term tasks, just as that the developments at the "high end" of immersive technology development will eventually affect longer-term socializing in online worlds. We will return to this in the concluding Chapter.

From Short-term Experiments to Long-term Relations

In the meantime, it is worth summarizing the different foci of study of the two most common types of systems and uses. Studies of short-term interaction (regardless of system) tend to concentrate on:

- Presence and copresence
- Mutual awareness and common focus of attention
- Collaborative task performance

Here the analysis of copresence and social interaction will in *any* case be closely tied to the specific purpose of the session, with all else being left to one side. For longer-term interaction in online worlds, on the other hand, the features that are typically analyzed are:

- Preference for avatar appearance and measures of how avatars interact on a large scale
- Identifying the social rules or conventions that apply
- Forms of governance of the world and patterns of behavior in online games or social spaces

These features relate to the online world, but there are also studies that relate uses of online spaces and games to the offline characteristics or demographics of users (Williams, Yee, and Caplan 2008).

Putting the two side-by-side allows us to notice several things: The first is that the social "role" of the participant is not important for short-term trials but rather is taken for granted: when participants interact briefly in an experimental situation, the question of whether the participants adopt certain roles or identities vis-à-vis coparticipants is "bracketed," even though the participants will feel compelled to follow the social conventions of particular roles (for example, to be a leader in a collaboration). This "role" that participants establish in relation to each other is of course critical to longer-term online interaction in online worlds, because the establishment of an avatar's personality or character and how this is expressed, for example, in the avatar's appearance is critical to the long-term interaction of people.

Conversely, for longer-term interaction in online worlds, participants will take "immersiveness" and task performance in terms of what they can do in the system "for granted." In these studies, the concern is not with immersiveness in the environment but rather with how partici-pants become immersed in the social conventions and acclimatized in dif-ferent social settings within the environment. Researchers in this case will look not so much at individual interactions one at a time or step-by-step (although there are some studies that take this approach; see Antonijevic 2008), as they do in studies of short-term tasks in immersive MUVEs.

In what follows, connections will be made between the two types of studies and their findings. Yet even with this broader scope than studies of the two individual areas, we can still see that the range of phenomena under investigation and that actually occur in MUVEs is quite narrow. The main features can now be summarized as follows: The absence of smell, taste, and touch is not necessarily something that is greatly "missed" in MUVEs. The exception is touch or collision detection, which will affect copresence and interacting with others in important ways, although what can be "imported" from real settings in terms of visual touch and how the conventions of visual touch are applied in virtual settings—whether avatars can go through things or other avatars or not and how objects can be manipulated—depend on the type of interaction.

As for the aural or audible part of the world, it would be nice to be able to make the assumption that good audio quality is sufficient to enable fluid interaction. Yet trials show that this assumption should *not* in fact be made—because poor audio is often the single-most important obstacle to fluid shared interaction and there continue to be debates over the best form of voice or text communication in online worlds (it can be mentioned that audio quality is also a key issue in videoconferencing—and we will return to this). Still, the obstacles to technical improvements in this case are not great, and in any case there is much more scope for rapid improvement than in relation to the visual environment (although it can also be mentioned that this is not just a technical issue; in the physical world, we are highly attuned to the direction of sound, which is difficult to recreate in a MUVE).

If we *could* assume that audio is as good as in a real setting or as in a telephone conversation, then (apart from audio as part of the atmosphere of the VE) we would be able to leave audio to one side as a question for research into behavior in MUVEs because voice communication is sim-ilar to offline communication—as long as we keep in mind the effect of having a voice attached to an avatar as opposed to a real body. The issues around the use of 3D sound (or spatial audio) have not been extensively investigated (but see Cohen and Wenzel 1995). For social interaction in VEs, we will need in any case to pay particular attention to how the voice(s) belong to avatars because audio can be implemented in different ways (including as spatial 3D audio).

If we had perfect audio *and* could leave the *modality* of communication to one side (text versus voice), then it would be possible to focus entirely on how the visual environment, including avatar appearance, affects the interaction. This is therefore an appropriate focus for research on the most common VEs because the visual environment is the largest part of what participants concentrate on. The key question thus becomes: How does the visual environment (including avatar appearance) and visual nonverbal communication influence being there together? This question, which will be tackled in Chapter 3, will entail comparing the visual conditions for interaction with those that apply to real face-to-face encounters.

Hence, to summarize again, we can see that there is a limited range of activities and environments in immersive MUVEs and in online worlds by comparison with real-world social interaction. Yet this will not be the only comparison: we will also need to compare interaction in MUVEs with other forms of mediated communication, and in the conclusion I will argue that this comparison is more important in certain respects than the comparison with face-to-face interaction or with real-world encounters and populations. At the same time, despite the narrow range of activities and settings, we have seen that being there together is complex, and the reason is that this a multidimensional phenomenon. If we think back to some of the examples that have been discussed—collaborating on a Rubik's Cube–type puzzle, being able to build something together in an online environment, rehearsing acting together—the differences are perhaps shaped more by *what* you are doing and *doing together* than by the experience of being *there* together—or being there *together*.

Before moving on, it will be useful to elaborate this point: Copresence is interesting to measure in relation to presence—how do they vary with each other? Apart from the relationship between the two, the usefulness of measuring copresence is unclear. Copresence is influenced by a number of factors, including how the level of immersiveness affects interacting with others (or the social relations between people), how habituated to the VE people are, how many participants there are, and what they are jointly aware of. Yet two examples can suffice to illustrate how difficult it is to separate copresence in the sense of coimmersiveness—from copresence in the sense of doing things together. First, when doing the Rubik's Cube–type puzzle in networked IPTs, we observed how several pairs of collaborators tried to shake hands together after successfully completing the task! (In other words, via a kind of visual or pseudo touch.) How best to understand copresence in this case: Is it because of a joint sense of achievement that participants try to shake hands? Or is it because they have become used to picking up cubes together, and are therefore used to following the conventions of working on a manual task in relation to visual blocks? Here is a second example: In a different trial in the same networked IPT setting, after spending more than two hours collaborating in various environments, it could be observed that participants would still continually lean toward their partner in order to hear him or her better, despite the fact that there was no 3D audio! I did this when experiencing this environment—much to my embarrassment when it was pointed out to me. Again, in terms of copresence, we could ask in this case: Would this kind of behavior stop after many lengthy sessions and one became more used to the fact that leaning is pointless? But if not after more than two hours, when? And how does this leaning toward each other affect copresence?

These findings already have (nonobvious) design implications: Would it be better to have audio in which leaning to hear each other better could be avoided altogether (for example, by giving participants earphones, which is technically straightforward and could improve audio but may be awkward for users to adjust to), or is it better to produce an environment in which "leaning to hear each other better" is as realistic as possible with a 3D audio environment (technically difficult, and it may be even more difficult for participants to adjust to in a VE setting, but this could provide a more natural context for social interaction)? Many other such examples could be given—yet the point again is that copresence is more about what participants *do together* rather than simply being aware of each other's presence.

These examples also point to the novelty aspect of MUVEs. As we become used to using highly immersive MUVEs more extensively, it will become more apparent—once the novelty of the situation "wears off"—what social or interpersonal conventions apply in these environments and what type of technology best supports these conventions. (Again, it can be mentioned that much the same applies to videoconferencing, as when people comment "after a while, we forgot that the technology was there.") Similarly, in online MUVEs for socializing, once the novelty wears off, the focus will be more on interpersonal relations per se and the constraints and possibilities of interacting with others and shaping online worlds. Thus the limitations—but also the possibilities—of MUVEs will crystallize: to what extent do others and objects need to be treated like real people and objects (avatar appearance, property relations, joint manipulation of objects, being able to pass through people and objects, the applicability of real-world conventions, and the like)?

The Phenomenology of Experiences in MUVEs

Against this backdrop of the narrowness of the range of experiences in MUVEs, it will be useful—before we move on to discuss various aspects in greater detail—to zero in on the experience of MUVEs in a different sense; namely, what do users of MUVEs actually encounter inside the VE? This focus on what is experienced in MUVEs is important for two reasons: one is to highlight again that there is a limited range in terms of what the user experiences, and the second is that (as we shall see later) the user has limited attention resources in terms of what to focus *on*. For these reasons, it will be useful to catalogue experiences in MUVEs from a phenomenological perspective.

It needs to be pointed out before we do so that phenomenology is not meant in the sense of a particular epistemology but rather an attempt to present phenomena in their "raw" form, capturing the user's experiences as they appear to him or her. This is a phenomenological approach insofar as it tries to capture the user's experience without letting the observer's categories get in the way. (This is a problematical notion, but as long as the problem is borne in mind, not an insuperable one.) Phenomenology is also sometimes associated with a social interactionist perspective, which puts the emphasis on the *meaning* that the experience has for the user, or an approach that makes this meaning "strange" or that concentrates on the micro level of individual actions and encounters rather than the level of groups and longer-term relationships (for a syn-thetic approach to micro-analysis of communication, see Bull 2002).

The point here is to use phenomenology in a broader sense, which is to catalogue the phenomena that the user encounters. If we examine the focus of the user's attention in VEs, we see that this focus has a limited range of things that it can be devoted *to* in VEs. A key concept that can be used here is "focus of attention," derived from Goffman (1959; see also Collins 2004; Turner 2002; psychologists have a similar concept, "atten-tion allocation"; see Klimmt and Vorderer 2003), In social interactions in face-to-face settings, this refers to the amount of things that can be focused on at any one time, given that attention is limited. The focus of attention can therefore be seen as a stream of experiences whereby the focus shifts constantly from one object of attention to another. Practitioners of phenomenological or social interactionist approaches often claim that it is not possible to generalize from particular contexts or that all phe-nomena are contextual.[10] Against this, it can be argued that there are patterns that commonly apply to social experiences—or at least to the types of experiences of VEs discussed here.

The Components of MUVE Experiences

Even though people's focus of attention is limited, they are very adept at managing this limitation and shifting their focus to cope with the ongoing stream of inputs, in VEs as in real life. Unlike in real life, however, the focus in MUVEs, as we have seen, is (1) very narrow in being focused on a few things and (2) constantly engaged because there is typically an ongoing reason for being in the VE. This point is worth highlighting: the difference between the experience of MUVEs and experiences in the physical world is that in the physical world, our focus of attention can be on other things—interiorized reflection, physical experiences of touch (for example, the discomfort of our seat), daydreaming while looking out the window, and the like. Obviously it is not possible to give an exhaus-tive account of our focus of attention in VEs—it is enough to notice that it is less varied than in the physical world. Second, in the physical world, our focus of attention may not be constantly or intensively engaged with various parts of the environment. This constant or intensive engagement is what may make MUVE experiences so tiring and seem longer than experiences in the physical world.

With this in mind, we can divide the experience in VEs into the following components: place (where?), task (doing what?),[11] and inter-personal interaction and communication (how engaged with others?). This is perhaps the most general classification of VE experiences, but only the last item applies specifically to *shared* VEs.

Place and Space

Whether one is surrounded by an immersive environment or engaged in a desktop environment, the focus of attention will continuously be engaged with the virtual place, either (1) automatically—one is pre-occupied with being in another place except for interruptions (a "break in presence"; see Slater and Steed 2000) or one has become so acclima-tized to the VE so that one temporarily "snaps out of it" and remembers that is one is simultaneously in a real physical environment or (2) the focus is taken off the environment and placed on the task or the other person(s), which supersedes the focus on place *without* disturbing it or (3) there is a conflict between these two foci such that the focus on place is interrupted (we will encounter some examples of such "tradeoffs" in Chapter 4).

The important point here is that the stream of inputs about place—or the focus on space (place and space have been used interchangeably here because, for the purpose of this argument, the focus on spatial objects entails a sense of place)—either occurs automatically or it is deliberately maintained, so that, except for the breaks or interruptions just mentioned, this is a continuous focus in VEs. A corollary is that a lot of attention is devoted to "repair"—not, as in real life, to maintaining the norms of what one expects from face-to-face interaction but rather to maintaining the norm that things are like a real place and avoiding that one's task and interpersonal interaction should interrupt this norm.

Task

We can limit tasks here for the moment to spatial tasks because these are the most common tasks in VEs—unless we regard communication as a task, but this is treated in the next section under interaction with others. With this limitation in mind, these spatial tasks demand constant and self-conscious attention. Tasks absorb attention because they involve either manipulating objects or monitoring the environment. This includes an awareness of where the body is in the environment, as well as an awareness of objects—which are both more focus-demanding in VEs than in real life (although arguably, perhaps this is a matter of becoming used to the VE: if one has a lot of experience in the VE, perhaps it is no more focus-demanding than in real life). This is where the intuitiveness of the interface and our ability to cope well with a stream of inputs are important: it is immediately easy to focus on a task in VEs, and yet at the same time this requires continuous conscious effort.

The explicit or highly conscious focus on a few things is one possible explanation why performing a spatial task—we can take the example of a Rubik's Cube–type puzzle that has already been mentioned—can be performed just as well in networked IPTs as in real life (Schroeder et al. 2001): heightened and more concentrated focus make up for the need to cope with a novel environment and therefore compensate for greater demands on the user's awareness in comparison with real life. Finally, navigation combines task with place, but again, a heightened awareness of the space that one locomotes through is both intuitive and more attention-demanding in VEs.

Interpersonal Interaction and Communication

Whenever VEs are shared with others, maintaining an awareness of the other(s) is also an ongoing and attention-demanding effort. A steady "holding the other in the visual and auditory field" is required and needs to be maintained—unlike in the physical world, where this activity is typically effortless. This is why if the other is not in one's field of vision, it is necessary to monitor whether they are copresent by means of an audio signal from them. Because we do not have the same kind of audio signals or peripheral awareness of physical bodies that we have in real life, the signals of copresence need to be more explicit. We know this because in MUVEs, silences need to be "repaired," lest they should be interpreted as an absence of the other(s) or lead to confusion about where they are or whether they are still there. This is particularly clear in an environment like OnLive Traveler (Becker and Mark 2002), an environment in which the main purpose is voice communication. We will encounter a number of other examples in the following chapters.

Awareness of the other person(s) is perhaps the most common problem in MUVEs for collaboration (Tromp, Steed, and Wilson 2003; see also Rittenbruch and McEwan 2007 for an overview of awareness research). The shift to focusing to another person is much more conscious than in real life because in the VE it is necessary to single out another person on whom one wants to concentrate and keep in focus—unlike in real life, where (again) we do this in a taken-for-granted manner, often via nonverbal communication by turning toward them. (This point also applies to shifting our attention from one person to another.)

If interaction with others involves more than communication—for example, in a shared spatial task—there is also more self-conscious movement of the self in relation to the other than in real life. This is partly because one needs to position oneself in relation to the other to be aware of them and partly because one does not want to cause embarrassment by walking through them or otherwise colliding awkwardly with them (however, this may change over time so that one no longer cares about this embarrassment after a while—again, we shall see examples later) and, finally, because one does not want to encroach on the other's space while at the same wanting to be in their field of awareness.

Changes over Time

So far, the focus of attention has been examined regardless of how it shifts over time. But in VEs, the focus also shifts as one becomes more familiar with the environment. There is likely to be a continuum of how one becomes acclimatized to VEs: short term, the initial few minutes when one experiences a novel place upon first entering the VE; medium term, when one gets used to what one needs to concentrate on; and long term, when one can ignore being in a different environment except for interruptions. However, this is a speculative way to understand acclimatization to the VE because we know little about this process.[12] Note, however, that *adaptation*, or "change over time," does not mean that presence and copresence weaken. Rather, it may be that the focus on— or awareness of—various dimensions of the experience weakens.

Nevertheless, an important difference between virtual and real in directing and allocating attention over time is that in real life, it is for the most part taken for granted how this is done. In VEs, there is a more deliberate process of doing this and hence also a deliberate focus on one input or another in a continuous stream. This deliberateness may become "less conscious" over time, and it is perhaps the key to adaptation to the VE.

Presence versus Staging the Self

This is a good point at which to take what may appear as a detour from presence, copresence, and the phenomenology of MUVE experiences, which is that there is a different way to interpret people's experiences—as role play, a perspective derived from Goffman and social interactionism.[13] This perspective applies particularly to VWs for socializing, but as we shall see, again, there are overlaps with immersive and collaborative VEs (and role-play also partly explains the difference between them, to be discussed shortly). From the point of view of role-play, when people interact as avatars, they are presenting themselves in the form of an idealized frontstage (as in the offline world). Frontstages can be seen, briefly, as the appearance that people try to convey to others of how they would like to come across. Unlike in the offline world, however, in MUVEs this impression management takes place via the avatar appearance and its behavior.

A number of points follow immediately: one is that there is a fundamental difference in how this presentation of self takes place between text- and voice-based forms of interaction. In text-based VWs, it is possible to craft a self based on self-description and a way with words, whereas in voice-based VWs, voice will dominate how one is perceived and will not leave as much scope for such self-crafting. It is for this reason that Walther's notion of hyperpersonal relationships (1996), discussed earlier, applies to text-based interactions but presumably less so to voice-based interaction.[14] Second, this concentration on the frontstage presentation of the self means that the backstage, which is where social actors can "drop" the frontstage performance and one can also reveal to others things that one would not want the audience of the frontstage to know, is, in the case of VE, so to speak, left behind in one's physical body sitting in front of the screen in the case of PC-based desktop VEs. This is why it is so important to create artificial backstages—such as the "whisper" function in Active Worlds or Second Life whereby avatars can hide their conversations from others. Another example might be spaces in the environment where one or more avatars can interact privately.

This leads to another point: one reason why avatars are often regarded as artificial is that they are situational identities—they are frontstages to which one's attention must be completely devoted while interacting with others in VWs. At the same time, they demand a kind of impression management that people are not aware of in their day-to-day face-to-face interaction—because they take day-to-day interaction for granted, while interacting in VWs may force them to reflect on the way they stage themselves.

We can take these ideas further if we see the environments in which these frontstages interact with each other as highly crafted stages. Take, for example, the difference between VWs like online games (such as World of Warcraft) and VWs for socializing (like Second Life). In the former, the world is highly themed so that people encounter each other as game characters, with buildings and landscapes designed to reinforce this impression. In Second Life, in contrast, most of the world has been created by users, and these environments are created to support the impression management of avatars. For example, many environments are recreations of real-world environments: Oxford and Harvard universities have recreated parts of their campuses because they are designed as learning environments, nightclubs are created for dancing together, shops are designed for retail, and the like. Or again, the houses that people build are designed such that they reflect the personality or in-world-adeptness of their avatar creators.

The notion of idealized frontstages also sheds light on why people most commonly want to appear neither as completely unlike their real-world appearances nor completely realistically: They want to appear in a somewhat idealized form, not unlike how we present ourselves in a number of other contexts such as social networking sites, résumés, and family photograph albums. The difference in the context of VWs is that people are possibly more keenly aware of how much is invested in their frontstage appearance and why real-world gatherings of people who have so far encountered each other only as avatars have a special poignancy.

Finally, these idealized frontstages help to clarify the similarity and difference between immersive VEs and VWs: in VWs, people also experience presence and copresence. And in immersive VEs, they also engage in presenting a frontstage in the form of their avatar. In immersive VEs, however, there is at once less of a possibility of managing one's frontstage—after all, one's full-size tracked avatar *is* one's self-presentation vis-à-vis the other—and even more reliance on this avatar for self-presentation (which is evident from the fact that one has no backstage to return to!).[15] In desktop VWs, in contrast, one experiences being immersed in one's character or one's managed frontstage self, while at the same time having a distance from it—after all, one still has the backstage "real" self behind the screen. This may also explain why people sometimes prefer to have a bird's-eye or camera view of themselves in VWs (rather than a first-person view), which gives them a perspective on how they are staging themselves, while this would not make sense in immersive VEs.

It can be added here that this is also where videoconferences differ fundamentally from both types of VEs: videoconferences, too, represent a staged self-presentation (people adopt certain poses, exaggerate gestures, and the like), but they are not idealized ones in the sense that they cannot be shaped as much as avatars. Nevertheless, users are highly aware of or self-conscious about how others are seeing them because a videoconference "meeting" is a highly staged event (and this is literally so in the case of videoconferences that include a picture of how the user appears, called "picture in picture"—a feature whose main function is to allow the user to worry less about how he or she is appearing to others on the screen).

This notion of an idealized or a managed frontstage can also be applied to copresence—or the Meadean "me" (after the sociologist Mead, who theorized that how we see ourselves depends on our view of how others see us). For example, the reason why people sometimes go through each other and sometimes do not perhaps depend on whether they "inhabit" their frontstages vis-à-vis others. The same applies to trust in long-term relationships in VWs: to what extent do people think that the idealized frontstages of the avatars that they have come to know do *not* so much represent the real-world selves of their owners but are frontstages that they can expect to behave as they have come to expect them to behave? In both cases, the extent to which frontstages should be respected cannot be seen purely from the point of one's own avatar. Instead, the sense of one's own frontstage self has been shaped by interaction with others, and what one thinks they expect from one's frontstage self—whether they expect you to go through them, for example, or whether they expect you to be trustworthy—and vice versa, and so on in a constant chain of interaction; in this case, in a virtual rather than a face-to-face physical environment.

In short, VEs, like face-to-face interaction, are based on complex role-play. This, incidentally, is not so much to do with identifying with one's online self or with creating an alternative identity; rather, it is situational. It is doubtful, for example, that people identify offline with the online persona or the presentation of themselves that they use online. But when they adopt the perspective of their avatar, they stage themselves as they wish to be seen by other avatars and in relation to how they think other avatars have come to see them.

Presence and copresence can thus be understood in relation to this staging of the self. The notion of presence as it has been discussed so far is related to VE technology and can be measured as a psychological or psychophysiological state. Equally, however, it could interpreted by the observer, and experienced by the user, as a state in which the user finds himself or herself as staging themselves in another place, which is also a product of the technology but which is difficult to gauge as a psychological or physical state. This other place for presenting one's frontstage can nevertheless be accurately described as a stage other than that which one is physically in; again, with all the consequences for copresence that follow: that is, that the avatar(s) that one interacts with are also present and that one interacts with them on—this stage.

Seen in this way, we can again distinguish the two types of environments: for desktop online VWs, experiencing a sense of place requires that one experiences the staged self as one that is navigating around in a place, a kind of "I am a camera" sensation.[16] In immersive VEs using an HMD, the experience of place is tied, for example, to looking down and seeing one's avatar body and seeing that one's movements affect the world, which is a way of feeling that one's staged self is a physical one (in the case of an immersive VE in an IPT system, of course, one looks down and sees one's own body). The same applies to copresence, which can be measured as a psychological state but equally as a state of experiencing others as "giving off a self" (again, using Goffman's drama-turgical language) or projecting a self—powerfully in terms of the phys-ical presence of another person in the case of an immersive VE (but only in relation to a few others) or powerfully in a social sense in an online VW where many others are presenting social selves of different stripes.

In terms of avatar appearance (to be discussed in Chapter 3), it is worth adding that although these are idealized *self*-projections, they are also highly dependent on the context—what *other* people appear like. In Second Life, for example, if one is among others who appear as outlandish-looking avatars, it could seem inappropriate to appear as a realistic-looking or very plain-looking avatar. Similarly, in an IPT envi-ronment with voice, there may be no choice about avatar appearance, so the idealized staging of the self needs to take place in terms of how one communicates via voice and describes oneself (if the interaction is between strangers who do not know each other offline) or what one "puts into" one's self-presentation in terms of how one collaborates. Again, this context dependence may seem to make the notion of ideal-ized self-staging seem too diffuse, but it should be remembered that all presentations of one's avatar self, including its communicative modality—make possible only certain types of self-presentations—and this includes the context of how *others* are presenting themselves. In MUVEs for socializing and gaming, this context is often playful and thus allows much scope. And in MUVEs for collaboration, not much attention may be paid to appearance, especially in the case of a spatial task where the bulk of attention is on the objects that are being jointly manipulated or visual-ized. Finally, in videoconferences, there is no possibility to depart from one's real appearance (although participants may be worried about what is going on off-camera).

The Phenomenology of MUVE Experiences in Context

At this point we can put MUVEs into the context of other media and return to the notion of presence and where the user concentrates his or her focus of attention. Klimmt and Vorderer (2003), for example, discuss entertainment media such as computer games and suspenseful films in terms of presence. And Ijsselsteijn (2003) places VR in the history of presence media, including various forms of screen entertainment. The difference between VEs and these other media, however, is that even if there is a first-person perspective on the environment, the focus of attention is absorbed by the events onscreen—as a spectator. This is similar with role-playing or videogames, where the attention is "drawn into" or devoted to prespecified events (goals, prompts for action) and these are responded to—rather than issuing from—the user.

Put differently, other media such as those described by Klimmt and Vorderer and by Ijsselsteijn also demand a constant focus of attention, but the attention is determined by the narrative; it is not self-initiated. This position will be contentious from the point of view that the extent to which the user controls the interaction will depend on the definition of interaction (online games, for example, have a high degree of interaction). Note, however, that there can be a high degree of presence with a low degree of interaction and vice versa in these other media. VEs, by their very definition, always provide both. This point is amenable to testing, and a possible hypothesis (discussed in another context earlier) is that the more interaction that issues from the user, the greater is the self-reported degree of presence. An easy way to recognize the difference between MUVEs and other media, however, is to imagine asking the user about presence and copresence if no self-initiated action or interaction has taken place in the VE—while this makes sense for other media, in the case of a VR system, asking this question is meaningless! This brings us back to the flow of the focus of attention in MUVEs and the need to maintain this flow in the light of the ongoing engagement with the environment.

The Structures of MUVE Experiences

With these components of the MUVE experience in place, it becomes possible to ask what they add up to. This could be labeled a phenomenological-*structural* approach, whereby all the components are related to each other and the interrelationships or structure of the stream of inputs is identified. Again, this is possible because the three components (place, task, other) plus their development over time provide one way to describe the vast majority of activities or experiences in MUVEs. The chapters that follow will focus on these main activities and experiences in more detail. Yet we have already seen how these experiences (from a phenomeno- logical point of view) fit into two types of dominant-use settings, and we also now have a sense of how the complex norms that govern the interaction within smaller and larger groups emerge. Again, however, the point of an exhaustive cataloguing is to highlight that interaction in MUVEs is not endlessly complicated in practice: even if we will not be able to tie all the structural elements into a single whole, at least it will be possible to bring them into a manageable frame for making sense of interaction in MUVEs.

At this stage, one implication of what has been said can be spelled out already because it will help us to think about interaction in the chap- ters that follow; namely, that it may be just as useful to think about what shapes the focus of attention in MUVEs as it is to think about realism and presence or copresence (which are discussed much more frequently). For example:

- Apart from the (dominant) visual environment plus the auditory signal from others who share the VE (partly because of the need maintain awareness of others), what kind of additional information, if *any*, will aid the user? Is this additional information distracting or superfluous for most MUVE applications?
- There will often be a tradeoff between attention devoted to place, to task/activity, and to the other person(s): more of one will not neces- sarily mean less of the other, but it may be necessary to balance them, or to put them in sequence, to avoid the user becoming disoriented or having an overload of information. Another possibility is that infor- mation lacking in one sensory modality may be presented in the form of another—for example, putting false but "natural" visual cues (for example, a "snapping" together of objects) in the place of auditory ones and thus creating an "illusion" of hearing touch without loss of presence. Such "false" cues may balance or enhance the focus of attention.
- Are there ways to overcome some of the problems that users face in VEs as opposed to real life? For example, could the "silences" that disorient the user about the presence of others be overcome by means of visual signals (for example, a warm glow of the avatar means they

are present, or a ghostly avatar means they have temporarily left)? Or can awareness of one's avatar be enhanced by showing the user a "mirror" of their own facial expression (Slater and Steed 2002)? Or, to take another example, is it possible to improve the distinguishability of objects by "unrealistic" means (vivid colors, highlighting of objects, semitransparent objects to avoid occlusion)?

These and other suggestions may or may not enhance presence and copresence, but they *may* make the environment more friendly in regard to the "focus of attention" or enhance "situation awareness," even if they are not "realistic." It can be noted that some of these improvements have been put forward for other reasons (such as usability), but it is also important to keep in mind that some of these "unrealistic" means of supporting people's focus in MUVEs may add complexity and may therefore be distracting. In short, the study of MUVEs has been preoccupied with being there and being there together—but improvements in MUVEs that afford being there together could also be made by concentrating on the possibilities and limits of the focus of attention instead. This may lead to tools that are not realistic but that do not detract from the other foci that the user is experiencing. This aspect is often ignored in the design of VEs.

In relation to presence and copresence, the components of MUVE experience raise several additional questions:

- Under what conditions will a mismatch in the focus of attention between the three components diminish presence and copresence? And, conversely, when is the user oblivious to such a mismatch?
- Under what conditions will the disruption to the flow of the focus of attention by forces outside the VE (noisy distractions) diminish presence or copresence?
- More generally, how can the flow of the focus on the three components (place, task, interaction with others) be structured over the course of the experience so as to maximize and maintain presence, copresence, task effectiveness, and enjoyment?

Put negatively: it might be argued that MUVEs are intuitive interfaces (which goes somewhat against the idea put forward here that MUVEs are highly attention-demanding and constrained by a limited focus of attention), and many points made here—about maximizing presence and copresence in view of the flow of the focus of attention, the need to get used to VEs, or the need to devote special attention to certain features unlike in real life—will disappear with more powerful systems and when we have become used to them. This objection overlooks that (1) there are technological limits to these systems, (2) there are limits to our sensory apparatus and to how our focus of attention can be distributed, and (3) the solution to build more powerful and complex systems may be less useful than designing tools that we can handle easily in terms of the phenomenological flow of our stream of inputs and activities.

Summary

We have seen that the range of experiences is quite narrow, with the visual part of the environment and how the user focuses attention on this environment—including the appearance of others—playing a central role.[17] As we shall see, while interaction in MUVEs is developing in many different directions, MUVE researchers are in the enviable position that there is a valuable research goal no matter how the technology develops in the future: how being there and interacting with others works in various devices for being there together. The differences from face-to-face interaction will continue to be a research question because being there and interacting with virtual others will always in certain respects be unlike interacting in real-world settings. So will the differences and similarities with other communications media, as these will compete with or complement MUVEs. The research agenda for MUVEs—what people do with each other and with objects within the environment, with what appearance and with what capabilities, and how these affect their effectiveness and enjoyment—is thus in a certain sense given.

NOTES

1. For criticisms of this view of new technologies, sometimes known as the social shaping or social constructivist approach, see Schroeder (2007a).

2. It is true that there are well-established VE system products rather than just prototypes. However, these tend to be for single-user VR system applications,

especially for training, rather than for multiuser applications. The exception here are military training applications, which involve many users, although I am not aware of studies that have been published about interaction in these environments or how they transfer to real-world skills in interacting with others.

3. A limitation of this book is that it does not discuss the various application areas such as therapy or education in any detail, although a number of references are provided. The focus of the book, however, is to pull together what we know about how people interact in VEs, and this topic (as opposed to usability of the systems for individual users) is rarely studied for these applications areas (some exceptions will be encountered later). It might seem that educational uses of MUVEs should be an exception here because there have been many efforts to use MUVEs for education. However, evaluations of the systems and lessons about how people interact in educational VEs are very rare (Wan-Ying Tay, a graduate student in the Department of Education at the University of Oxford, is currently pursuing research on this topic).

4. For an example of regular classroom uses, see Nesson and Nesson (2008).

5. Slater's thoughts about presence and its measurement have evolved, and there has been a lively debate about presence measurement (for a recent view, see Slater 2009). Many contributions on this topic can be found in the journal *Presence: Teleoperators and Virtual Environments.*

6. Some early and influential images represented either one or two VR users with their five senses immersed in the environment (see Biocca and Delaney 1995; Steuer 1995). This was highly misleading. A more accurate representation in terms of existing and foreseeable systems would put two or more users into an audiovisual space, navigating and picking up (visual) objects. In other words, there were too many senses and not enough emphasis on the representation of the environment (including the other users).

7. Position-sensing interfaces or body input has been far less developed commercially than other technologies but has recently become popular in the form of the Wii game (http://wii.com/). With the development of a way of connecting this game to VWs such as Second Life (Au 2008: 224), this way of linking users by means of "visual touch" could become widespread.

8. In relation to how sensory experience affects presence and copresence, it can be mentioned that when several sensory modalities are used in social VEs, they will have different weights attached to them. Sallnas mentions (2004: 49) that philosophers, psychologists, and people in general generally regard "touch" (or haptics) as the "reality sense," partly because it is more difficult to fool than, say, vision. She also points out that "in the use of haptic interfaces, touch is usually active rather than passive" (2004: 51). Yet she also finds that voice is more important for social presence than haptics (2004: 80). Indeed, her own and other studies show that when haptics is added to a visual-only condition, presence and social presence are increased, but that when haptics is added to a visual and

audio condition, there is no effect on social presence, which, as Sallnas puts it, means that the effect of audio "overshadows" the effect of haptics (2004: 60). Perhaps haptics is a reality check for objects, whereas voice is the reality check for humans—or for interacting with people.

9. One study, for example, had participants walk on a plank across a deep virtual pit (Meehan, Insko, Whitton, and Brooks 2002) and measured their heart rate and found that this was indeed stressful for them.

10. The problem of not being able to generalize from micro-contexts of interaction in phenomenological or ethnomethodological studies of interaction is well known. The approach taken here is that this kind of "particularism" or relativism can be overcome, in line with Collins' (1988: 263–300) and Turner's (2002) ideas.

11. To "doing what," one might add, "doing it how well?" This will be discussed in Chapter 4.

12. There is research on short-term adaptation in cognitive ergonomics (see the discussion in Spante 2009), but this addresses narrower issues than adaptation to the VE over the longer term.

13. See the references in Note 10 for accounts of Goffman and social interactionism.

14. "Presumably" is used because this has not, to my knowledge, been investigated.

15. An interesting way to think about this point (which was made by a reviewer of the manuscript) is to think about how an immersed person would see himself or herself in a "virtual mirror," which exist in various VEs: a person using an HMD system would see the full-body avatar in the mirror, and presumably be much more surprised at his or her self-representation than would someone with a desktop system, who is used to "staging" himself or herself. A person in an immersive IPT system could be shown his or her real body *within* his or her own system but could also be represented as an avatar body in the mirror, in which case, again, the fact that the person was "staging" himself or herself in the form of a full-body would come as a surprise to that person.

16. I have described the environment as an "I am a camera world" (Schroeder 1996: 109, 111) in the case of an immersive technology that allowed the user to fly through the world.

17. A reviewer of the manuscript helpfully pointed out that "narrow" is perhaps the wrong word: "narrow" applies, foremost, to the elements of analysis of interaction involved, which are currently narrow in the sense that interaction is often limited to certain tasks or forms of socializing, and to the visual and auditory experience. "Less varied" or "less rich" could be another way to put it.

3

Avatar Bodies and Virtual Spaces

Now that we have a sense of the technology and the experiences it provides, it is time to turn to the content of multiuser virtual environments (MUVEs): How do the spaces of VEs and the appearance of avatars, especially faces, shape social interaction within these environments? As has been mentioned, the realism of avatars and spaces is a key factor in the experience of being there and of being there together. At the same time, it has often been pointed out that the focus in technology development on realism is misleading: an abstract or fantastical space, for example, can afford a sense of being there in another place, just as a cartoon-like avatar with realistic behaviors can make for a powerful experience that someone is in the same environment with you. In any event, the visual landscape or built environment, and the extent to which nonverbal communication and interaction can take place with representations of users—these are the most distinctive components of MUVEs that set them apart from other technologies.[1] This chapter will therefore provide an overview of the different forms that bodies and spaces take in MUVEs and how they affect interaction.

Virtual Spaces

We can begin with an inventory of the appearance of virtual environments (VEs) or virtual worlds (VWs).[2] The most common VEs consist of models of the real world, that is, recognizable landscapes and buildings and rooms, or representations of real-world objects to be manipulated, and the like. Online worlds, especially for socializing and gaming, typically also contain many fantastical elements. There are of course many worlds that have elements of both. The reason for mentioning these options is that if we add abstract models, then these—plus realistic and fantastical environments—exhaust the range of options, and it is therefore useful to think about the environments as lying within a certain range. It can also be mentioned that even though visual environments have just been divided into fantastical, abstract, and realistic environments, what is common to all of them is that the worlds need to be designed in such a way that we at least know how to get around in them. And finding your way around immediately raises another point about the appearance of worlds (see Chapter 8 for the social aspects of this issue) and which concerns the vast and interconnected nature of the environments: How do developers cope with connecting spaces or worlds within one system? How do users cope with spaces in which it is hard to know how far they extend, for example? Or how durable they are?

A final general point is necessary: The idea that it is in principle impossible to represent a visually realistic world can be rejected. The only limits here are the limits of human visual perception, and in this respect, it has been shown that a graphical display could be powerful enough to trick the eye into perceiving a three-dimensional (3D) image as being real (see the discussion in Schroeder 1996: 27–28). Furthermore, the possibility of creating visually realistic 3D environments has been improving rapidly. Many worlds, particularly landscapes for military training, for example, are highly detailed and realistic. On the other hand, many VWs are rather simple or cartoon-like, which is mainly due to the fact that it takes a lot of effort to create visually rich worlds. Again, there is a range, and it will be useful to explore how this impacts on the users and on how they interact. In any event, apart from realism, one theme that will need to be explored in this chapter is how various environments are designed to cope with users being able to find their way around in them and experience it as a space or world in which they can do things.

The Examples of Active Worlds and Second Life

How will VWs ultimately appear? Here we can think, apart from the examples we have already encountered, about the VWs depicted in science fiction. The answer is that they will appear partly like the real world, in providing enough world-likeness to enable users to orient themselves and carry on their activities (again, it needs to be borne in mind that this will often not require "realism"—users will be perfectly at ease in fantastical environments). Partly, these environments will be subject to the technical constraints and possibilities of the system and to the effort required to develop it. Apart from this, however, VWs are constrained only by the imagination of those who design and build them, which is why they are often regarded as amazing in terms of their creativity: at their best, people have used the technology to create attractive and interesting spaces. On the other hand, VEs are often disappointingly dull and unoriginal, and many consist of recreations of existing buildings and of details that serve no purpose in VWs (although they may, of course, be useful for orientation purposes).[3]

One way to get a sense of the appearance of the environment is at the hand of a concrete example: Active Worlds (AW). This VW can serve as good example for two reasons: it is one of the oldest online VWs for socializing, and it is one of the few worlds that users have been able to build almost entirely on their own and thus shape their own environment. In fact, although there are a number of other VWs where users have been actively involved in building and introducing features into the environment, AW users have contributed more extensively to building their own worlds than in any other VE for socializing—with the possible exception of Second Life (SL). Since SL has recently become more popular, however, it will be useful to make comparisons with SL at various points.

It should be pointed out immediately that everything that will be said about the AW environment—the characteristics of time and space, property, the manipulability and malleability of the world, and navigation—applies in some form to all shared VWs. The key difference between AW, which is primarily a text-chat world, and other MUVEs is that some MUVEs are designed with audio so that spaces need to be organized in such a way that, for example, people are within hearing distance of each other. This will have a number of other implications for the appearance of the environment, but these can be treated later in the context of communication (see Chapter 6).[4]

Some brief history and background will be useful: AW was one of the first public (free) online VWs for socializing, opening to the public in 1995.[5] The small company that developed and maintained AW had its ups and downs, like many small Internet start-ups. Still, AW had a steady number of users and also sold the software so that others could develop their own AW universes, such as for educational purposes. Note that separate universes immediately prompt a question that was mentioned briefly and that also applies to SL: Should a world or environment consist of a single interconnected space, or is it sometimes preferable to build an environment (or world, or universe) that is separate for various reasons, such as to restrict access to a certain population (children, for example, so that they are not exposed to "adult" content) or to ensure that only certain features go into the design of the world? One potential solution to avoid this choice can be mentioned straight away; which is to allow some kind of interconnection and transfer between worlds. A number of efforts in this direction have been under way to do this.[6]

To return to AW: The software has by now gone through a series of iterations.[7] Still, what has remained the same is that once users download the software onto their PC, they are free to explore the vast spaces. Here we can briefly note one way in which technical and social characteristics are interrelated, which has a profound impact on the nature of visual environment (the following is based on Schroeder, Huxor, and Smith 2001): AW is based on streaming technology, which means that once the software is installed on the user's PC, the new parts of the world that come into the user's field of view are seamlessly loaded onto their computer via the Internet.

This streaming technology is only one option. A different technology was used in the Blaxxun system, whereby whenever a user enters a new room, the whole room has to be downloaded to the user's machine. This option thus limits the size and complexity of the geography of the virtual space, although it has the advantage that not as much as information needs to be transferred as long as the user remains in one place. In short, there will always be tradeoffs involved in online VWs: how much of their content resides on each user's machine, and how much resides on a central server?

It can be seen that this is fundamental design decision, and the decision is not just about a technical tradeoff but also a social one about how much power the world's owner-developers have in VEs as opposed to users (we will return to this). The technical part involves how the content of the world or the space resides on each user's machine and how much of the world or space needs to be updated as the user moves around and interacts with it. In other words, this is a tradeoff between bandwidth and graphics rendering power. But the technical tradeoff is intertwined with a social one: How much can the world or space be changed by users? If other users build or change objects and if the world is not static, then these changes need to be seen and be available to all other users. The two sides are connected, and they also apply to immersive worlds. Furthermore, even with greater computer graphics power and more bandwidth, some element of a design decision remains about how much the users can interact with and modify the world depending on what part of the VE is on a central server or a local machine. Finally, it can be mentioned that part of the solution in SL has been to divide the world up into parcels (or sims), so that only certain spaces within a certain area are updated in this way. The size of the spaces, again, entails a tradeoff, in this case between the volume of space in which people can interact and what can fit into these spaces (see also Au 2008; Boellstorff 2008: esp. 89–117).[8]

With this we can return to AW. The first world on the AW server, AlphaWorld, was a flat plain larger than California in terms of an equivalent real-world space. Users then, as now, orient themselves by means of a Cartesian coordinate system, with ground zero at the center and the world measured out in meters from this point. Because users can fly, there is also a height dimension. Rendering in this case is based on the user's viewpoint, which gives them a view, set by default to 60 meters, of objects up to 60 meters away. If the user has a faster or slower connection or computer, they can set this range of view farther or closer.

The entry point to AW provides signposts for first-time users about where they can go next. The same applies to SL: Orientation Island, the place where one enters SL, provides a user guide and information about the features of the online world. Interestingly, these places of entry do not provide a guide to social norms (even though it has been thought that it might be useful to do so; Boellstorff 2008: 123). Again, this sets online worlds apart from gaming, where users will have an introduction—by means of a trailer movie with the back story of the game and other introductions to the rules—about their roles and the aims of the game.

Apart from the geographical layout, AW divided its users into monthly fee-paying citizens and non–fee-paying tourist categories (in 1997) and moved later to allow tourists only on a short-term basis. Again, this has been a standard feature of online worlds, including SL, where fee-paying users are allowed more privileges than those who do not pay fees. (There are also completely free worlds such as OnLive Traveler, whereas others, especially online games, only allow fee-paying users except for brief trial periods.) Up until that time, tourists as well as citizens could build in the world, although tourists were restricted to certain areas. Still, this was a unique feature of AW—that users could lay claim to ground, usually by putting down areas of grass and placing objects on them, which could then not be deleted or moved by other users. This feature was unique in comparison to other VWs at the time, such as Blaxxun and OnLive Traveler, though in the Habitat system, for example, people could decorate their rooms by buying objects for it. Boellstorff (2008: 96–97) says that less than 1% of things in SL have been produced by Linden Lab, the creators of SL; the rest has been built by users.[9] In any event, the process of claiming land and building was rather simple, a process of marking an object and copying (or cloning) it and giving it certain "object properties" (Figure 3.1).

An interesting development that raised some issues around virtual property was that at one point, some users began to use software called *RoboBuilder*, which was designed to claim land automatically. This enabled

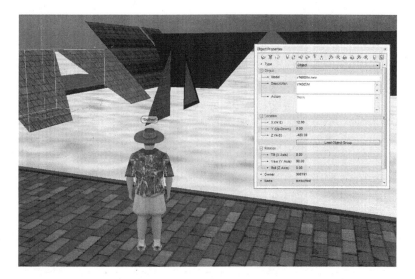

FIGURE 3.1   Building in ActiveWorlds. (Image courtesy of Andy Hudson-Smith.)

users to occupy large amounts of space, and as a result the use of such tools was banned in AW. (SL similarly had to outlaw "copybots"; see Au 2008: 133; Boellstorff 2008: 214). This highlights a key issue relating to property, which is that even though in principle land is "endless," in practice, restrictions need to be imposed so that people do not produce endless *private* spaces. Other issues include the balance between premade objects and the extent to which they can be modified, the persistence of objects, how the rights to objects and land can be transferred, how to deal with aggressive moves to control land or property, and similar issues.

Regarding property and building rights, AW maintained the policy of allowing anyone to build in certain areas and restricting building and ownership to citizens in other areas. What property rights ultimately amounted to in AW is unclear: what if the company experienced technical difficulty or went bankrupt and had to shut down the servers? (Again, parallels could be made here with other online spaces where people keep digital content, such as photo-sharing sites or shared document spaces.) Still, in VWs, there are also ways to counteract this possibility—if AW disappeared, the creations might be saved in another place, and if the AW universe broke down, other universes might survive or take its place.

Similar questions surrounding property have arisen in SL. The notion of property in SL is reinforced by the fact that if you own a place, it is possible to exclude others from it ("ban lines"), but these are rarely used, reflecting the widely held belief that SL is a shared world (see Boellstorff 2008: 95–96). Some "islands," on the other hand, require registration to enter (such as Oxford University's island in SL). Another common way to preserve some exclusivity is to use "sky builds": having places high up at "cloud level" to stay out of sight.

A separate issue concerns the extent to which objects can be imported into and exported from AW. This includes the question of whether objects designed in another software program can be brought into AW. There are some examples of such programs (see Hudson-Smith 2002 for an early example), and again, this is a wider issue for all VWs, which partly concerns software standards and compatibility and partly concerns ownership of objects (and copyrighted material) and of space in the world.[10] As an aside it can be mentioned that it has been very popular to display personal photographs, which are imported, in galleries and homes in AW and in other worlds.

Another interesting issue, this time in relation to transportation, that caused controversy early in the development of AW concerned how one should travel through the world. The issue was fundamentally over whether one should be able to teleport, either by typing in coordinates or by going into teleportation stations that take you directly to another place. This method of travel was opposed by some AW users, and the discussion was partly influenced by the science fiction novel *Snow Crash* by Neal Stephenson (1992), in which teleporting is not possible because this would undermine the realism of the VW. For example, it could be disconcerting to have people materializing out of nowhere next to you (Stephenson 1992: 42), and similarly one might not get a realistic sense of place if one could go directly to certain places without having to get there via others. In AW, the issue was resolved in favor of teleportation, although in different worlds of AW, owners still have the possibility to disable teleportation.

The travel and transportation issue has been handled differently in different systems. Some systems have teleportation or similar metaphors—clicking on links, taking a virtual vehicle, typing in coordinates or place names related to maps, and the like. As in AW, the geographical environment in SL is shaped by the flying and teleporting capabilities (Boellstorff 2008: 95). SL also used to have telehubs (places you could go to transport from one place to the other), but it has adopted the more common mode of avatars teleporting from one place to another (by typing in the geographical coordinates of the place you want to go to). This is perhaps the clearest instance where different technological capabilities directly shape what users can do or how they experience the environment.

A different constraint exists in games[1] such as World of Warcraft, where a player may have to earn game points to be able to use faster modes of transport such as airships. This is one of the areas where VWs are very flexible and there are many options, although in the case of gaming, again, the constraints relate to the rules of the game. At the same time, there are tradeoffs for each option, and because the VWs need to be consistent, it is not possible to leave the choice to be made from one moment to the next. As for how the environment shapes navigation, apart from the "faux" transportation systems of virtual vehicles and the like, in PC-based environments like AW there is a tendency to stand immobile in small groups unless one is exploring. And in AW and SL, it is possible to fly, and this is useful for getting to places quickly, obtaining an overview, and avoiding distraction on the ground level. (Flying is also possible in some immersive VEs, but this also highlights a contrast between VWs with onscreen avatars, where it is easy to fly, versus having a full-size and tracked body in immersive VEs, which makes this form of navigation more unnerving!)

"Teleportation" might seem "cheating" in a place like AW or elsewhere, but it could also be an efficient way to travel to a target in an application or a VE where this is a key task. Still, as Börner and Penumarthy point out, "real world cities are approached from their periphery, on roads with signs displaying the names of the city, nearby cities, major interstates, etc.; VWs are entered at their center. Hence visiting a new 3D VW is comparable with being blindfolded, driven (here teleported), and dropped off in the middle of an unknown city. The resulting "lost in space" effect is amplified by the fact that users are typically unaware of the size and layout of a world, existing interaction possibilities, or major places to go" (2003: 188). This applies not only to cities or to VWs but also to entering many VEs that are not overviewable, with their absence of doors or entryways.

Apart from space, users in VWs like AW from around the world need to be able to orient themselves to a common time-frame. In AW, time has been set as Greenwich Mean Time minus two hours, named Active Worlds Standard Time (AWST) or Virtual Reality Time (VRT). In a similar way, in SL, the standard is pegged to the U.S. Pacific time zone. This has no doubt been a useful convention in AW, for example in planning meetings, although it is not clear how much people make use of this. For example, in first encounters, participants from different parts of the world will often enquire about what the (real, offline) time is for the others. If we consider "time" more broadly, as historical change, AW undergoes quite rapid changes—for example, areas have been built up and then left abandoned quite quickly, or their popularity rises and declines quickly.

From Geographies to Social Patterns

Apart from the geographical and physical features of AW, it is important to identify different social milieus. So, for example, certain places have a more suburban feel—separate houses where users visit each other— or the feel of a busy urban center with many shops and services and many avatars. Others have the feel of a natural wilderness or of vast empty spaces. These social atmospheres can also be linked to different landscapes. For example, a world like "Patagonia," with its beaches and thatched huts, has fostered a "relaxed" or "party-like" ambience, unlike the "seedy" and futuristic "nightlife-in-the-big-city" appearance of "Metatropolis," which has often been a place for deviant or aggressive behavior.[11] There are also different "national" atmospheres in the worlds associated with particular languages or states, and in this case certain features of the landscape or the built environment—clichéd national monuments or styles—reflect the national culture and may reinforce the users' sense of being "at home" in certain parts of their world.

Apart from milieus in the sense that different areas in AW have a particular atmosphere, there have also been attempts to create distinctive "communities." Sherwood was one such and had several interesting features: One was the utopian aim of the community. Sherwood was created to "craft a community space for the purposes of beauty, function, and personal expression" (Damer 1998: 142). People had to apply to enter and build in an area set apart by a wall, and within this area an attempt was made to develop an environment where certain commonly espoused rules were to be followed and a particular style of building was to be shared. The Sherwood community developed quickly, with many features of a real-world community (newspaper, help patrols, public buildings, and the like). There were, nevertheless, problems with vandalism and verbal abuse. Still, the idea that new communities with their own rules could be established in VWs or in parts of VWs has been a common theme in AW and SL.

In AW, it is interesting to notice that the way in which areas have become built up has followed several real-world patterns: development from a center outward, clustering of buildings in certain areas, and the emergence of different themes or styles in different places. Some central spaces, especially ground zero in the most well-developed area of AWs central world AlphaWorld, looked from above like a city, in contrast to Sherwood, which looked more like a mixture of suburbia and a modern-day attempt at a medieval village. The other link to make here is to science fiction, because many VWs have taken inspiration from science fiction novels and films. A good example is the Metatropolis world in AW, which looked a lot like the science fiction film *Bladerunner* (1982), which was in turn inspired by the architecture in the early German science fiction film *Metropolis* (1927). Other non–science fiction themes include the architectural styles of different parts of the world, such as recreations of iconic real-world monuments and landscaped gardens.

It can also be mentioned that many features of the built environment in AW—kitchens and toilets in houses or streetlamps and road markings on streets—are not functional but are for display or to provide a real world–like atmosphere. Compare this with the Sims Online (which shut down in 2007; but see Steen, Davies, Tynes, and Greenfield 2006), an online VW where some of these features like kitchens and toilets were included as part of a game-like narrative or for the purpose of engaging users in role-play activities. Again, this a good place to recall that the features of AW apply to all kinds of different virtual spaces, including immersive ones: in many immersive spaces such as architectural walk-throughs and even models for scientific visualization (for example, molecular visualization), there will be many elements of the visual environment that are not functional or that provide functions unlike in the physical world (for example, markers to indicate a "background" horizon to support orientation in models for molecular visualization).

If we return to the appearance of online worlds, a key feature that distinguishes the different types of worlds is how they implement the maintenance and creation of rules within the environments. This feature applies to all online VWs, such as SL, Sims Online, There, and games like World of Warcraft—which vary in that the rules are in some cases more and in others less dictated by the developers. There is thus a continuum from rules and environments shaped by users to rules and environments that are shaped by developers, and all VWs have a mixture of the two. VW environments also share, however, that there is a lot of idealism about the kind of social and geographical environment that can or should be created, as well as a sense that this idealism has to be compromised in practice. The example of Sherwood in AW was given earlier, but there are others in SL (see Au 2008; Boellstorff 2008). The parallels with real-world "alternative" or "pioneer" communities come to mind here (and are discussed in Schroeder, Huxor, and Smith 2001).

A related leitmotif governing VWs is the frontier mentality. Some areas and buildings in AW look like log cabins in remote woods, an image that is somewhat at odds with the futuristic science fiction aesthetic just mentioned and with the high-tech appeal of VWs more generally. But there is also an elective affinity between this frontier mentality and VWs, although perhaps this applied especially to the Internet boom years (late 1990s through 2001), when all Internet-related opportunities seemed to be associated with a gold rush mentality (see also Turner 2006: 207–262). Yet even now, worlds like SL are still regarded as lands of opportunity. VWs have always been associated with the image of an open frontier—and to some extent with good reason because their spaces present many new possibilities: These are new worlds to explore, there is plenty of land to build on, and there are opportunities for new creations of all types. At the same time, the frontier is often described as lawless, untried, and unstable in the sense that the new digital domain brings together people from different backgrounds, and so its rules and forms of interaction seem more open and fluid (for further comparisons to the "frontier," see Schroeder, Huxor, and Smith 2001: 579–581).

Apart from how users make use of these novel opportunities (which, as we shall see in Chapter 5, are also quite limited), a key question concerns the popularity of different places or where users spend most of their time. In AW, this is easy to see because there is a list of users in different worlds in the universe. SL and other online spaces have implemented similar "Where are the other users?" functions, as have online games. But popularity also depends on where new entrants enter the VW and go from there—for AW, the Gate and AlphaWorld, and for SL, Orientation Island. Popularity is also a question of the milieu or atmosphere of different places, which may relate to language, special interests, knowledge of which other people frequent particular places, and the like. In AW, there have been tiers of popularity among worlds, and although the popularity of particular worlds has waxed and waned, there were some constants—such as the popularity of the place of entry.[12]

The *use* of the space also displays certain patterns. Although it is in principle possible for limitless amounts of people to meet in an endless amount of space, in practice avatars cluster in certain popular places and the number of people who engage each other—except at special events like parties or conferences—tends to be restricted to small groups of avatars who can monitor each other's conversations and movements. Holding large-scale events poses considerable logistical challenges, although successful conference-type events have been held (Damer 2000). The clustering of avatars who are communicating with each other will be dealt with more extensively in Chapter 6, and especially in the discussion of how many conversation partners can effectively monitor each other and maintain awareness of each other. Still, it is worth pointing out that certain spaces will be more conducive to avatars engaging with each other than will others.

Clustering of participants takes place in relation to activity: If users have a common focus of attention (an object to build, a board game to play, or a room in house to stand in), they need to stand so as to be able to see the same object, but apart from this, they will stand around within sight of each other but in a way that is spatially much more freely organized than in a face-to-face conversation because in the text-based world of AW, nothing hinges on being within earshot of each other (and nonverbal gestures can be counted as a common focus of visual attention). This contrasts with worlds with audio such as OnLive Traveler, where being within earshot keeps groups more closely together and keeps groups smaller.

If we go one step further, it is possible to identify certain roles or different "types" of users in AW that are related to the geography of place (in doing this, there is an overlap with the next section about avatar appearance, as well as links to Chapter 2, where "roles" where discussed). Some of the different roles here might include "bully," "friendly helper," "prankster," "deviant," and others.[13] The difference between online games and online social spaces is that in a social VW, these roles are created by users. In AW, for example, there are almost no predefined roles—the only such roles are "gatekeeper" and "peacekeeper," roles for which one can volunteer and which entail helping novice users and enforcing certain rules of conduct. But "gatekeepers," for example, will tend to carry out this role near the Gate, where people enter AW. Similarly in SL, certain users have been designated with special names and have volunteered to help novice users and monitor the world for untoward activities.

Apart from these roles, a key distinction is to divide the population into "newbies" versus "regulars" or "insiders" versus "outsiders" (see Schroeder 1996). Along the same lines, we could distinguish between more active and more passive users, where the more active ones build, participate in newsgroups, engage with creating new features, and perform similar activities, while more passive users engage more casually and behave as visitors. Or again, "groups" can be related to various interests in different places, such as religious worlds or areas, worlds for education, worlds with a permanent "party" atmosphere, worlds for builders, worlds for "deviant" behaviors, and other interests. There are obvious parallels here with real-world stratification or differentiation—except that this is much less complex in VWs. The different groups or communities or subcultures will be discussed at greater length in Chapter 5—here, the point is simply that these groups tend to congregate in different places, which is partly fostered by the appearance of the environment.[14]

One can also distinguish between formal and informal rules or norms of social interaction. Gatekeepers and peacekeepers in AW, for example, have the task to enforce certain codes of conduct by threatening to expel users who use aggressive language or who annoy other users. This way of dealing with rule enforcement harks back to the "wizards" in multiuser dungeons or MUDs (see Pargman 2000). Apart from this in-world rule enforcement, there are also certain rules that are enforced by the system developers on one side and rules that have emerged among users in certain places on the other (for example, in relation to vandalism in Sherwood).

In addition to these formal rules, many informal codes of behavior have emerged in the interaction between users, and some of these will be identified later (in Chapters 5 and 6), including introductions of new languages, greeting behaviors, codes for helping each other, and the like. At this point, however, we can turn from individual features of AW to more complex social dynamics that shape the overall appearance of the environment. And the most general characteristic of the AW population is that it became more self-organized over time—despite the fact that there has been a large amount of "churn" in the population (again, the same applies to SL). There are many examples of self-organization apart from those already mentioned, including newsgroups, parties, and elections for the best-designed world. Another interesting example is the AW Historical Society, which had a homepage and a museum (see http://mauz.info/awhistory.html under "history links"), including images of "historic" moments in the development of AW as well as maps that chart the growth of the AW world. In other words, some basic social institutions emerged. Here we need to return to the point that there is a difference between social rules or institutions that are built into the design of the system by the system's designers or operators, such as the "gate-keeper" role in AW—or, to take a different example, the money economy in SL—and the institutions arising from the populations in the VEs themselves, like the museum and others just mentioned.

It is also possible to identify some changes in the attitude of the population toward the system that took place over time. Initially, for example, the policy of "gatekeepers" in "cracking down" on deviance provoked widespread dissatisfaction, especially among "insiders" or "regulars," and led them to urge other users to boycott the use of AW. Another example was the introduction of fees for "citizenship" in 1997, which led many users to become disgruntled. This policy caused some built-up areas to be abandoned or turn into "ghost towns." Interestingly, the disgruntlement in the discussions among users died down fairly quickly, although it is impossible to tell whether those who were disaffected simply no longer used the world, leaving the field to contented fee-payers.

The switch to fee-paying citizenship is also an interesting chapter in the development of AW because it might have been expected that many users would simply remain non–fee-paying "tourists," especially because relatively few citizens seemed to be making use of the "building" privilege that was the main advantage of citizenship. But it seems that the majority of users who ventured beyond short visits to AW became citizens. And when being a "tourist" was restricted to a short free trial, the population nevertheless remained stable or decreased only somewhat. In short, populations were wedded to places.

Another development was the increasing commercialization of AW. One aspect of this, citizenship fees, has already been discussed. But there were a number of others: the increasing use of advertising hoardings, themed worlds related to products (a "Godzilla" world was created to promote the blockbuster film), the offer of a CD-ROM for faster and higher resolution graphics, and the "sale" or "leasing" of whole worlds. In 1999, there was also a shopping mall world ("@Mart") where users could buy and sell products in a virtual space. And finally (again, in 1999), the company was floated on the stock exchange (previously it was known as Circle of Fire and at this point became Activeworlds.com, Inc.), which can be seen as further step in commercialization.

There are parallels between how AW divided the population into "citizens" and "tourists" and divisions of "class" or "status" in the real world. Similarly striking was how AW was carved up into worlds, especially worlds with the names of real countries ("France," "Russia," "Japan" etc.), just as the real world is divided up into nation-states. At the same time, these parallels should not be taken too far: for example, there has been no money economy in AW—as there was, for example, in WorldsAway (the successor to Habitat) and in SL. And there were no "passports" or "customs" barriers between worlds (apart from the citizenship fee and building restrictions that have been mentioned) or separations between national cultures (again, apart from the different atmospheres in different worlds, and the fact that speakers of the same language often prefer to socialize in the same world; see also Chapter 6). But the main divide between citizens and tourists in AW has perhaps been that "citizens" sometimes treat "tourists" with mild disdain because of their "inexperience," although it is difficult to gauge how widespread this sentiment is. In any case, it is difficult to weigh this "snobbery" against the welcoming and helpful attitude that "citizens" or "insiders" often have toward "tourists" or "newbies" (see Spante 2009). In other words, the divide is not between material resources and cultural capital—like the divisions of class and status in the real world—but rather one between insiders and outsiders. And this division has been noticed in many other online worlds (Boellstorff 2008; Taylor 2006).

The connection between social behavior and the built environment is not straightforward. Aside from the public squares, for example, there were two main types of houses or dwellings in AW, depending on whether they were "public" (sometimes provided or encouraged by the system developers) or "private" (built by participants). The public buildings and spaces, such as museums and parks, were often designed with "civic" or recreational functions in mind. But in practice, the main use of public squares and public buildings was to provide central places for socializing and for displaying public information. The main function of houses built for "private" use, on the other hand, was to give builders a sense of having their own place and "showing off" to visitors. Hence a common form of socializing that takes place in relation to private buildings is that builders invite others to their "homes" to show them its unique features and engage in more private conversations than in the "public" spaces. In this respect AW is similar to the text-based MUD LambdaMOO, for which Schiano and White (1998) found that regular users spent most of their time in the private spaces that they had "built."

VW systems like AW allow system developers and builders a lot of freedom in creating spaces and places to socialize. But as we have seen, the spaces in AW have also reincorporated many features of the geographies and forms of social interaction from the real world. There is thus a balance between the utopian visions that influenced parts of the AW geography and patterns of building and socializing that follow "real-world" constraints more closely. The utopian and science fiction elements in AW have remained a strong influence, but there have also been increasingly commercial pressures in this VW that have shaped the appropriation and use of land. So, for example, the myth of an open frontier, of a vast expanse of land with unlimited opportunities, was important for the initial patterns of land development but also came under increasing pressure. It has to be remembered here that although virtual land may be in "unlimited" supply, land or space that is shared with others is subject to the constraint—to put it in the language of e-commerce, "if you build it, will they come?" In other words, there may be plenty of space, but who is there to interact with? The fact that there are indicator mechanisms for locating other users in AW and SL does not solve this problem: places still need to attract users.

The diverse "atmospheres" in AW have allowed different groups of users to find their own favorite places and ways to socialize. What is perhaps more important is how the social relations in AW as a whole have been shaped by geography: despite the division into many worlds and types of spaces within worlds, users still congregate in certain worlds and concentrate in central areas for general socializing, especially where newcomers enter the system. The use of far-flung or private places is reserved for one-to-one conversations or other special interest activities. Further, AW is no longer the only universe of its type since the developers sold whole worlds (or "universes") for others to develop. Thus, there were other universes, such as OuterWorlds, which had a different character but still had the look and feel of AW.

This differentiation of virtual spaces has implications for the dispersion of users: how, for example, are these similar to and different from the space-time patterns of human dispersion and mobility in the "real" world? And if VWs are different and more "open," could they create possibilities that avoid some of the current problems of mobility of "real"-world geographical settings such as congestion. As we have seen, many of the features of real-world social and geographical relations have become transferred (albeit in modified form) into virtual geographies, while other features of transportation and settlement are more malleable and subject to faster transformations.

At the most general level, then, the patterns described here can be seen as a process whereby populations become acculturated to new environments and follow the logic described in historical geography. So, for example, one could see the development of AW in terms of the historical geography of Friedrich Ratzel (as summarized here by Osterhammel): "With 'increasing culture,' peoples become more settled … they dig themselves literally into the ground"—as we have shown in AW through the appropriation of land and building—"and at the same time increase their mobility by means of the technological progress of modern transport" (1994: 65) or, in this case, developing the nature of "mobility" in virtual spaces.

But despite this "acculturation," the balance between settled social and geographical relations in this new setting remains very open, as do the norms of social behavior in AW and other such online worlds (as we shall see later). Users from different backgrounds are constantly being thrown together in an open and relatively "lawless" space, and although they will no doubt keep socializing in a cosmopolitan and unstructured way, there will also continue to be a further differentiation of the geographies of VEs, both within and between VWs, and with it the acclimatizations of users' modes of social interaction to these environments.

As we have seen, there are many points of overlap between online VEs with large populations and immersive VEs for small groups. Hudson-Smith (2002), for example, points out that there is a build-and-abandon attitude in AW, and this applies to the landscapes and built environment in other online VWs, too. The same could be said for immersive VEs, because many VEs are developed and built, often at great cost in terms of effort, only to be used for a few demonstrations, after which they are abandoned and never used again. This observation has implications for the design of VEs: for example, why not engage in recycling?

Still, it is worth recalling here that in terms of visual appearance, these large-scale online worlds and immersive VEs for small groups are currently for the most part different: online worlds cover vast spaces and contain populations of avatars and they are experienced on PC screens. These worlds are designed for long-term socializing. Immersive VEs feature life-size avatars and are often designed to a particular level of realism, and they have small spaces to support particular tasks. The appearance of the two is therefore usually quite different. But again, the distinction is not a hard-and-fast one: online worlds or parts of online worlds are being devoted to particular tasks (the teaching areas in SL, for example), and immersive VEs are sometimes used for socializing and gaming, at least in experimental uses (Persky and Blascovich 2006). The two have many elements in common—such as that avatars need to appear in such a way that others can interact with them or that the environment is navigable.

Environments with large populations often have extensive and varied landscapes, such as the hundreds of worlds in AW—or islands or regions in SL. Perhaps the easiest way to make this point (for those who are not familiar with online worlds) is to say that it would take many days to take a tour to see the various sights and become familiar with the social milieus that can be found in the many worlds that have been built in AW or SL (or World of Warcraft, WoW). Again, however, this point immediately leads to another, which is that there is a sameness to online VWs after a while that strikes anyone who has wandered around extensively in large-scale worlds such as AW, WoW, or SL.

Another feature that can be mentioned is the mixture in the environments of elements that imitate the real world as against those that depart from it, or real versus imaginary VEs. Examples of "realism" include the way that the layout of densely populated areas imitates real-world cities, the resemblance of many buildings in AW to real-world buildings, and the furnishing of many houses with chairs and tables (which often serve no function apart from decoration or orientation). Examples of the "imaginariness" in AW on the other hand are the frequent use of all-glass transparent buildings, buildings that imitate science fiction or that were built in the sky, and objects like waterfalls or flames in unlikely places.

In experimental VE settings for small groups, the appearance of the VE is typically related to the application area: visualization, collaboration, acting rehearsals, and the like. There are also some highly realistic environments for training and games; military simulations and Internet-based games like Quake and Doom are good examples of the latter. These may have a higher degree of "realism," but they are often restricted to a particular functionality: the user must follow certain rules (in a game) or manipulate the environment by means of certain tools or weapons, even if these games can also be quite social.

Thus, a classification of the appearance of VEs could be useful that would link the appearance of the environment to how users interact with them: What features must the environment have to enable particular types of social interaction? This is an issue that goes beyond joint navigation or way-finding (Munro, Höök, and Benyon 1999), and there is often a mismatch here, especially in that many environments are too complex for novice users' needs. It may seem obvious, taking a broader view, that the appearance of the environment will affect not only navigability (the issue that has been most studied so far) but also how users interact with each other in more subtle ways. A key feature, mentioned in passing in Chapter 2, is how much the appearance of the environment detracts from—or allows the user to focus on—interaction with other users. Finally, it can be mentioned that there is an obvious contrast between online spaces and other types of communications media— namely, that "media spaces are different from the videophone model in that they provide a range of functionality, are ubiquitous, and have a persistent presence" (Sellen 1997: 102).

The Solidity and Manipulability of Avatar Bodies and Virtual Spaces

One issue that affects both the appearance of the world and of avatars is their solidity. For example, how should two visually represented objects— or avatar bodies—interact with each other?[15] The options for visual bodies are limited; they are that:

- Bodies simply pass through each other.
- Collision detection is built into the system, such that the two bodies cannot pass through each other. (This option needs to be visualized in

the mind's eye: what happens in this case is that the visual representations of users are not allowed to overlap so that they "push" each other around.)
- The two bodies have different capabilities; that is, one can move through the other, and the other cannot.

The last scenario deserves to be spelled out: Imagine two actors on a TV screen who interact onscreen while the real actors simultaneously make them move (as in a two-player video game). This leads to a situation in a shared VE whereby one person can, for example, move another avatar around. The practical implications are, for example, that you are able to "eject" an avatar from its place. Or in a task with three persons, one avatar has the capability to move the second, and the third can see that the first has the power to move the second.

Now among the three options, for most situations—except where one person should guide others through a training scenario or similar situation—the third option is not desirable, not just because of the power imbalance, but because it would cause disorientation on the part of the person that can be moved around. In effect, their position tracking (or how they moved their avatar bodies with their mouse) would not work if the other person was able to move their body.

That leaves the other two options, which can quickly be reduced to the first for most scenarios that can be envisioned, because collision detection whereby avatars can "push each other around" is not useful for many applications. The exceptions are where the application requires that the avatars cannot go through each other, for example, because they collaborate such that their bodies should not overlap—imagine a training session for going across a river together by means of a log where only one person can fit at a time.

The main drawback of "transparent" bodies that can pass through each other is the sense of unease that people have in doing this. But this is something that one quickly becomes used to, even though, as we shall see (in Chapter 4), moving through each other sometimes causes embarrassment and sometimes does not. So, for example, in one of our trials, although the individuals were not aware of their own appearance, they seemed to respect the avatars of others, trying to avoid passing through them and sometimes apologizing when they did so (Steed, Spante, Heldal,

Axelsson, and Schroeder 2003; see also Slater, Sadagic, Usoh, and Schroeder 2000).

Similar considerations apply to the relations between avatars and the visual landscape, with the difference that it is of course desirable that avatars should be able to move around and manipulate objects. Here the question can be put this way: What parts of the environment should be manipulable? The most common way this is implemented is the following: there is a range of things that the user *cannot* manipulate—the background landscape, buildings, and the like—and another range of objects that *can* be manipulated. The latter will include middle-sized objects—such as furniture, objects to build with, objects to collect (in a game, for example), and the like. Note that we have assumed that the user has the freedom to move around in the world, pass through things, and "fly," although in AW, SL, and other worlds, there is typically a mixture of walls, for example, that one can pass through and others that are impassable. In short, VWs are half-realistic worlds in the sense that the visual environment can be navigated in a way that does not correspond to real-world navigation while others are real world–like.

Another solution that can be envisioned is to make the manipulability of things as true-to-life as possible. Yet a simple run-through of this solution shows that it is not feasible, mainly because the objects are all visual—which does not correspond to the real world. And since the environment is not realistic in any case (there is no touch, for example), it will not make sense to make objects and features of the environment as realistic as possible. Still, there are bound to be tradeoffs here: people can cope with some types of non-naturalism and not with others; they will need a certain amount of "stability" as against "flexibility," and it will be practical, from the point of view of system capabilities and user needs, to implement certain constraints and possibilities rather than others. Note, incidentally, that one problem that we will also come across in Chapter 4 on collaboration (where it is much more important) is known as the "floor control" problem: When two or more people are working together, who has control of the object that they are working on?

Finally, it is worth mentioning that many commonly used worlds are visually very simple and will consist of, say, a flat plane or room in which there are a few objects that can be manipulated, perhaps against a simple background of the plane or room that cannot be manipulated. In other words, before we get carried away thinking of VEs in the same way as we think of the complexity of our real-world environment, it is worth remembering that VWs are typically radically simplified versions of it, even if they can also be visually very beautiful, imaginative, and complex. It is also worth considering that the various options that have been discussed have implications for the way in which online spaces can be changed and, related to this, what parts of the space can and cannot be owned. In any event, as we have seen, there are various options for VEs that have different possibilities and constraints, and these will be suited to different applications contexts.

Avatar Appearance and Realism

Avatar appearance has been examined in many studies. In her review of "avatar fidelity," Garau makes the simple point that "one of the major drawbacks of CVEs is the relative paucity of avatar expressiveness compared with live human faces on video" (2003: 22). This problem has two dimensions: "the avatar's static appearance (visual fidelity) and dynamic animation (behavioural fidelity)" (2003: 22). A number of points can be made immediately: first, visual fidelity and behavioral fidelity are not mutually exclusive. Second (a point that was made earlier), there are only two options for the future of MUVEs: either they go in the direction of fully video-captured and/or motion-tracked users, in which case the user is "realistically represented"—and if the environment is also realistic, this will not be a VE, but a 3D video environment—or the avatar is computer-generated and *controlled* by the user. In this case, the users will be able to shape (and need to be aware of) how they look, to control the parts of themselves that are tracked, and navigate with their bodies.

The reason for spelling out these two options is not just that they presage two very different types of MUVEs, but in this context, as Garau points out, "full manual control over an avatar's actions would introduce an unacceptable cognitive load" (2003: 23). In other words—imagine that, apart from controlling head and hand movement by means of trackers (the most common option in immersive VEs), the user would also need to "manually" (individually or separately) control their tracked feet or could use a tracked little finger to pick up objects. It is easy to see that this would be difficult for users (note that a video-captured avatar's little finger is unlikely to be usable for picking up objects). The same applies if these different body parts would not be tracked but needed to be "steered." In short, computer-generated avatars either need to be simple, use mechanisms to track facial expressions or body parts, or they need to not be too difficult or complex to control or steer. At this point, it will suffice to bear these options in mind—we will return to them at various points.

Against the general background of these options, we can pursue some detailed findings about realism or fidelity. Garau investigated this topic for her 2003 doctoral thesis. She found, for example, that avatars with high realism and inferred eye gaze (programming the avatar so their eyes are not static but gaze in a human-like way) had high ratings for acting as if in a face-to-face situation (2003: 162). However, there was a difference: the greater "face-to-face" effectiveness (or social copresence) only worked in the condition when a higher realism avatar was used. In the case of a lower realism avatar with this realistic inferred eye gaze behavior, the effect was negative; that is, reducing face-to-face effectiveness (or social copresence). Garau concludes that this "suggests a need for consistency between the visual appearance of the avatar and the type of behaviour [in this case, inferred eye gaze] that it exhibits" (2003: 162).[16] In other words, users need to have consistency in avatar appearance, not realism only in some aspects and not in others.

Garau also measured responses to avatar agents (avatars programmed to act like humans) encountered in a virtual library that were more and less life-like (static versus moving agents, moving when the user got close, and speaking when the user got closer). She found that people experienced more of a sense of copresence with the agents with more life-like attributes (2003: 194–197). She also discusses how "none of the participants reported responding to the avatars as if they were 'really' people. However, many expressed surprise at the fact that they had respected some social norms despite the fact that they knew that the avatars were computer-generated" (2003: 206). This finding is supported in other studies where people interacted with life-like agents (for example, Blascovich 2002). Finally, it can be mentioned that one possible explanation that Garau does not consider in this case—in addition to the life-likeness of the agent avatar's behavior—may be the particular social setting. People know that in a library, they are not supposed to move about and should be quiet, so this may have influenced results about how lifelike they regarded their encounters with different avatar agents.

Overall, Garau concludes that "findings suggest that a cartoonish avatar with minimal behaviours can begin to positively affect perceptions of interaction. The caveat is that its behaviour should reflect some of the ongoing interaction, and the level of behavioural realism should be aligned with the photorealism of the avatar's appearance" (2003: 214). Note that this applies to *adding* behaviors to cartoon-like avatars—adding speech and movement to avatar agents in an exploration task in library, and adding random eye gaze or inferred eye gaze and realism to an avatar "talking head" in a negotiation (or conversation) task. As Garau points out, it remains to be seen whether these findings can be generalized to other settings or to uses that are longer-term than her brief experimental encounters. Still, this brief summary of some of her findings can give an indication of the types of investigations and issues that concern research into avatar realism.[17]

Realism is not the only issue in how avatar appearance affects interpersonal interaction. For online worlds, for example, a key issue is what kinds of choices of avatar appearance are possible in the environment. The choices of developers will often determine the range of avatars available, but in some cases the developers also allow users to modify their appearance. And the choices of both will have certain technical and social constraints and possibilities (for example, what kinds of conventions are there?).

In AW, for example, apart from the basic choice between avatar tourists and citizens, the avatar choice for citizens has been restricted to a range of choices that represented certain "types." These avatars further had a small range of expressions—"happy," "angry," "jump," "fight," "dance," "wave," and the like. In SL, on the other hand, users are able to customize their appearance not only by avatar types but also by going through a menu of features and selecting parts of their avatar appearance (hair and eye color, clothes, and so on). The range of options in online worlds with computer-generated avatars (as opposed to captured realistic ones) is between being forced to adopt a particular avatar appearance at one extreme and being able to customize your appearance as you see fit at the other extreme. Note, however, that the choice of complete avatar customization, even if it can be technically enabled by the system, is still subject to the social constraint of the kind of avatar that others will want to interact with.

At this stage we can ask a basic question: How realistic do avatars need to be for people to work together or socialize? The short answer is not very realistic—*unless* nonverbal cues are required for the ongoing interaction. "Ongoing" is necessary here because, as argued earlier, over longer periods, participants can compensate for the absence of these cues by means of "hyperpersonal" communication or otherwise adapting to the absence of nonverbal communication. Further, realistic avatars are often not necessary for collaboration and socializing *insofar as* the interaction revolves around objects or other kinds of social interaction that are not focused on facial or bodily cues (if we remember the division in the previous chapter into focus on the environment, on the task, and on the interaction with others). Having said this, clearly avatar appearance *does* make a difference to the *way* people interact.

This is a good place to mention that avatar appearance is one of the most interesting areas where MUVEs can be used to study human behavior in an experimental way (see also Chapter 7). Bailenson and Beall (2006), for example, have undertaken a series of studies of how users react to different virtual selves. They found, among other things, that people react differently depending on how the extent to which their own appearance is "blended" in with the appearance of others. Or, again, Lok, Naik, Whitton, and Brooks (2003) showed that the realistic appearance of one's own avatar does not enhance the sense of presence in certain circumstances. These and other research uses of MUVEs will be discussed later.

Returning to avatar appearance apart from experimental uses, it needs to be stressed that in addition to visual realism (or form similarity), avatar appearance also depends on behavioral realism (or behavioral similarity). Both types of realism have been shown to produce higher levels of copresence in experiments (Bailenson, Beall, and Blascovich 2002), and we have already encountered some findings by Garau (2003) that behavioral realism is more important than form realism. This finding is reinforced in studies by Bente, Ruggenberg, and Kraemer (2005), who found that even cartoon-like avatars with minimal levels of behavioral realism elicit responses from research participants. Furthermore, avatars recognize emotion even when a simple block, with different colors representing the "block-face's" emotion, can be treated in a human-like way (disclosing personal information to it) and its emotions can be recognized (Bailenson, Yee, Merget, and Schroeder 2006).

The debate about which is more important—realism in appearance or in behavior—will continue (Garau 2003: 54). But it will also depend on the context: Realistic behaviors are mainly related to body language, and although findings have generally shown that behavioral realism is more important than visual realism (with important implications for the agenda of developing MUVEs, which has tended to focus on visual realism), it is possible to imagine circumstances where a static realistic face is more important, such as, (to take a somewhat artificial example) when it is necessary to pick out avatar faces in a crowd of similar looking avatars. Avatar representation will thus always involve tradeoffs (technically and socially), both for visual realism and behavior. But although it may be possible to "do with less" from the point of view of the technology, it is also ever less "expensive" to provide realism, with eye gaze and facial expressions the most difficult hurdles to overcome (eye gaze is also, incidentally, the most difficult problem for videoconferencing; see Vertegaal 1998).

Yee, Bailenson, and Rickertson (2007) undertook a meta-analysis of studies of the realism of human-like faces of embodied agents and found that subjective measures (asking people) produced a much stronger effect in terms of realism than objective or behavioral measures (such as task performance). They also note, however, that these kinds of studies are difficult to interpret because characteristics of facial expressions apart from whether they are realistic may play a role: for example, faces that "appear unnatural or disturbing", or the difference between a photograph and a cartoon face (which may be highly realistic).[18] It can be added here that for facial expressions, adding visual features is not always useful and may be counterproductive: Showing another person's face is mainly beneficial when the interaction is social and less so when the interaction is instrumental.

There are also interesting insights from online worlds to draw on. For example, the developers of Microsoft's V-Chat system (see Cheng, Farnham, and Stone 2002) found that people would like to be able to have greater control over their avatar representation or have input into its design. This demand from the users has been found in a variety of online worlds (Taylor 2002). Meeting this demand, however, has a number of technological challenges: one is to provide the user with the tools to create his or her own custom avatar. Another concerns network capabilities (which has already been mentioned in connection with the environment): in shared VEs, should each avatar representation permanently reside on each of the other users' computers? This would create problems for computer memory if there were hundreds or thousands of unique users. Or should each new avatar only be downloaded when it is used? This would avoid the storage problem on each computer but would require lots of bandwidth. (Much depends here on the complexity of avatar appearance or the amount of data required by each avatar. The same point could be made in relation to other objects in the environment.) Finally, a few customized avatars may not be a problem, as in the case of small groups, but in larger populations there will be a tradeoff between unique and complex avatars and technological capabilities. As it stands, in most MUVEs there is only a small number of custom avatars or avatar parts to choose from—although customizing avatars and importing avatar appearance into environments have become common in some systems.

As already mentioned, people prefer to have a single consistent avatar representation. Boellstorff reports (2008: 128–134), as others have found, that in SL, people often use a second alternative avatar ("alts") for interacting with others. Yet the very fact that these are called "alts" is indicative of their main purpose: they are used when one wants to undertake activities that one does not want others (who would normally recognize an avatar's main identity) to know about. In other words, these are supplemental to a main identity that one wants to be known by. A further interesting finding about SL is that, according to Au (2008: 67), the vast majority of users choose not to reveal any information about their real-life selves in their clickable profiles, which remain mostly blank. So on the one hand, users choose consistent online representations, but on the other, most users do not want to disclose their real-world identity.

No doubt technical solutions will continue to make progress and influence avatar appearance. It is possible to anticipate, for example, that avatars will feature a mixture of computer-generated representations and real-time video images of users (Hirose, Ogi, and Yamada 1999), so that avatars will range from cartoon-like, as they are now, to very realistic.[19] But, as Cheng, Farnham, and Stone also found (2002), users may want avatars that are neither too abstract nor too realistic. Similarly, in SL, most people choose human-like avatars, although there are also subcommunities of people who choose different appearances to set themselves apart. Au, for example, reports that there is a group of like-minded avatars, an interest community, who have chosen a fox-like appearance called "furries," which he says account for 6% of all avatar appearances (2008: 75; cf. Boellstorff 2008: 184). Apart from these specialized avatars, it is too early to say how much avatar customization will in fact be demanded by users in systems where they are given a choice.

Perhaps a mixture of "off-the-shelf" or ready-made avatars and customized solutions will emerge in VEs. In the meantime, there are several studies (Blascovich 2002; Garau 2003; Slater and Steed 2002; Slater, Sadagic, Usoh, and Schroeder 2000; Taylor 2002) that provide insights into particular aspects of how avatar appearance affects social interaction. But apart from effects of avatar interaction on individual encounters, what would need to be considered—over the longer term— are issues such as the influence of the persistence of avatar appearance in different conditions. For example, what kind of persistence do users need in order to recognize each other over repeated encounters? And what kind of diversity of avatar appearances is needed within both small and large groups for participants to be able to distinguish between them— and what diversity can they cope with? These kinds of question remain unexplored.

Avatar appearance is an area where users will be particularly careful about how the medium works, choosing the medium in which they are best embodied, or choosing the best embodiment for particular circumstances. Cheng, Farnham, and Stone found that people in the 2.5D V-Chat online environment did not want to be represented either as too "cartoonish" or too realistically as a humanoid, liked to choose their own avatars, and liked to interact with certain avatars rather than others (2002: 98–100). Similar findings, that users avoid certain unappealing-looking avatars—just as they avoid avatars with off-putting names—have been found in qualitative studies (see Chapter 5). In the real world, of course, it is often impossible to make the choice of who we interact with.

One other issue must be mentioned in relation to appearance, namely anonymity and deception (it will reappear later in Chapter 8). The idea that people misrepresent their identity is common in discussion of online worlds and has been investigated, including in experimental work. However, the importance of misrepresentation has been exaggerated. In text-based online interaction, for example, it has been argued that "anonymity is not an issue": "some online contexts will do little to make the self-categories associated with offline selves relevant, and these will be most likely to result in identity play, deception and other behaviors divorced from social contexts. Other contexts will make those categories more relevant, and will invoke self-representation and behavior consistent with embodied versions of the self" (Baym 2002: 68). That is, avatars will either misrepresent the user, but in the context of nonserious interaction, or they will represent the user faithfully. As we have seen, users tend to prefer somewhat idealized representations of themselves, and their departure from this preference will be within the constraints of the aims of their interactions with others.

Avatar appearance can, to anticipate the concluding chapter, be put in a much broader context: How people present themselves digitally—that is, what information about themselves they display (iris scan, résumé, medical information, photograph, or other representation on a social networking site [the list here is potentially very long])—are sometimes regarded as people's online "presence" (or "copresence") and identity. Similarly with the online space: In online worlds, people can often shape the environment, its appearance and rules, but they also use a range of environments that are not quite worlds but rather spaces in which they interact with others. In short, from full-size avatars and immersive worlds, to lesser digital self-representations and spaces, these ranges of phenomena will need to be considered if we are to understand our manifold online interactions.

There are by now various findings about the extent to which avatar appearance and the appearance of online spaces enhance presence and copresence (see Chapter 2) in the sense of a psychological or measurable state, but they do not yet add up to a body of knowledge that applies to a wide range of contexts. What we *do* know is that these features make it into a medium that affords users a more powerful sense of being there and doing things with others—*in the general sense of affording a greater attachment to people and places*—than other media. A different way to put this is that whereas presence-generating technologies allow the sense of another place and communication technologies allow people to exchange messages, MUVEs allow a combination of the two—to engage in communication and interaction in another place and with the people in it. Finally, in relation to the visual appearance of the environment and of avatars, researchers and developers will continue to have realism in the sense of perception as a goal. Yet, as we have seen, realism is of limited importance, less so than making the environment navigable and habitable and the avatars suitable for social interaction.

NOTES

1. The reason for narrowing the environment and people in it to visual appearance (audio will be treated in Chapter 6), as opposed to the other senses, has been explained in Chapter 2.

2. Again, *worlds* and *environments* will be used interchangeably, with the proviso that *worlds* makes more sense in the context of elaborate large-scale places, whereas *environments* is more suited to smaller and simpler spaces and models.

3. It can be noted in passing that online games like World of Warcraft are generally considered more aesthetically pleasing or sophisticated than SL, which is more cartoon-like. This is partly because of the resources that go into a game and partly because SL is user generated. This greater sophistication applies particularly to features like lighting and shading, the movements of avatars, and the detail in buildings and landscapes. But this contrast only raises a further question: What is more important—a beautifully prerendered environment, or a less beautiful or less technically polished environment that has been created by its inhabitants? (It needs to be added that the two are not mutually exclusive.)

4. It is of course possible to use AW, like any text-based world, with a separate audio channel.

5. See the history pages of Mauz at http://mauz.info/awhistory.html (last accessed February 16, 2009), as well as Schroeder, Huxor, and Smith (2001).

6. These efforts have surfaced in the mainstream press, but they also seem to have been abandoned. However, the issue is bound to arise again insofar as people want to take their avatars and objects from one world into others.

7. I adopt the past tense here to describe AW in the mid- to late 1990s when most of my participant observation took place. I have not followed AW since then, although it still exists and many features described here have remained the same. This was for a time the largest VW for socializing, consisting of hundreds

of worlds (500+ at the time our 2001 article was written; see Schroeder, Huxor, and Smith 2001).

8. One of the reasons that online games like World of Warcraft has graphics that are much smoother than SL is that the graphics are on the user's computer and so do not need to be downloaded. Again, the drawback is that World of Warcraft users cannot change the world and its objects.

9. In this respect, online VWs are examples of user-generated content, the most famous example of which is Wikipedia. See Benkler (2006).

10. Hudson-Smith (personal communication) says it is much easier to export and import objects into AW than into and out of SL.

11. Nardi and Harris (2006: section 4.4) similarly found in World of Warcraft that there are certain areas that are known for players misbehaving; that is being aggressive and using unpleasant language. This seems to be common in certain areas of online VWs (Boellstorff 2008; Schroeder, Huxor, and Smith 2001).

12. As we shall see in Chapter 7, one unique and useful feature of VWs in general is that the movements of people and their activities can easily be captured; see Harris, Bailenson, Nielsen, and Yee, 2009; Penumarthy and Boerner 2006.

13. These "types" can be separated from the "player motivations" of different types of players (see Yee 2006).

14. See Bardzell and Odom (2008) for an example of how power and stratification plays out in the subculture of the Goreans in SL (see also Chapter 5).

15. To the reader who is not familiar with VWs, it needs to be mentioned that since it is impossible for both bodies to have force feedback, as there is in the real world, there is no straightforward or realistic solution to implementing touch, or haptics, in VEs. A system in which two or more bodies have force feedback, and could therefore engage with each other like in the physical world, is of course *technically* not out of the question (although it would currently take a vast amount of effort). For two collaborators using haptic systems, this has already been studied (Sallnaes 2002). Nowadays, virtual touch via haptics typically consists of the force of two handheld "points" (or "tips" that can push things) collaborating with each other, such as in moving a virtual object. As an aside here it can be mentioned that virtual bodies being able to touch each other was, of course, the scenario that led to a lot of speculation about virtual sex, which, for better or worse, is impossible unless there are complex sensor and force-feedback mechanisms.

16. As will be discussed later, much progress has recently been made in capturing and representing eye-gaze (see Steptoe et al., forthcoming).

17. It would be interesting to examine how much body, and how much face, we need to have a realistic sense of another person via an avatar. Some relevant work has already been mentioned. In the Eye CVE experiments (Steptoe et al. forthcoming), gestures and nods but, most important, eye gaze, but no other facial expressions, were possible, with important implications for facilitating object-focused collaboration. On the other hand, from videoconferencing systems we

know how interaction in 2D videoconferencing works with full faces, but these systems have severe limitations on the use of gestures or nods or use of the space around the user. Comparison between these different configurations will ultimately tell us about how much face, and how much body, are needed in different settings.

18. Yee, Bailenson, and Rickertsen formulate the conclusion of their meta-analysis as follows: "A visual representation of an agent leads to more positive social interaction than not having a visual representation. On the other hand, it appears that the realism of the embodied agent may matter very little" (2007).

19. A VW that has come online recently, Twinity (http://www.twinity.com/en; last accessed February 16, 2009) combines photorealistic images of people's heads and details of real cities (in this case, Berlin, for example) with more virtual elements.

4

Collaboration

Working together or collaborating at a distance has been one of the main areas envisioned for how multiuser virtual environments (MUVEs) will be used. Yet barring a few niche applications and trials, the practice has remained far behind the vision. Later (in Chapter 9) we shall see why this also applies to videoconferencing. In this chapter, the focus will be on these VEs, and various findings will be reviewed about how people collaborate in MUVEs—or collaborative virtual environments (CVEs), which makes more sense in this context. Broadly speaking, immersive VEs for collaboration have tended to be for single users or small groups at a single site or with a single immersive system—in other words, non-distributed collaboration whereby people visualize models together while standing in the same physical space. This is an area where it makes sense to use an immersive environment: an environment where a model, for example, can be inspected and changed in virtual before committing to real resources, or where complex information needs to be displayed in a large space—such as oil exploration or automotive design. Nevertheless, evaluations of the usefulness of these systems, typically used in the private sector, are rare and the systems are expensive. Collaboration in desktop MUVEs, on the other hand, is more common, but confined to education and similar conferencing-type uses in online worlds. This chapter will examine *distributed* collaboration, in desktop VEs but mainly in trial uses of networked immersive systems.

Distributed Work—Distributed Research—Distributed Collaboration

In examining MUVEs for collaboration, it is necessary to look briefly at the broader area of distributed work, where extensive research has been carried out. Kiesler and Cummings summarize the findings about distributed work as follows: "Research suggests that the presence of others increases attention, social impact and familiarity… distributed work that causes people to be out of one another's sight may also lead to their comparative inattention to coworkers, a lower level of effort, or an increase in free riding" (2002: 63). In relation to MUVEs, this statement could be interpreted either as implying that face-to-face work will remain superior to distributed work, or that, other things being equal (which for our purposes can be taken as the suitability of the system to the task), the aim should be to enhance copresence for CVEs.[1]

What is it about face-to-face relations that make for better collaboration? Kiesler and Cummings point to talk: "to the degree that a distributed work group lacks chances to talk face-to-face, it also lacks the most direct and easy route to cooperation and coordination" (2002: 64). They further argue that "sharing social settings in physical space affects the similarity of people's expectations and experiences and influences the likelihood of establishing a shared territory" (2002: 65). Hence they "hypothesize that the effectiveness of remedies for physical distance in work groups will depend on the degree of existing social distance or cohesion in the group. If existing cohesion is high… then mediated communication technologies provide a plausible remedy for the lack of close physical proximity" (2002: 72), and if cohesion is low, then not.

To my mind, these points are not conclusive. First, the question of social relations in distributed work is not so straightforward: if Walther (1996) is correct in his findings about hyperpersonal relationships (which were discussed in Chapter 2), then this should also apply to work settings. Or again, should we assume that Kiesler and Cummings' arguments should also apply, for example, to the telephone? To be sure, Kiesler and Cummings' findings can be observed in many instances when comparing face-to-face with distributed work. At the same time, more and more collaboration is taking place in various mediated formats.[2] Furthermore, anyone who regularly calls and sends e-mails to collaborate with others at a distance will have made the observation that collaboration and communication with *some* people under *some* circumstances are *easier* in terms of both the task and the interpersonal relations, and this applies both to people whom one knows already as well as to people with whom one has only collaborated online.

One reason why Kiesler and Cummings and also Olson and Olson (2000) conclude that face-to-face collaboration is superior is because experimental settings have shown this on many occasions. Yet experiments provide limited evidence about a world in which many and varied types of distributed collaboration have been steadily increasing. In this chapter, all that can be done is to provide some counterexamples from the world of MUVEs. We shall return to the larger issues of working and other mediated relationships in the conclusion.

One example where distributed collaboration has been used extensively, even if mostly on a trial basis, is for research. As Sonnenwald points out, scientific collaboration has been regarded as an area of great promise for CVEs, but few of these systems have been evaluated (2003: 151). Studies of distributed scientific collaboration generally have consistently found that co-located researchers collaborate more and better than distributed ones (Rittenbruch and McEwan 2007), or that "distance matters" (Olson and Olson 2000). Yet the various phenomena associated with being there together—working with strangers, working in synchronous mode via "copresence" tools (at least in the sense of awareness), collaboration in distributed teams (Wuchty, Jones, and Uzzi 2007)—are becoming more common. It seems then that at the macro- level of changing practices, researchers are adopting and adapting to the tools for distributed collaboration despite difficulties.

On the other hand, there is the micro-level of "situation awareness." Sonnenwald says that the information required for "situation awareness" involves "contextual, task and process, and socio-emotional information" (2006: 64). She discusses situation awareness for a case of pairs of users jointly using an atomic force microscope via a haptic device shared across two desktop systems to carry out a lab exercise, both in distributed mode and sitting side-by-side. Here, one of the key issues is one that we have encountered; managing "floor control"—or in this case, who controls the (in this case haptic) tool to manipulate the three-dimensional (3D) environments? An important finding in this study was that collaborating first in the virtual (distributed) condition and then side-by-side was better in terms of task performance than the other way around (Sonnenwald 2006: 75). This finding can be compared with our study of a molecular visualization task where two people worked together in an immersive setting and in a co-located desktop setting (sitting doing the task shoulder to shoulder), with some groups using immersive first and the desktop task second and others in the reverse order (Axelsson et al. 1999). In this case, there were differences in the extent to which they enjoyed the collaboration more in the immersive as against the desktop condition, and they also thought they communicated better in the immersive setting (which goes against what might be expected), but they thought that they collaborated better using the desktop systems.

Collaboration by means of videoconferencing will be discussed later. But one videoconferencing study that can already be mentioned (again, by Sonnenwald and colleagues) examined a group of researchers over a (relatively) long period (fifty meetings over a period of twelve months). The study involved the participation of 110 researchers, faculty, and students, who had weekly and other (less frequent) meetings of 1.5 to 2 hours with twenty to thirty participants, testing a videoconferencing system that was improved over the course of the project and included shared slide (PowerPoint) presentations. The study was thus unusual in investigating everyday uses of this technology—in other words, not a laboratory trial.

One conclusion of this study was that: "Video conferencing may work fairly well in situations where people are separated across physical distances and a face-to-face meeting is not possible, or where visual information needs to be shared and acted upon...[but] there is something about physical distance that is maintained by the video medium which inhibits discussion, and thus video conferencing, as it is presently constituted, may not be appropriate for brainstorming and conflict resolution" (Sonnenwald et al. 2003: 118). Another finding was that in current systems, much technical and organizational effort was needed to get the systems working properly, although in this study there were also continual efforts to remedy technical "glitches" and improve the workings of the system—so that technical problems, insofar as they could be overcome, were not an issue in this trial (Sonnenwald et al. 2003: 119–121). A further finding to highlight that will be relevant to CVEs as a meeting technology is that these meetings were regarded as too formal (Sonnenwald et al. 2003: 132–133). This may, as the authors of the study point out, have advantages in leading to more preparation and thus more effective meetings, yet it may also lead over the longer term to preferences for face-to-face meetings.

This study is cited here partly because for videoconferencing meetings in general (apart from research collaboration), there are few studies that have results for everyday or regular uses of this technology (Finn, Sellen, and Wilbur 1997). And in relation to CVEs for meetings among researchers, there are few studies. A different perspective is provided by considering which functions can be added to support collaboration? As we shall see (in Chapter 6, Communication), one requirement of shared spaces is that they provide common ground so that people can achieve joint understandings of what they are doing together. For example, when Kraut, Gergle, and Fussell compared an audio-only task with performing a task with a shared visual space, they showed that "collaborative pairs can perform more quickly when they have a shared view of a common work area," and this applied most when the tasks were visually complex (2002: 39). They conclude that "less complex visual tasks, especially those in which objects and spatial relationships are static and easily lexicalized [identified by name], an audio-only connection may suffice" (Kraut et al. 2002: 39). This comparison of audio with audio-plus shared workspaces points us to the fact that sometimes less is more, but also alerts us to pay attention to how visual the task is.

Collaboration requires copresence (or social presence), and in MUVEs, much of what is missing are the social cues of nonverbal communication. Yet Sallnas' studies of collaborative tasks (drawing on earlier work by Short, Williams, and Christie [1976] on social presence) found that "meetings involving attitude change or negotiation or involving getting to know strangers were found to be more sensitive than other situations regarding which communication medium was used. Yet in many situations, such as problem-solving interactions, the omission of nonverbal cues had little effect on the outcome of the task" (Sallnas 2004: 25). In other words, it is not just a question of object-focused versus person-focused task, but also the *type* of task that is important.

Put differently, and if we use the term "awareness" we can distinguish between being aware of another person's activities or of their emotive state (which is perhaps closer to social presence). This makes it possible to conceive of various combinations that are possible whereby shared spaces make us aware of one but not the other. Another dimension that arises from a study mentioned earlier was that "leadership was conferred by immersion" (Tromp et al. 1998: 59; see also Slater, Sadagic,

Usoh, and Schroeder 2000). This study introduced another distinction that needs to be borne in mind, which is between "unfocused collaboration, where the individual monitors the other participants' activities without getting involved, and focused collaboration, where individuals work closely together" (Tromp et al. 1998: 61). Task and personal relationships are thus key dimensions to consider separately but also in terms of the balance between them.

What if we focus purely on the technology? For example, when is it better to have a larger display? This is a key question that will bear on the difference between immersive displays versus PC-based displays. Tan, Gergle, Scuppelli, and Pausch (2003) compared a reading comprehension task and a spatial orientation task on a large wall-size screen and a desktop-size screen. If a larger and a smaller display are compared at a constant visual angle (in other words, if the size of the display is the only difference between the two), the finding was that display makes no difference for the reading comprehension task (as might be expected). For the spatial orientation task, on the other hand, the study found that the "benefits" of the larger display "extended only to the task that allowed easy access to egocentric representation and strategy" (2003: 218; see also Pausch, Proffitt, and Williams [1997] for similar results with a search task). In other words, large displays only help if you have a first person perspective and use it. This is important for VEs because a key feature of both head-mounted display (HMD) systems and immersive projection technologies (IPTs) is that they provide these types of large displays.

More generally, a number of studies have found that people using MUVEs have problems with perception of the space around them—including awareness of the environment and of others (Rittenbruch and McEwan 2007). In many situations this will not make much of a difference, but it *does* matter where spatial accuracy, mutual awareness, and tightly coupled object-related collaboration are required. From the point of view of how object-oriented and environment interaction affects social interaction, there will obviously be frustration on the part of users if the task-related interactions are not going well (Heldal, Steed, Spante, Schroeder, Bengtsson, and Partanen 2005; Roberts, Wolff, Otto, and Steed 2003; Tromp, Steed, and Wilson 2003). But from the perspective of *social* interaction, as opposed to improving the object and environment interaction of MUVE design, it may also be that the difficulties with interpersonal relations fade into the background and thus do not seem problematic. Finally, we shall see again and again that the problematic nature of the task performance or social interaction is something that users (as opposed to researchers) may not be aware of.

What about "realism" and collaboration? Again, harking back to the argument made in Chapter 1, it depends on the task: Bowman, Kruijff, LaViola, and Poupyrev, for example, note that "often nonrealistic techniques have better performance than those based on the real world" (2001: 102). And if this applies to selecting and manipulating objects (the focus of Bowman, Kruijff, LaViola, and Poupyrev), the same applies to other forms of interaction within the VE, to the appearance of the VE, and to social interactions. Hence, Bowman, Kruijff, LaViola, and Poupyrev (2001) make a recommendation for user interface design: "Consider 'magic' interfaces in the place of 'natural' ones when tasks require productivity and efficiency. Natural interaction should be used when a replication of the physical world is important" (2001: 107). (By "magic," they mean special "powers" for the user beyond a one-to-one mapping between body movement and the interface tool, such as using a "laser" pointer to select an object.) Now the reply here might be that the whole point of VEs and MUVEs is precisely to provide natural or intuitive interfaces or realism rather than "magic"! Yet as I argued earlier, "natural" interfaces and "realism" are not necessarily a single end-state, and users often have no problem with unnatural or unrealistic environments or forms of interaction. Hence, realistic interfaces and forms of interaction may not be the best way to think about the future of MUVEs as a medium for collaboration.

VEs for collaboration at a distance, as mentioned earlier, are a special case of MUVEs, and they are treated separately in the research community.[3] Indeed, as mentioned earlier. the label that is commonly used is *collaborative virtual environments* (or CVEs), However, here, as in the rest of the book, the distinction between collaborative and other MUVEs is sometimes hard to maintain: how, for example, should we regard players collaborating in an online game or, to take the opposite case, a task that involves not so much effective working practice as interpersonal understanding? Nevertheless, instrumental tasks have different dynamics from MUVEs for leisure and socializing. Still, it is possible to speak of collaboration in the context of online social spaces, and the point is often made that work or instrumental applications need to be made engaging as well as effective.

A variety of tools for collaboration at a distance are in use (see the contributions in Hinds and Kiesler 2002). For most people the most common experience is voice over the telephone; for a few, it is video-conferencing; for still others, it is instant messaging and a variety of web-based collaboration tools. Only immersive virtual environments, however, allow users to share the same space, and nonimmersive ones allow some degree of interacting in the same space (as do shared workspaces). In either case, workaday uses of CVEs need to do two things: allow people do things together in spatial environments and allow them to bridge distance. The distinction in relation to what they do together has already been made in Chapter 1, between videoconferencing-type or "talking heads" CVEs on the one hand and CVEs that are mainly designed to allow the user to take advantage of the space on the other. The latter includes environments for visualizing and navigating through complex information, walkthroughs of buildings and landscapes, or manipulating objects.

In the context of collaboration, it is worth asking whether the two very different types of CVEs—roughly, for interpersonal interaction and for spatial interaction—will converge or will follow separate paths of development and use. It may, for example, be that spatial VEs will be largely confined to single-user applications. Or it may be that even if shared spaces in which people jointly explore and manipulate the space become important, they will be confined to certain niches of work or collaboration. Finally, it could be that "talking heads" systems far out-weigh the uses of systems for sharing the same space.

Against this backdrop, if we consider the difference between a 3D video-captured representation of real-world phenomena and a 3D graphical representation of a world (the two end-states presented in Chapter 1), we can note immediately that it has not so far been feasible (except for some small-scale attempts) to capture anything more than the immediate surroundings of users by means of video-capture (mostly room-size environments, although there are cases of larger captured spaces). Hence the space (in Table 4.1) under "Spatial Interaction" in the top row of "Immersive captured" CVEs is empty. And although *immersive*

TABLE 4.1   Types of multiuser virtual environments for collaboration.

	Talking Heads	Interacting Tracked Bodies	Spatial Interaction	Large Heavily Populated Spaces
Immersive Captured	High-end videoconferencing	Blue-C	Empty	Empty
Immersive Generated	Strangers and Friends Rubik's Gazebo	Strangers and Friends Rubik's Gazebo	Strangers and Friends Rubik's Gazebo	Empty
Desktop Captured	Access Grid Netmeeting Skype Video	Empty	Examples of people moving 3D Video objects	Empty
Desktop Generated	Online Traveler (if used for collaboration)	Empty	Object-focused interaction (ie. furniture, Hindmarsh, et al. 2002)	Online Spaces for gaming and socializing used to collaborate

computer-generated environments have been used for larger spaces such as buildings and landscapes, the systems (this also applies to immersive *captured* systems) have not so far, unlike VEs on desktop systems, been used for larger groups or populations (larger than a handful of people, perhaps two dozen in videoconferencing systems). Hence, there is an empty right-hand column for the top two rows. Finally, as discussed in Chapter 3, in computer-generated environments, one of the main issues has been to create realistic-looking facial expressions (and especially eye gaze)—which is an issue in captured environments only insofar this eye gaze needs to be displayed accurately.

For collaborations that consist primarily of communication, talking heads plus some social cues via bodies are all that is required. In video-conferencing, talking heads are normally sufficient except where work materials are needed. But the question in this case is whether these work materials need to be shared within a shared space by the participants, or if these materials can be separate from the talking heads. There is also the further question about where to draw the line between work and socializing, and it can be mentioned that a number of attempts to create shared and persistent 3D spaces that not only support distributed work but also promote distributed sociability (Churchill, Snowdon, and Munro 2002) have not been successful. (One guess here as to why this might be is that people do not have the possibility to split their attention between the distributed others and their immediate work environment.)

Now the argument has been made that tools for distributed collaboration do not match up to being there together face-to-face, but this argument, as we have seen, is too simple. We will return to the reasons in the case of videoconferencing in Chapter 9. IPT and HMD systems, on the other hand, have the advantage that they can represent both objects and people at a one-to-one scale. Further, the user's position is known—typically their head plus several tracked points such as the dominant hand. Having to wear trackers is obviously a drawback of immersive systems, just as the need to go to a special room is a drawback of high-end videoconferencing systems. The advantage, however, is that simple tracked avatars can create a highly expressive representation of another person.

But while the user's motion is conveyed in real-time, in CVEs it is still difficult to provide real-time information about appearance (as we have seen in Chapter 3). Two systems that have begun to do this are the Office of the Future project (Raskar et al. 1998) and the Blue-C system (Gross et al. 2003). The Office of the Future project used life-size videoconferencing technology and simulates the situation of being across a desk from the other person (see also the discussion of the related National Teleimmersion Initiative in Chapter 1, and Sadagic et al. 2001 and Towles et al. 2002). The Blue-C system, mentioned in Chapter 1, is an example of a system that manages to combine 3D video of the person with an immersive display format. The system works by switching from transparent to opaque, so that the walls serve both as a display for the user and can capture him or her when the walls are transparent. The two systems represent the video-captured end-point discussed in Chapter 2—compared with a computer-generated avatar and world (although neither system captures the user's gaze). Yet while both systems have been used on a proof-of-concept basis, the value of having both video-captured people and objects in a shared working space has not been extended to practical settings (which could indicate that the technology is not mature or sufficiently inexpensive or that it has limited usefulness).[4]

In the context of collaboration, it is worth noting again that eye gaze and facial expression are in many cases critical for interpersonal interaction, and bodily movement and gesture are needed for successful instrumental interaction. From the real world we are aware of the power of "first impressions." But this is not always important and may not apply to bodily avatar appearance: in many circumstances, people seem to be able to cope with highly unrealistic avatars or do not pay much attention to them, such as when they are engaged in joint tasks that focus on objects or on the environment (Heldal et al. 2005a).

In terms of collaboration, instead of having a sense of being there together, it may be more important that people are able to interact with the other person(s) and with the environment. For instrumental tasks (as we shall see), it may be particularly important that people "compensate" for missing cues—for example, when they cannot see certain parts of their interaction with each other, they may be able to put this part of interaction into words. Conversely, they may use exaggerated body movements to underline something they are saying. Some examples will be given later in this chapter, but under what circumstances people do this has not been systematically investigated, and this "compensation" is something that people will often be unaware of. Furthermore, "compensating" is possibly the wrong term, because users are also able to ignore the absence of many cues: it would be easy, for example to list a host of visual and auditory cues that users do not comment on as being "missing." Conversely, they are able to make creative use of the "superpowers" that CVEs afford them without finding this remarkable—for example, picking up oversized objects.

For work involving orientation, the environment must provide this. Again, certain cues in the environment may be missing in a way that is different from real-world environments: for example, when people walked around in a landscape where many features such as a horizon were lacking (this study will be described shortly), people complained about not knowing whether they had been to particular landmarks before and found it difficult in general to orient themselves (Steed, Spante, Heldal, Axelsson, and Schroeder 2003). In the equivalent real-world scenario, it is much harder to experience this kind of confusion because so many cues in a landscape tell us where we have been (a horizon, for example, or having a sense of how objects are typically positioned in relation to each other, or the physical experience of having traversed a space). The use of landmarks and various other tools for orientation (for example, footprints to mark where one has been; see Munro, Höök, and Benyon 1999 for these and other examples) have therefore been suggested as means to overcome these problems. Moreover, they can be relatively easy to implement and can compensate for missing cues, but again, research on the circumstances in which these are needed and effective is still at an early stage.

Apart from objects and the environment, a key question is interaction with others: What is the relation to the other person(s)? Are they people with whom one is familiar or people with whom one is interacting for the first time (Steed, Spante, Heldal, Axelsson, and Schroeder 2003)? What is the task? (Perhaps it is unspecific socializing, in which case it may be inappropriate to call it a "task.") And finally, but not least, what is the size of the group? If, for example, one is interacting with a larger group, it is difficult, unlike in the real world, to monitor the behavior of several copresent others simultaneously (whereas in the real world, this awareness is relatively easy). When one is interacting with several other people in the VE, does the attention that one can pay to any one of them become "diluted"? (This is much more likely in a VE because mutual awareness is more difficult.)

Interaction with others can, moreover, be important in different ways. For example, in the various settings of the Strangers and Friends trial using networked immersive environments to be described later (Steed et al. 2003), there were many occasions when the tracked bodies and gestures were critical to joint coordination, but the absence of eye gaze and facial expressions was not an important obstacle in this set of tasks. The key point is that in *immersive* collaborative systems, the task is likely to be one in which people have to focus their attention on the space and the objects in it—otherwise these systems would not be used in the first place! Thus, the other person's avatar body will be used for joint orientation, but in these settings people do *not* focus on each other's facial expressions. Furthermore, they will not need realistic-looking bodies; it will be sufficient to be able to follow the other's movements and gestures—the appearance of their body is irrelevant in these tasks (Steed et al. 2003).

One way to underline this point is by noting that if there is more than one other person in the immersive space, the most important feature of the avatar bodies of others is that the user should be able to tell them apart, not what they look like. This is easy to implement: for a small group of tracked life-size avatars, their bodies can be distinguished by means of different colors (Mr. Blue, Mr. Green, etc., or giving them different color shirts, as in the image on the cover of this book).

If we now add that immersive spaces are likely to contain only a small number of (not co-located) people at any given time, it is possible to specify a simple core requirement of immersive spaces for collaboration: for instrumental tasks, the aspects of the environment that facilitate joint orientation and manipulation should be adequate to the task (whereas appearance of the avatar, including expression, is relatively insignificant). Where tasks mainly involve interpersonal communication, facial expressions will be important, but it is unlikely that facial expressions will play a dominant role in a shared immersive space: after all, people will not spend much time in close face-to-face contact in spaces where they mainly focus on the objects and the place. Eye gaze is mainly useful in spatial tasks in immersive spaces to indicate whether people are looking at something that one's collaborators are interested in (and there are means to make eye gaze apparent in MUVEs that go beyond those in face-to-face interaction—such as providing an exaggerated view of where a person's eyes are aimed at, or providing a "laser pointing" view of where the eyes are aimed at).

In immersive spaces then, the need for expressive faces (including eye gaze) depends on the task: the virtual office where one collaborates with another person in trauma counseling, training for public speaking, or acting sessions (where facial expressions are critical) will be quite different from the environment that is required for joint molecular visualization or vehicle design (where joint orientation and referencing objects are most important). Perhaps an avatar face with the possibility to express only certain emotions or only certain acknowledgements of the other person's effort will not only be sufficient in the immersive space but superior—because it will reduce the "cognitive load" in the task.

Collaboration can thus be related to the two end-states that have been discussed in Chapter 1: for instrumental distributed tasks, there will be advantages and disadvantages of computer-generated as opposed to video-captured environments. Even completely computer-generated artificial worlds can be designed so as to put constraints and possibilities into the environment with which the users are familiar and at ease, and as we have already seen, users are able to accept certain "unnatural" features of CVEs, adapt easily to others, and find yet others impossible or difficult to cope with.

The contrast with a video-captured environment is that people will be certain of another person being there (they are, after all, being captured), while in a generated CVEs, mechanisms need to be put in place to ensure that users are "really there": an immobile avatar, for example, may have temporarily abandoned his or her avatar, or another person may have taken their place unless their voice has made their persistence identifiable. In workaday settings, the fidelity of the environments may be selectively applied to certain parts of the environment, such as facial characteristics (realistic or enhanced in some way) that convey essential information but leave out a host of information that is conveyed in face-to-face settings. Similarly, environments may be designed to facilitate easy orientation and mutual awareness by means of various "artificial" features such as maps or locators of other persons.

Before going into detailed examples that illustrate various particular facets of collaboration, it is possible to give an overview of some key issues: how does interaction differ from face-to-face interaction? How easy or difficult it is to perform certain tasks *together*?

So far, we have seen that:

- Users find it difficult to adjust some behaviors to virtual settings, such as using gestures.
- Spatial tasks with objects can be accomplished very successfully, although for joint navigation the space needs to provide the means for orientation.
- Where the focus of attention is on objects and on the environment, the absence of social cues plays a lesser role. This stands in contrast to communication-focused tasks, where social cues play a strong role.
- Compared to face-to-face communication, certain social cues get filtered out, but others get "filtered in"—that is, nonverbal communication is made explicit by means of verbalizing it, or the absence of certain behaviors is compensated by adding other behaviors.

Two conclusions can thus be anticipated: networked IPTs are easy or intuitive to use and effective for highly spatial or visual tasks, but for interpersonal encounters, networked IPTs provide greater awareness of users than desktop systems but otherwise have similar possibilities and constraints. For collaboration, the single most important distinction to make at the outset is thus about the mix of spatial and communicative behavior and how different systems and environments support these, especially in view of what users can and cannot get used to in these settings. These points will be fleshed out in the examples given later.

Tasks, Collaboration, and Systems

The Rubik's Cube

The Rubik's Cube trial has been the most extensive test to compare and evaluate different systems for performance of a spatial task. In this trial, we compared pairs performing a Rubik's Cube–type puzzle in various configurations: IPT-IPT, IPT-HMD, IPT-desktop or IPT-D, desktop-desktop or D-D, and face-to-face or F2F (see Figures 4.1, 4.2, 4.3, and 4.4).

The details and findings have been reported elsewhere (Heldal et al. 2005a; Schroeder et al. 2001; and Heldal, Spante, and Connell 2006 also examined single users). Here the point is to highlight some of the main ones. First, we can look at performance. Figure 4.5 shows the cumulative percentage of pairs that completed the task by the given time for three of the trial conditions (IPT-IPT [ITI], F2F [Real], and IPT-D [ITD]).

For IPT-IPT, eighteen of twenty groups completed the task within 20 minutes (mean = 8.82 minutes, standard deviation [SD] = 4.61 minutes); for ITD, six of twenty-two groups completed the task within the time limit (mean = 15.00 minutes, SD = 3.10 minutes); and in the F2F condition, all groups completed the task within the time limit (mean = 5.75 minutes, SD = 3.72 minutes). The difference between IPT-IPT and F2F was not significant, and allowed us to conclude, as mentioned, that doing this type of task in immersed distributed mode is as good as doing it face-to-face or in the real world. Importantly, this is also a task in which two people collaborating can do this task in many respects better than a single user, either in IPT systems or in the real world (Heldal et al. 2006a).

FIGURE 4.1   Rubik's Cube–type puzzle being done in an IPT system.

FIGURE 4.2   Person doing Rubik's Cube–type puzzle on a desktop computer.

FIGURE 4.3   Persons doing the Rubik's Cube–type puzzle face-to-face.

FIGURE 4.4   Rubik's Cube–type puzzle in various stages of task completion.

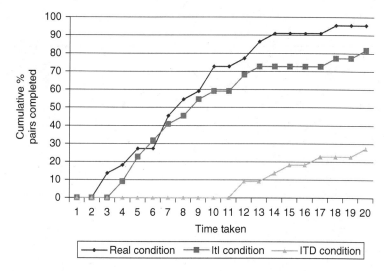

FIGURE 4.5   Cumulative percentage of pairs of participants that completed the task.

This is important because it rules out the possibility that our findings apply to a task that would be easier to do alone than collaboratively. In addition, there were also important findings for presence and copresence, which support the idea that those using more immersive systems reported a stronger sense of presence and copresence than those using less immersive ones.

If we compare different systems in terms of using the same or different systems, the immersive systems (two IPTs) are better than an IPT connected with an HMD system (we did not test two HMD systems, and so the poorer performance in IPT-HMD setting may be to do with the asymmetry between the partners). And asymmetry of systems must play a role because the D-D partners performed better than the IPT-D partners! This might change if the partners were informed from the start about the difference between the systems, but what we also find is that partners in asymmetrical IPT-D settings divide the labor between themselves without being aware of the difference—so, for example, the desktop partner asks the IPT partner to move the cubes. It can be noted immediately that there are practical implications of these findings: upgrading only one system to an immersive one when the other person is using a different (HMD or desktop) system may be counterproductive. Steed and

Parker (2004) also found that selection and manipulation of objects are better with IPTs as opposed to HMDs, and this advantage has been confirmed in other studies (Heldal et al. 2005b). So two key factors can be identified straight away as being critical: asymmetry and immersiveness of the system.

But we can also ask: *how* are the three types of systems or combinations of systems—IPT, HMD, or desktop—most effective for spatial tasks?[5] For example, immersive (IPT or HMD) systems are not always most effective: desktop systems can be more effective than immersive environments for problem-solving when visualizing large-scale and complex molecules because an overview may be needed and particular molecules can be referenced and related to one another (Axelsson et al. 1999). Moreover, this is not just a matter of the immersiveness of the display but also of the interaction styles and devices (Steed and Parker 2004).

Hence performance in a networked immersive (IPT) setting is as good as doing the task in a real-world setting, especially compared to a setting linking an immersive and a desktop system. Yet as soon as people use two different systems, their collaboration becomes unequal. And participants report unequal collaboration if they use different (immersive and desktop) systems, despite being unaware of what type of system the other participant was using.

Yet questionnaires do not tell whole story. For example, even when participants gave answers in our trials (on Likert-type scales) that showed that they experienced different systems in different ways (for example, in terms of how presence and immersiveness are related), they did not indicate (on the Likert-type scales) that they experienced collaboration differently in the different systems—even though their performance was quite different in the different systems! Similarly with self-reports about collaboration when open-ended questions were used, in which participants did not discriminate accurately between the various systems. In other words, directly asking the subjects about their experiences of collaborating does not necessarily provide a good understanding of how well or poorly they collaborate or how they experience collaboration.

A different way to evaluate collaboration is to examine the best and worst performing pairs (details in Heldal, Steed and Schroeder 2005). When this is done, we find for all the different combinations of technologies (F2F, IPT-IPT, IPT-D, IPT-HMD, and D-D) that the experience of solving and collaborating on the Rubik's Cube–type puzzle is enjoy-able (as might be expected) for the best performing pairs—they enjoy working with a stranger in the case of the F2F setting. For the worst performing pairs, on the other hand, it is characteristic that there are misunderstandings and frustrated communication in the MUVE setting, or not working well together in the sense of getting on with each other in the case of the F2F setting.

If we examine the best and worst performing pairs in greater detail, what emerges about the worst performing pairs is a distinction between the D-D condition, where the technology was difficult to use (although this also made it challenging and fun), versus the F2F setting where par-ticipants had different ways of going about things or were temperamen-tally not suited for working together (reserved and domineering people working together, for example). In the IPT-D setting, partners would work in an unbalanced way (for example, the immersed partner snatch-ing the cubes from the desktop partner), whereas in the pairs of immer-sive settings (IPT-HMD, IPT-IPT) there were misunderstandings about who is doing what. In other words, there are subtle differences in the experience of collaboration for each pair of technologies—and for how the face-to-face collaboration is experienced.

In terms of technical difficulties, the heaviness of the HMD and the difficulties of handling the cubes via the devices stand out. Several par-ticipants working on desktop systems in the IPT-D setting also com-plained about problems in manipulating objects and the device to do this (3D mouse)—more so than those in the D-D setting. This suggests that participants in the IPT-D setting were somehow aware of the benefits that their immersed partners had (even though they did not know what system the other was using).

Still, the self-reports by participants about collaboration were often "off the mark." For example, the participants divided the work between themselves—one person doing much of the talking and one doing most of the manipulating of the cubes. Yet they were not aware of this and estimated that they contributed equally to the task. It is easy for observers to pick up on these differences and problems, and these can be checked against the participants' responses to see if the observer's evaluation can be validated. Still, users find it particularly hard to discriminate the differences in the affordances of the different systems (Heldal et al. 2005a).

And while it would be possible to inform them beforehand, this would limit how the trials could yield insights into the different experiences of the systems for collaboration (and knowing that one's partner has a different system might also impose an additional cognitive load on the collaborators).

One advantage that IPT systems have is that they allow users to manipulate objects in a 3D space. So in one study, we compared the advantages and disadvantages (or successes and failures) in immersive systems with the findings of a study which examined object-focused interaction using a desktop-based collaborative VE system (by Hindmarsh, Fraser, Heath, and Benford 2002; Hindmarsh, Fraser, Heath, Benford, and Greenhalgh 1998).[6] To anticipate, the comparison shows (as might be expected) that collaboration is better supported with the IPT system than the desktop system, but it also shows specifically where this is the case and also some of the shortcomings of IPT systems.

The study by Hindmarsh et al. (1998—henceforth simply "the Hindmarsh study") provided an in-depth analysis of collaboration in an object-focused task with a desktop VE system. The main reasons for problematic interaction in this case were visual discontinuities caused by the desktop screen, and hence the study refers to "fragmented interaction." The study involved sets of two and three participants who spent ten minutes familiarizing themselves with the system and thirty minutes performing a furniture arrangement task. The main problem doing this task—imagine a 3D room with furniture on a PC screen that you have to rearrange with one or two remote participants—was the fragmented interaction due the narrow field of view. This forced participants to compensate for the problems by explicitly describing actions and phenomena. Another problem was reduced peripheral awareness, which hindered being able to coordinate actions. Hindmarsh et al. (1998) therefore identified several problematic factors: the limited field of view (FOV), the lack of information about the others' actions, as well slow and clumsy movements and difficulties in doing things simultaneously.[7]

The Hindmarsh study provided the point of departure for analyzing the data from a trial (Heldal et al. 2005b) that used questionnaires (with Likert-type scales and written answers), debriefing interviews, and video and audio recordings of the sessions. The trial also allowed us to select a number of examples of successes and failures that could be analyzed in depth.[8] In the study, participants had to interact with the virtual objects in the space and with each other to do several tasks. For the comparison with the Hindmarsh et al. study, however, we concentrated on the two most object-focused tasks: solving a Rubik's Cube–type puzzle and using Lego-like objects in a Modeling World to build a sculpture together.

The Rubik's Cube–type puzzle task has already been described briefly. The Modeling World environment contained 96 shapes (square blocks, cones, etc.) in six different colors. The subjects were told to make a building or a model of a building to be entered in an architectural competition (see Figure 4.10 below). At least three colors were to be used and the building had to be a single object, their joint "architectural masterpiece." The two tasks provide a nice contrast in that the Rubik's Cube–type puzzle task had a definite goal, whereas the modeling task was much more open-ended. Also, in the Rubik's Cube–type puzzle task, the virtual space was small, roughly the same size as the IPTs (3 m × 3 m) and participants did not have to move about in the space, whereas in the Modeling World, the virtual space was much larger, 14 m × 14 m, and they therefore had to navigate and orient themselves more.

Now it should be remembered that although the IPT system *can* overcome the problem of the limited FOV of the desktop system, there is a limitation to the IPT system in that it is not completely immersive (for example, most systems, including those in this trial, have no ceilings, and there are the encumbrances of wearing joystick and glasses). Second, even though full size, the representations of the users are not perfect: subtle movements, and also eye gaze, are not transmitted by the medium, and gestures with the nontracked arm are not conveyed. Third, the system can be slow and clumsy in representing movements and the objects and the environment. And finally, being able to do things in parallel with the other person can be poorly rendered in an IPT system (we will encounter several examples shortly).

One important and frequent form of interaction in this trial was coordination, and in this respect participants often used gestures to refer to items. However, there were several cases, as in the example that follows, when one person used the nontracked hand to point with, and in the next moment changed to the tracked hand. Even if this kind of behavior generally did not create a particular problem for the other person; it happened quite often and occurred throughout the sessions and is bound to affect how people collaborate in an object-focused task:

L and G were working together with the puzzle, standing almost opposite to each other. G asks L what colors she has on her side and L answers and points with her nontracked and tracked hand, on several occasions.

G: "So ... what color do you have on these ... the other side there?"

L: "Oh, the thing is ... ehhh .... Well, this ... [*points with nontracked hand*] is blue here, then we've [*points with the tracked hand*] got white here and here [*points with nontracked hand*] it's orange. However, ahmm [*sits down and looks at the cubes from beneath*] ... we can't leave the two [*points with nontracked hand*] like that because we've got yellow and ahmm ... yellow [*points with tracked hand*] here and red [*rises, stands up*] on the other side so that's already violated."

G: "Aaah!"

Example 1. *Alternating gestures with the nontracked and tracked hands.*

Participants would sometime realize that they were pointing with the nontracked hand and change to the tracked hand. The next example is where one of the participants wants to help his partner to move one of the Rubik's Cube–type blocks and realizes that this gesture cannot be seen and verbally comments on this:

G: "Here, here ... against me ... Do you see my ... Of course, you can't see my hand ... Damn, I'm waving with my real hand ... Hmm."
[*L makes G aware of the need to use the tracked hand.*]

L: "Sure, yes ... If you point with the joystick hand I'll see it!"

Example 2. *Using the nontracked hand to point.*

What is interesting here is that people made this mistake over and over again, and in the course of several hours. There were also frequent examples of misunderstandings when one person was pointing (correctly) to an object but the partner thought that the reference was to another object nearby. This could be solved, as noted in the Hindmarsh study, by having a "laser-pointer" (as people have for pointing to things on screens in lecture rooms).

Another set of examples concerns people verbalizing their actions, which allowed both partners to better tackle problems. Note how this relates to Chapter 6 (on communication) as participants are using two communication channels (verbal communication and nonverbal communication using indicative gestures) to make their actions explicit. The Hindmarsh study also noted that desktop users needed to compensate for some ambiguity in the situation (which they called "compensating interactions"), especially when people could not see something clearly. In the desktop environment, they could verbalize what they could not do with gestures.

In the IPT settings, in contrast, a typical example is a verbal confirmation of a gesture to establish a mutual understanding about the location of objects or where they should be put in relation to the other's embodiment or to other virtual objects; such as "See the blue cube on your left side." In contrast to the Hindmarsh study, such utterances usually did not compensate for ambiguities but rather supported the general flow of conversation. This is because in the desktop systems, pointing would take a relatively long time, whereas in the IPT systems a simple gesture can be made (on a desktop system, pointing involves the use of keyboard and mouse).

One limitation in object-focused manipulation with the IPT system is that two people cannot hold the same object at the same time. That means that to give to each other an object, one person has to let it go and then the other to pick it up (recall the discussion in Chapter 2). At the same time, there are advantages to the fact that in the IPT, objects in this case did not have gravity. The following example is only possible because the cube hung in the air while the object was being handed over:

> [G and L are standing side by side; G is to the right, working with the cubes.]
>
> L: "Do you have green and orange somewhere?" [G looks for it among the cubes he has on his right side.]

G: "Aah, I think I saw it somewhere here ... Hmm, green and yellow ... Uh..."

[G finds the cube he is looking for, and hands it to L who takes it.]

G: "Here we have green and orange ... Um, orange. Here you are."

Example 3. *Handing over the cubes to the partner*.

Another phenomenon that could be observed was about the "gluing" function of small social phrases. There are several examples when participants were working independently, but from time to time they would ask each other, "What are you doing?" "Everything is all right?", "Are you there?" This, together with the possibility to quickly take a glance at one's partner, contributed to maintaining the flow of interaction. This "gluing" function also applies to mutual monitoring: many examples could be given where the participants are working in parallel, quite silently, but also follow each other's movements throughout this time and are thus able to follow on from one another's actions.

The full-size bodies in the IPT systems, unlike using desktop systems, function to inform the partners about (1) one's position and (2) the direction of movements and gaze direction—and (3) they can be used as a reference object. For example, participants would often refer to the Rubik's Cube–type puzzle by its position as being close to a part of the embodiment such as legs, arms, head, or shoulders. And even though the cubes had different colors on their sides, it was easier to refer to a cube as "that one by the side of your leg" than to indicate the colors that would not necessarily have been the same as the partner's (because of the different view). An example is the following:

[G has some difficulties with placing objects close to the ground.]

G: "OK, L, for technical reasons we have to start the building at chest level."

L: "OK..."

[They start to build and L offers to fill in missing pieces underneath if G wants him to. L then places a block at approximately chest level and says:]

L: "I'll put things where you can reach them then ..."

Example 4. Using embodiment as reference.

This example clearly shows how the partners can work together on object manipulation in a way that would be very difficult in a desktop situation, especially in terms of awareness of body and relative distance and scale.

Still, there could be confusion about how to interpret left and right, as in the following example, even when the position of the object is indicated in relation to the avatar:

> *[L and G are facing each other and have right and left on different sides, thus the misunderstanding.]*
>
> L: "Now we have blue on your left side. Blue on your left side."
> G: "You mean right ... oh ... yeah, towards ..."
> G: "Your left?"
> L: "The left side!"
> G: "OK, OK, sorry."

Example 5. Referring to the partner's specific side.

What we can see in these examples is that IPT systems can overcome many of the constraints of desktop systems but also have some lesser constraints of their own. The IPT system allows much intuitive collaborative interaction, and this also allows people to concentrate on solving the task together. Participants frequently manipulated the environment while speaking to each other, whereas with the desktop VE systems, they often had to concentrate on one *or* the other. Still, other problems such as pointing with the nontracked hand remain common in the IPT system.

Collaborating in IPTs even works well for complex and tightly coupled tasks. To illustrate this, we can examine a different task where pairs of participants build a gazebo (Figure 4.6).[9]

The task involved close collaboration to fit planks and supports together and required both participants to carry objects and fix parts *together*. In this case, the wide FOV, control of gaze (at least roughly where the other person is looking), and accurate representation of pointing support the efficient referencing of objects. A typical conversation

FIGURE 4.6   Building a gazebo together. (Image courtesy of Dave Roberts, Salford University.)

between two collaborators—Bob and Lara in this case—engaged with moving a heavy beam using carry tools, can illustrate this:

> Bob: "Hey, let's move this beam over there." *[Points with his hand to the beam in front of him and to the left.]*
>
> Lara: *[Rotating to see Bob and then follows his hand movements.]*
>
> Lara: "Ok, I will take this carry tool here." *[Points to the tool and moves to pick it up.]*
>
> Bob: "I'll take the other tool then. Where is that?"
>
> Lara: "Just next to you."
>
> Bob: "Ah, OK." *[Rotates and picks up the tool.]*
>
> Lara: "I have my end of the beam now."
>
> Bob: "Yup, I am right with you. OK now, let's move it over there."
>
> Lara: "I am following your direction."

Here we can see how verbal and nonverbal communication are used in a nuanced way while referring to objects and places within the environment. For example, a participant might point to an object and say "let's pick that up" and then rapidly turn and point to a place in the environment, saying "and take it over there." Another example is a participant simply taking an object and telling the other participant to do the same. These gestures happen very fluidly and there is an implicit assumption on the part of the participant performing the gesture that their collaborator will see and hear the gesture immediately. This type of fluidity in the collaboration also occurred during the Rubik's Cube–type puzzle, but in the Gazebo we see that the same also applies to handling objects together and when building a predefined object together.

For way-finding, it was interesting that in the Landscape task (see figure 4.7 below), pairs often got lost because the horizon was similar (and there was no lighting and shadow to indicate the direction of the sun). Walking or exploring together in the Landscape also resulted in different ways that avatar bodies were treated: sometime partners would run "through" each other's avatars, and on occasion, this would cause embarrassment ("Sorry, I'm running through you again"), but at other times the same pairs might not notice this. It seems when people are concentrating on objects or manipulating them together, they don't notice interfering with each other's avatars, while when they are aware of the other's avatar when walking around not concentrating on anything else, avatar "collisions" are noticed.

A different perspective on collaboration in IPT systems emerges if we break the interaction down into the following elements: social

FIGURE 4.7   The Landscape Task.

interaction, interaction via technology, and interaction in order to reach the goal.[10] This enables us to single out what users are concentrating or focusing on (if we recall the discussion in Chapter 2 about these different elements, and how focus on several of them can be a strain in MUVEs) and how this contributes to task performance. Many examples of hindrances and enabling features could be given, most of them having to do with shortcomings of the technology: poor audio, bumping into the walls of the display, being unable to identify objects, and the like. Some of these problems will be solved with improved technology. Here we can concentrate on where these problems illustrate important aspects of interaction and collaboration in shared immersive spaces.

One aspect that participants are able to handle easily is that they treat objects as being solid (having mass)—or not—as the situation requires, and alternating between these two states. When solving the WhoDo mystery (to be discussed shortly), for example, participants would sometimes go through objects like chairs and tables, but at other times would walk around them or pick them up (by clicking on them with the wand joystick). Or again, for the Rubik's Cube–type puzzle, the participants handled the cubes almost like real objects even though they had neither mass nor gravity. This means that a participant could mark (click on) an object, move it to her or his partner, and leave it (the object would stay suspended in the space), while the other "took it" and moved it where she or he wished. This is clearly hard to do in nonimmersive CVEs.

Another interesting phenomenon is how people handled each other's avatar during these tasks. The typical pattern was that they would comment on each other's avatar (and ask about their own appearance) when they started working together, go through the other's avatar when necessary during the course of the task (occasionally being embarrassed by this and saying "excuse me" and the like), and then treating the other person's avatar as if it were "real" or solid again at the end of the sessions (we also saw that they did this during the Landscape task).[11] The most amusing part of this was that after successful sessions, many of the pairs "shook" each other's hand (tried to move their virtual hand to the partner's hand), others waved good-bye to each other at the end of almost every task, and one pair lifted their hands over their heads and tried to "high five" each other. Recall that similar phenomena apply to desktop online worlds when people gesture to each other as if touching the other's body, and even in videoconferencing sessions people wave to each other.

Another noticeable phenomenon is how participants would use brief utterances—"Great," "Precise," "Cool," "Fine," "Perfect," and the like—to give each other feedback on the collaboration, even though the partners seldom reacted to these phrases (note the difference here with text-based worlds, where utterances without reply are impossible because they would be seen as rude). These utterances also kept the interaction going because longer periods of silence could be confusing if partners did not know whether their partner was listening, intentionally or unintentionally ignoring their comments, or experiencing a technical failure. Keeping a running commentary on the task was also useful to make explicit to the partner what you are doing (though occasionally this could lead to similar problems as in videoconferencing systems when there are "overlapping conversations," which is even more difficult in desktop text-based systems). Thus making one's actions explicit is important not only for social interaction and awareness, but also for managing the task (explaining where you are, which part of the task you are doing, and the like). Nonverbal communication—gestures, making your partner aware of what you are doing with your movements, and locating the partner in relation to your own position and activity—all these features support collaboration. The main features that are missing are facial expressions and gaze.

An interesting phenomenon that we have already encountered (and will encounter again) is that participants are often not aware of the kind of technology their partner is using. For example, one of the IPT systems used in the trial had only three horizontal walls, whereas the other had four surrounding walls, which meant that the person with three walls often needed to do tasks differently. This, however, went unnoticed.

As for navigation, when people are in IPTs together, they locomote in strange ways: for example, they "fly" backward and forward with a joystick to fetch objects, and they notice or ignore each other in ways that depart from the real world such that one person may ignore another who has technical difficulties. Now this type of behavior that departs from face-to-face interaction is typical when working together in distributed mode and immersively. The reason for highlighting it is that we are often able to cope with this easily; this kind of "unnatural" behavior that breaks the rules of face-to-face behavior in the physical world is unproblematic. (This also applies to other technologies like telephones and online games—some of the conventions of collaborating with others, even if they are "unnatural,", are easily mastered.)

In general, it can be seen that in certain ways, people easily accept the nonrealistic nature of immersive spaces and adapt to certain aspects (moving through people) and fail to adapt to others (pointing with the nontracked hand, as seen earlier). These characteristics furthermore have design implications, and also implications for understanding social interaction in MUVEs. As for the latter, it is particularly noticeable that people tend to break with social conventions—moving through the other's avatar—when their focus is on the task or in the middle of the session—whereas they follow social conventions (shaking "hands") or moving around the avatar at the beginning or end of the task when their focus is on each other.

One limitation of networked immersive systems is that they have not been used or tested during longer periods or in routine situations.[12] Yet another limitation is that trials of these systems typically involve strangers, people who don't know each other, whereas in most uses of computer-mediated communication, people work and interact with people they already know.[13] Hence we carried out an exploratory study to address both limitations (reported in Steed, Spante, Heldal, Axelsson, and Schroeder 2003). Pairs spent more than three and one-half hours together inside the same virtual space almost continuously (even though they were in different countries) and performed five different collaborative tasks. This allowed us to examine their interaction over time as well as their experience of different tasks. The pairs consisted of two sets of friends, people who knew each other well (or mutual history pairs), and three sets of strangers (or zero-history pairs), and some of the tasks were sociable (that is, they focused not just on achieving a defined objective but also involved open-ended creativity and exploration), whereas others were mainly spatial tasks. All tasks were highly interactive and collaborative—which is the main advantage of networked immersive VEs.

The study included qualitative observations, questionnaires, debriefing interviews, and making video and audio recordings of the sessions. The tasks took a minimum of twenty-five minutes and a maximum of seventy minutes, with short breaks between tasks. The tasks (we have encountered these before) were:

1. Rubik's Cube–type puzzle puzzle, using a small-scale version of the popular Rubik's Cube–type puzzle with eight blocks with different colors on each side so that each side would have a single color (that is, four squares of the same color on each of the six sides).

2. Landscape orientation—the environment in this case was a small townscape with surrounding countryside ringed by mountains. Subjects were instructed to familiarize themselves with this landscape and to count the number of buildings. They were also told that they would be asked to draw a map of the environment at the end of the task.

3. WhoDo—this task was based on a popular game, in this case the "who-dunnit" board game, ClueDo. The subjects were asked to find five murder weapons and five suspects in a building with nine rooms. They needed to locate the murder victim's body and find and eliminate weapons and suspects.

4. Poster World—this environment consisted of a room with ten posters stuck on the walls. The posters each contained a list of six sentence fragments. When all the fragments were put in the right order, they would make a popular saying or phrase (see also Slater, Sadagic, Usoh, and Schroeder 2000).

5. Modeling World—this environment contained ninety-six shapes (square blocks, cones, etc.) in six different colors. The subjects were told to make a building or model of a building to be entered into an architectural competition. They had to use at least three colors and the building had to be a single object. The result was to be their joint "architectural masterpiece."

The tasks therefore ranged from an almost entirely verbal task with a fixed goal (Poster World) to an open-ended task that involved lots of navigation and manipulation of objects (Modeling World).

The detailed findings about how people collaborate across the five tasks and in strangers (zero-history) versus friends (pairs who knew each other well) are reported elsewhere.[14] Here it will suffice to draw attention to a few points. First, it was surprising (or unexpected in relation to what we thought we might find) how similar friends and strangers were

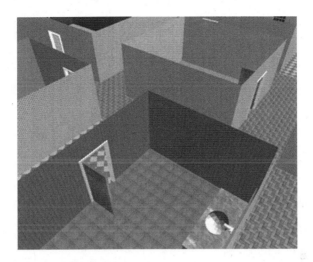

FIGURE 4.8   The WhoDo Task.

FIGURE 4.9   The Poster World Task. (Image courtesy of Anthony Steed, University College London. Note that this image is from a different trial involving three rather than two participants.)

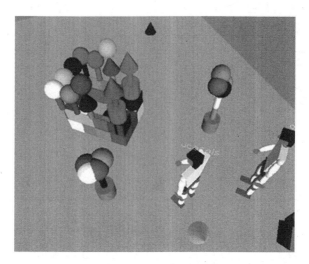

FIGURE 4.10   The Modelling World Task.

in terms of their interactions with each partner and how they handled the tasks. Yet when asked to rate their awareness of their partner's intentions or wishes, strangers reported lower mutual awareness than friends—and this is borne out by observations. Comments made by the two groups of participants also shed light on these differences: from strangers, "cool to be able to work together" but also "the lack of body language makes communication harder"; and for friends, "good to have her with me."

To the question, "What did you find hardest to do together with the other person," the answers from strangers included "to make him understand my ideas," and from friends, "difficult to agree" and "get him to understand which direction I meant." Our own observations add another dimension to this point: mutual history pairs engaged in more "small talk" that was unrelated to the task. Still, on the whole, there was little difference in their ability to perform the task together, and we concluded that this absence of a major difference could itself be seen as a significant finding: it may be that for these kinds of spatial and environment-related collaborative activities (unlike a videoconference focusing on verbal discussion, perhaps), whether people are strangers or friends plays little role. Note how this differs from what people often say about videoconferencing—that it is much easier when people already know each other face-to-face.

In terms of the difference between the tasks, we found that how participants rate the pleasantness and difficulty of the tasks did not correspond to the order of the tasks (which was the same for all participants); in other words, the later ones were not regarded as less pleasant or more difficult because of fatigue. But participants found the most open-ended and sociable tasks the easiest and most enjoyable, which suggests that the less sociable and more "closed" (closely coupled and instrumental) tasks are regarded as less enjoyable and harder in this setting. Again, note how this contrasts with a point often made about videoconferencing; that a more structured organization of meetings is more enjoyable and easier than more open-ended and unstructured encounters.

The main technical problem that was commented on was display quality, especially for one of the displays that used a screen with poor contrast. What is notable here, as in our other trials using immersive technology, is that the technology apart from the display quality (which has since improved considerably) works well. And as we have already seen, certain tasks, such as moving around and manipulating objects, are regarded as easy. What was hard was negotiating tasks—keeping track of the other person and coordinating who is doing what. As we saw earlier, these coordination tasks have also been found hard for desktop or nonimmersive CVE systems, but in these systems, navigating and manipulating objects is also difficult. Note also that keeping the flow of conversation going and complex negotiation are not difficult tasks in similar real-world situations. In networked VEs, however, like in videoconferences, these tasks are hard because the absence of face-to-face cues and poor voice quality do not allow for flowing conversation. And again, physical bodies and environments allow us to keep track of other people's locations easily and accurately, but in shared IPTs the lack of a detailed and rich visual environment with bodies that make noises and the like means that it is difficult to monitor one's partner.

One pair of strangers deserves a special mention because unlike the other pairs, they reported that they did not enjoy doing the tasks together. Unlike the other pairs, who introduced themselves to each other, acknowledged what the other was doing, faced each other, and shared jokes—this pair consistently failed to communicate difficulties and did not establish much common conversational ground. This, we suspect, was to do with the fact that they were unable to establish a rapport with each other at the start, and although they carried out the tasks just as easily, the failure to create a shared enjoyable experience persisted throughout the tasks. We can surmise that even though CVEs may lend themselves to effective collaboration, they may not be able to cope well with interpersonal aspects of collaboration if these get off to a bad start. This finding can be related to Walther's (1996) argument that online relations need more time than face-to-face relations to establish themselves, and they depend on what partners are able to "put into" the establishment of a relationship. It may also be, however, that networked immersive systems, unlike text-based computer-mediated communication (as in Walther's case), do not allow for an adjustment of mutual impressions, because the focus is more on the task and the environment in this case (rather than focusing on mutual understanding by communicating).

For the other pairs, the experience was different: their interaction was very friendly, included a lot of small talk, and they kept each other aware of what they were doing. And there are examples of pairs (unlike the bad rapport pair just mentioned) that improved how they handled their collaboration over time. For example, during the WhoDo task (where a lot of coordination about looking in different rooms is required), one person said: "I will stand in the room now so tell me what you are up to so that we don't have to run around." Or in the modeling task, one person said, "Now I also want to wander around and see how this house looks." These are examples of making explicit to the other person what they may not be aware of, unlike in an equivalent F2F situation.

Again, it can be stressed that these were highly collaborative tasks and that it was surprising that the technology coped well with allowing the pairs to work together. Nevertheless, with the possible exception that partners who were friends were more aware of the other person's intentions, there were no major differences between the pairs of strangers and friends (which we had expected).[15] There were, however, differences between the tasks, so that more sociable and creative tasks were reported and observed as being more enjoyable and easier than purely instrumental or spatial ones. This is curious, because in the latter set of tasks, the absence of interpersonal cues is not so critical. It may be, however, that the open-ended and creative nature of the former types of tasks overrides the need for interpersonal cues, although more research would be needed to confirm this hunch.[16]

These findings can be put into the context that many aspects of the technology such as displays are likely to improve significantly. In this light, it becomes clear that the problems of collaboration that have been described here are much more to do with the social part of the interaction, and that technological improvements are required above all in the communication of facial expressions. Still, for spatial tasks, immersive technology is appropriate even for longer periods (although it is also important to think about the physical part of this setting—for example, that people need to sit down to rest or that users may feel as if they are under surveillance when they spend so much time inside the virtual space). Still, the tasks in this study were such that they provide good demonstrations of collaborative tasks that can be carried out in immersive VEs even though they are difficult in the real world, or they can be done more effectively or enjoyably in the virtual world.

Finally, it is interesting to think about the different forms of adaptation to VEs that take place with these longer uses of MUVEs. As we have seen, sometimes people adapt to the environment, whereas at other times there is no adaptation even though there ought to be. It is also possible that some forms of adaptation take place at the expense of each other: For example, if one gets used to teleporting or flying, one might not be able to adapt to having an awareness of virtual spaces as one might have if it was necessary to traverse spaces on foot. Over time, it may become "automatic" to use CVEs in certain ways, as has happened with other devices.

Long-Term Collaboration

A different way to examine longer-term interaction or collaboration in online worlds is by means of quasi-experimental research. One question that can be asked in light of the absence of studies of longer-term uses is, How do people who already know each other work on different tasks together over a series of sessions? To investigate this, we undertook an exploratory trial within our own group of researchers, organizing ten one-hour meetings in Active Worlds (AW) among four participants (the author and three colleagues).[17] The aim was to explore both technical and social problems over the course of these meetings. One feature that set these meetings apart from commonplace uses of AW and systems like SL is that we used voice communication in addition to text.

As mentioned earlier, the longer-term uses of MUVEs have hardly been investigated. For immersive systems, the study that involved pairs collaborating over the course of more than three hours that has been described earlier in this chapter is among the few. Williams and colleagues followed the longer-term uses of online games (see Chapter 5, Williams 2006; Williams, Caplan, and Xiong 2007; Williams, Yee, and Caplan 2008). In the course of our ten sessions, we found that the main technical problems were related to voice communication. We also found that technical issues and issues involving the design of the VE, which have been the focus of much research on VEs, were much less important than specific social issues, including awareness of each other and structuring the organization of the meetings. We also found that we—as participants—adjusted to the constraints of the system over time, and in this sense adapted to it.

Much of the previous research on long-term uses of MUVEs is about issues such as nausea, human factors, and ergonomics (Stanney, Mourant, and Kennedy 1998), importing virtual behavior into real-life situations, and addiction (frequently discussed in the popular literature on VR and in relation to online games; see Lee and Peng 2006). In technologies *related* to VR, the following have also often been discussed: computer and Internet addiction (Shotton 1989)[18] and "cultivation" theory for television (users get a distorted view of reality with prolonged exposure; see Shanahan and Morgan 1999). Other studies related to online behavior are concerned with physiological or psychological effects, and these are reviewed in Nilsson, Heldal, Schroeder, and Axelsson (2002). This also applies to "adaptation," which can, for example, result in motion sickness or eye strain, especially with immersive systems. Here the term "adaptation" is used in a more general way, to indicate how the interaction changes to accommodate itself to the VE setting.

The main previous study that involved multiuser communication tasks in a desktop setting repeatedly over weekly sessions over the course of four years was the COVEN (COllaboration in Virtual ENvironments) trial, the main aim of which was to enhance the usability of the technology (see Tromp 2001 and Chapter 7). The findings showed that (because desktop systems were used) neither simulation sickness nor ergonomic problems were of major concern. It also proved easy to learn skillful ways of navigating and to adapt to the non-natural way of manipulating objects. Nevertheless, the trial was experienced as mentally tiresome and stressful, which could simply be because it is more exhausting to concentrate one's attention on the VE and on others in the VE than in similar real-world encounters. Also, there were problems with the audio and with orientation in the VE that continued over the course of the trial, and the participants also did not seem to get used to inconsistencies in worldview between the users. Finally, special functions were added to overcome the difficulties in communicating (a mechanism to form a group, graphical sound waves to indicate visually which avatar was speaking, and so on). In sum, the key problem in having networked meetings in small groups in desktop systems over the longer term revolved around coordinating with each other rather than around the environment.

For our trial in AW, we got together for ten one-hour meetings, with one meeting per week, to carry out various activities together. We filled out a questionnaire after each meeting covering key technical and social issues in MUVEs (for details, see Nilsson, Heldal, Schroeder, and Axelsson 2002). Of course, carrying out the trial among a group of researchers meant that we were not "unbiased subjects." On the other hand, we were able to comment on the system as expert users. Another unusual characteristic of the trial was that all four of us knew each other very well before the trial—we had all been working in the same department for more than a year and knew each other as both colleagues and friends. This is an advantage insofar as it is a common everyday scenario in terms of how people collaborate in distributed mode. Finally, two of the four participants were familiar with the VE, having spent more than 100 hours in AW, whereas the other two had spent a total of less than two hours in the VE previously. As we shall see, this is an important difference.

Again, the study and the results are described in detail elsewhere, including the tasks. The tasks can be classified into four different types: (1) *planning and decision-making*, (2) *teaching and learning*, (3) *collaborative building*, and (4) *joint exploration*. We found that, overall, there were no major obstacles to using AW for long-term collaborative meetings and tasks. Once we look more closely, however, there were a number of specific features that were problematic.

The most common technical problem during the trial in relation to long-term use was audio. This is very similar to what was found in the COVEN trial.[19] We used an audio technology that was complementary to AW because voice was not available within AW at the time (1999) with press-to-talk technology. This allowed us to speak one at a time. Internet telephony has of course progressed considerably since then and is often used with newer systems like SL. Despite this, audio is still problematic in Internet telephony and in videoconferencing systems (as we shall see in Chapter 9).

As for the sense of presence and copresence, it is evident in using a system like AW over a long time that this is not so much something that one remains aware of but rather fades into the background and depends on what one is *doing* together. Further, and this is a point we have encountered in Chapter 2 and will return to in Chapter 9, it is difficult to distinguish between copresence and awareness in this setting.

Similarly, avatar appearance is not important in this context. We changed avatars only occasionally, mainly for fun, and little attention was paid to this. We have already seen that when the focus is on the collaboration (as opposed to when people get to know each other for the first time) avatar appearance is less important. One interesting feature of the trial was how users' personalities, although initially "backgrounded," increasingly came into the foreground over the course of several online meetings. Put differently, personal characteristics "shone through" over the course of time. For example, there was sometimes frustration that things were taking too much time or about not having a clear goal, but sometimes also great enthusiasm for the tasks which seemed to relate clearly to our "real" personalities. This point is striking because we were not aware of it during the meetings themselves, but it emerged clearly when reading the questionnaire responses, especially for later meetings.

Push-to-talk voice technology meant that only one person could speak at a time (this problem is not unique to VEs, but can also apply to Internet telephony). This entails getting used to waiting for others when they are talking and an absence of verbal feedback while speaking. Hence, strict turn-taking in the conversation is needed. This does not get easier over time, but we became somewhat used to it. Turn-taking problems have been widely discussed in research on computer-mediated communication (as we have seen earlier in this chapter). In online desktop worlds, the key problem for collaborating is that it is very *difficult to express ideas, emotions, and opinions* in a VE: more effort is needed than in the real world. You have to be very explicit in what you say and refer more clearly to the objects and actions that you mention than you would in the real world. This is something that you get used to—and even though the difficulty does not go away over time, participants improved in expressing themselves in a suitable way.

It can also be mentioned that text communication was used in the trial in two ways: (1) as a back-up when other (voice) communication failed (this includes both when audio fails and when you cannot say anything because the audio-channel is busy) and (2), less commonly, to emphasize or clarify a word or a topic. The whisper function (text directed to one person only) was rarely used, mainly to not disturb participants with issues that were not relevant to them. Gestures or extra functions for nonverbal avatar expression (like "happy," "dance," and "wave" buttons that allow you to change avatar appearance in AW) were used very rarely. They were tried out initially, mainly for fun, but more or less died out over the course of the sessions.

In our sessions the participants were not really looking at each other's avatars and had difficulties in keeping track of others and what they were doing. This makes collaboration and coordination problematic. Experienced users seem to bother a lot less about a low degree of awareness, perhaps because they have become used to not being aware of others in this setting. The same applies to orientation and to the inconsistent or perceived inconsistent behavior of others (for example, flying, passing through objects, and so on).

For collaboration, a key difficulty was structuring the session. It is tricky to get joint agreement in a group and discussions take a longer time (though if we compare some asynchronous text-only collaboration, computer-mediated communication may be better than face-to-face meetings, see Scott 1999). In online worlds, it is difficult to know when someone would like to take a turn speaking or when they are satisfied with what has been said. Again, the lack of nonverbal cues is a key barrier. And although we had intended the sessions to be unstructured, the need for greater coordination became increasingly obvious over the course of the sessions. This finding is consistent with the findings of the COVEN trial.

The main problem in coordination is awareness. The problem lies in trying to organize your activity with others (does the other person want to do what you want to do? Which tasks are best divided into groups, and which can be done together?). It is more difficult to organize activity in small groups in VWs than in real meetings. One way to avoid this, incidentally, is to keep down the number of participants working together. It often seemed that pairs work better than groups of three or four. And it was valuable to have a leader organizing and driving the meetings forward—yet at the same time the lack of cues caused difficulties for leadership, such as in not providing the leader with adequate information.

Collaboration and coordination are particularly difficult in expressing ideas related to space. When discussing common objects, there is a need to understand the space; for example, knowing where to put an object or in which direction to look. (This is a major difference with collaboration in immersive VR systems, as seen earlier in this chapter.) In the VW setting, there was often confusion and difficulty in understanding each other, but this occurred mainly in relation to building things *together* and exploring places *together*. In relation to objects, there were some problems with object ownership while building (it is not always clear who has taken ownership of an object). It seems that the best results were often achieved when everyone was working on their own (and reconvening for updates) rather than collaborating—and next best when working with one other person—with little awareness of the others. The implication is that the question of which activities can be carried out effectively *collaboratively* still needs much investigation.

Overall, some of the difficulties mentioned diminished over time. In other words, an "adaptation" to the environment took place, and this also applies to coping with the need for greater coordination (and the lack thereof). Nevertheless, the lack of mutual understanding became more of a problem rather than less of one, at least in terms of our awareness of this. The two users who were less experienced with the system also expressed more frustration about this than the skilled/experienced users.

Again, the trial highlighted the centrality of social rather technical problems, and technical problems also become "backgrounded" over the course of time—one adapts to them in the sense of ignoring them—while social problems are increasingly "foregrounded." A number of recommendations for design follow, such as better tools for awareness and turn-taking. For example, an "I am currently not available" indicator for one's avatar appearance, as was implemented in the software of the COVEN trial, with the avatar lying "sleeping" on the ground, would be useful. Or an "arrange this group in the optimal configuration to see each other" function would improve meetings or instruction/teaching sessions (there have been experiments with this, but it is also potentially a "coercive" way to handle other people's avatars). Above all, however, there might be better means to allow avatars to make thoughts or feelings more explicit to enhance the collaboration.

Summary

As we have seen, it is possible to do a range of tasks together in immersive spaces—not just manipulating objects and visualizing complex models but also exploring spaces, building, rehearsing acting, and many others. This point can be put negatively: Immersive spaces are *not* useful *unless* the tracked body is used to *do* something, such as moving in relation to the objects or interacting with them. If bodily motion and interacting is not used—that is, if the objects are simply being pointed to and the environment navigated through by pointing—it is better to display the 3D space on a large two-dimensional screen. This point may be obvious, but it is often ignored by developers of immersive 3D models and also by people who use IPT technologies and stand immobile while navigating with the joystick.[20]

On the whole, however, immersive spaces *are* useful for collaborating on spatial tasks. Even tasks that can be done better together on desktop systems, such as molecular visualization, might work better in immersive spaces if, for example, it was possible to zoom in and out of the model rather than just flying in and around it. The main aspects that immersive spaces support poorly are facial expressions and awareness of where people are gazing. And collaboration on interpersonal tasks such as negotiation (Garau 2003) or acting rehearsals (Slater and Steed 2002) can be supported in MUVEs but will require suitable means for presenting persons' facial expressions.

Again, it can be noted that there not many examples of larger numbers of people collaborating in immersive MUVEs,[21] but there is no practical reason, apart from the technology being expensive (and that a person is typically required to run an IPT system while someone is using it), why such immersive gatherings should not become more common.[22] This is an important point that relates to future technology development: it used to be thought that network bandwidth constrained distributed immersive (and desktop) CVEs. Now, however, it is the technology for immersion—plus user demand for being immersed—that is the constraint on the future of immersive places to collaborate (and socialize).

NOTES

1. As Jää-Aro points out in his thesis (2004: 28), no one has been able to show that *presence* enhances task performance.

2. One indication that collaboration in MUVEs is a popular activity is that sandboxes—which allow people to build things together—are popular places for socializing in SL (Boellstorff 2008: 99).

3. The following is based on an unpublished paper with Anthony Steed.

4. The workings of shared video-captured environments for collaboration apart from those that immerse users (that is, those treated here)—sometimes called "media spaces"—are now documented in Harrison (2009).

5. The following is based on Heldal, Steed, and Schroeder (2005).

6. This section is based on Heldal, Steed, Spante, Bengtsson, and Partanen (2005b).

7. Fraser (2000: xi), whose thesis examined object-focused collaboration, similarly points out that the "peculiarities of object-focused CVE interaction… includ[e] difficulties in: peripheral monitoring and gaze direction; misleading user representations; organising actions for their visibility by others; 'seeing what others users see.'"

8. Details can be found in Heldal et al. (2005b); only a small part of this study is reported here.

9. The following is based on Steed, Roberts, Schroeder, and Heldal (2005).

10. This section reports on the findings of Heldal, Brathe, Steed, and Schroeder (2006).

11. It can be mentioned that both how people treat objects and how they treat avatars (passing through them or treating them as if they were solid) raise issues for the study of presence and copresence; namely, how is it possible to have such different experiences that nevertheless do not seem to have a detrimental effect on the experience of presence and copresence?

12. This section is based on Steed, Spante, Heldal, Axelsson and Schroeder 2003; see also Spante 2009.

13. These shortcomings have been identified for studies of computer-supported-cooperative work (CSCW) and computer-mediated communication (CMC) in general (Scott, 1999).

14. Details are given in Steed, Spante, Heldal, Axelsson, and Schroeder (2003).

15. It might be interesting to see if this result holds up even for cases where partners have photo-realistic images of each other, which might enhance the familiarity between "friends" but also lessen the "estrangement" among strangers.

16. For a different scenario of four "friend" collaborators using a desktop system, see the discussion in the next section, where more structured tasks were found to be in some respects more enjoyable (Nilsson, Heldal, Schroeder, and Axelsson 2002).

17. Wadley and Ducheneaut (forthcoming) undertook an exploratory study of object-focused collaboration in Second Life—in this case, building together in groups of two or three and doing this for one and one-half hours or longer. They found, among other things, that avatar bodies were little used in this task—much of the time, avatars were "parked"—and that, rather than working together, the task was "modularized" in the group. That is, as in our sessions (Nilsson, Heldal, Schroeder, and Axelsson 2002), a division of labor took place whereby individuals would work on subcomponents of the task alone and then assemble the whole building together only at the end. Put differently, unlike in immersive VEs where two or more people can perform closely coupled tasks together (Roberts, Wolff, Otto, and Steed 2003), this kind of work is too difficult in desktop-based nonimmersive VEs. Wadley and Ducheneaut suggest that it may be more useful to support collaboration in 3D spaces like Second Life by making the objects easier to handle collaboratively (for example, making sure it is clear who has control of an object by highlighting this) rather than, for example, making avatar gestures more realistic.

18. As Boellstorff points out (2008: 177), addiction is not a useful way to describe user behaviour (as is often done in the press), although as Yee (2006) has shown, many users think they spend too much time in online worlds, as people do for other activities.

19. According to Anthony Steed, who was coordinator of COVEN (personal communication, January 25, 2001).

20. For IPT systems, it is common for users not to use the technology to its full extent—one often has to tell users to move their head, body, and hand

(to pick up things) to experience the 3D capabilities and about the ability to interact with the environment.

21. There are exceptions, such as Waterworth, Waterworth and Westling (2002), although this was a highly coordinated performance.

22. It may be difficult to build or co-manipulate or navigate together in larger groups (Nilsson, Heldal, Schroeder, and Axelsson 2002). When there are more than two people, avatars tend to split into groups. One way to appreciate this point in a roundabout way is that it is very easy, for example, for a teacher or instructor to tether one or more avatars to them, and thus demonstrate how to build or find a place (Dodds and Ruddle 2008), which is difficult to do in the same way in the real world.

FIGURE 1.1   Avatars solving a Rubik's Cube-type puzzle in an IPT system. (Image courtesy of Will Steptoe and Anthony Steed at University College London and Dave Roberts of Salford University.)

FIGURE 1.3   Two people collaborating remotely on virtual objects as if they are sitting across the table from each other, from the National Tele-immersion Initiative. (Photograph courtesy of Amela Sadagic, Henry Fuchs, and Herman Towles.)

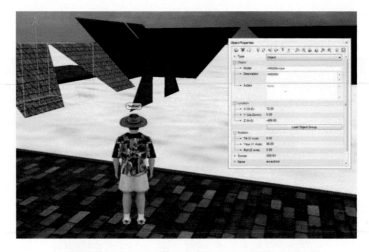

FIGURE 3.1   Building in ActiveWorlds. (Image courtesy of Andy Hudson-Smith.)

FIGURE 4.6   Building a gazebo together. (Image courtesy of Dave Roberts, Salford University.)

FIGURE 4.7   The Landscape Task.

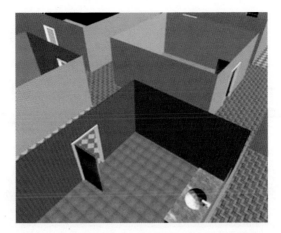

FIGURE 4.8   The WhoDo Task.

FIGURE 4.9   The Poster World Task (Image courtesy of Anthony Steed, University College London. Note that this image is from a different trial involving three rather than two participants).

FIGURE 4.10   The Modelling World Task.

FIGURE 5.1   Oxford University in Second Life (Image courtesy of Eric Meyer)

FIGURE 6.1   OnLive Traveler

FIGURE 9.1   High-end videoconferencing system

5

Social Life in Online Worlds

This chapter will examine how people interact in large-scale persistent multiuser virtual environments (MUVEs). Indeed, it is anachronistic to use the term MUVEs in this context because these VEs are mainly places for socializing and gaming. In this chapter, I will therefore mostly refer to virtual worlds (VWs) because the purpose of these online spaces is to provide an ongoing place for social interaction among a large population of people represented by avatars. As mentioned in Chapter 1, there has been little overlap between research on immersive and experimental MUVEs compared with research on VWs for socializing and gaming, and the two have also been quite separate in terms of the developer and user communities as well as in the public mind. One of the arguments of this chapter, however, is that this distinction is not always useful: many issues apply to both.

It may seem odd to consider issues such as copresence in online desktop VWs alongside the same issues in immersive MUVEs because desktop VWs evidently use less immersive technology. Yet this may be so because copresence is typically discussed in the context of psychological experiments. If we switch to the more neutral terminology of "being there together," this seems equally applicable to both immersive MUVEs with two users and large-scale highly populated places containing large populations with their connotation of sociability. Online gaming clearly fits both "being there together" and "copresence," although the gaming element should (as argued earlier, in Chapter 2) be put into a separate category.[1]

Another reason to consider them together is that many VWs have been used for collaboration in the narrow sense of workaday applications and in the broader sense of educational and similar uses. Still, the most widespread uses of online VWs has been for gaming (and even VWs like Second Life [SL] are sometimes referred to as "social games"). And it is appropriate to characterize the socializing and gaming uses of online VWs (although not the educational and commercial ones, for example) as falling within the domain of leisure and consumption of ICTs (Schroeder 2007: Chapter 6). Yet we should beware of regarding socializing (or establishing social relations via online games) as frivolous or unimportant—as in the saying about SL: "Don't these people have a real life?" As work on the social history of the telephone, for example, has shown (Fischer 1992; Schroeder 2007: Chapter 6), people's social or sociable ties can be equally important in the case of new technologies as the ties and relationships in the realm of "serious" work. And it is mainly a prejudice in favour of face-to-face relations that prevents us from seeing mediated relations as being rich and rewarding—a point we will need to return to in the conclusion. In any event, I will use VWs when referring to persistent online VEs for large groups, and these VWs, unlike other types of MUVEs, have recently become popular spaces for people to spend time.

The History of Virtual Worlds

Persistent online VWs have been around for some time, since the late 1980s for two-dimensional (2D) worlds and the mid-1990s for three-dimensional (3D) worlds.[2] It is intriguing to think about the history of these VWs because, apart from the offline interactions among developers and users, the material for a history of such VWs would consist of the sum total of online events within it, which could in principle be completely captured or recorded for research. In some cases, extensive periods of recorded events exist for entire worlds, and these are increasingly used for social science analysis (see Chapter 7). In any event, it is worth bearing in mind that the history of VWs is quite limited, beginning (if we restrict ourselves to 3D worlds providing a first-person perspective) to a small number of worlds since the mid-1990s.

These ideas about history can be taken further: Some online games and social spaces such as EverQuest or Active Worlds (AW) have persisted over time and thus constitute persistent and lasting worlds. Other online games and social spaces, however, like Blaxxun and V-Chat, have come and gone. Still others have become updated and so forced players or populations to migrate from one world to another. In short, the history of VWs already consists of different paths of social development, raising a host of issues—for example, what should be done with deserted spaces (Hudson-Smith 2002) and how should players end their involvement in the game or space (Jakobsson 2002)? Another set of issues revolves around how players or users of social spaces should be able to migrate from one world to another and transfer their identities and belongings between worlds (discussed in Chapter 3). Again, these are issues that we will return to later, in Chapter 8.

If we take these thoughts to their logical conclusion, we might consider how a history of the online world differs from the history of an offline social setting. Again, one difference is that in online worlds, it is possible to record all the events within the world. Another, however, is that there is fundamental difference between two types of VWs: those, like AW and many social spaces, where users shape the world, and those in which this shaping is not possible, such as most gaming VWs (although some gaming VWs allow limited customization of houses and avatars and the like). This is an important issue for MUVE development generally, and recalls the distinction (made in Chapter 2) between predefined player roles in online games as against avatars that represent the user. The differences between predefined roles and predefined uses of spaces in online games and user-created spaces and user-defined roles in social spaces make for quite different social dynamics.

It can be added immediately that shaping the world includes not just building things but also engaging with developers about features of the VWs. In AW, examples of features that were implemented because the users asked for them are the functionality for being able to "locate" other users (by typing in their name), and the "whisper" function. AW has been an ongoing VW since the mid-1990s, and although it has had a small number of concurrent users—numbering in the hundreds in its early days and recently fewer—its features and social characteristics, despite many changes, also show many continuities. How the dynamics of such longer-established VWs with smaller populations compare with much larger recent ones like SL only time will tell; as mentioned in Chapter 3, the main difference between AW and SL to date has been population size.[3]

Roles and Frames

At this point, it will be useful to develop a more systematic approach to social interactions in highly populated VWs. One such framework that builds on the phenomenological analysis in Chapter 2 is to start with interactions on the micro-level of roles and frames and to build up a picture of the larger social world by aggregating these smaller-scale interactions.[4] To begin with, the initial step of a micro-interaction (or Goffmanian) analysis is to look for the focus of attention in the encounter between people. In MUVEs (as we have already seen), the degree of focus (and distraction) relates to presence and copresence—or, to put into somewhat different language, to the bandwidth of the frame of interaction. So, for example, some VEs are (initially) so visually rich as to overwhelm the user, whereas other VEs are abstract or information "poor," leaving the user to focus on the task or on the interaction with the other participant(s). In other words, once the user turns from the visually rich space to other users, the focus is on what people *do* together. As this point, the question becomes not so much "How present do users feel?" but "Where is their attention focused in the VE?"[5]

A brief contrast with immersive VEs will be useful because, as we have seen, in certain small-group situations such as our Rubik's Cube–type puzzle trial, there is a high degree of focus on the task and the focus on interpersonal relations is secondary. In other immersive settings, such as the acting trial reported by Slater and Steed (2002), there can be a high degree of focus on interpersonal relations because the situations revolve around interaction with others rather than a shared practical or object-related task. Still, in these immersive VEs, the focus is on bodily expressive interaction. Moving further away from immersive settings and into PC-based interactions among small close-knit groups and where avatars have developed long-lasting interpersonal relationships, we see that the focus is still on the regular interaction with a few avatars (see Hudson-Smith 2002; Jakobsson 2002; Schroeder and Axelsson 2001). In these settings, most of the attention is paid to how participants present themselves to others, not so much in terms of avatar appearance (because we now have moved to text-based graphical environments) but through conversations and to how the rules of relationships are enacted. This is not contradicted by the fact that much of the conversation through which these relationships are formed may be about the spatial environment (because that is the setting in which the conversation and mutual self-presentation takes place, except inasmuch as the conversation relates to the offline world). All this is to say that there is a continuum from "close" encounters in immersive spaces where much revolves around the bodily interaction with a few others, to the larger spaces and groups where the focus revolves around the relationships formed by (often chance) encounters.

"Focus of attention." applies not only to how the user perceives or engages with the environment and other users, but also outside of it—how much distraction there is away from the frame of the VE. With a head-mounted display (HMD) system, for example, the world around the user is almost completely "shut out," although it has often been noted that cables for the equipment and other offline obstacles may distract the user. Or again, an immersive projection technology (IPT)-type system, which may provide a greater sense of presence in terms of "place" than an HMD system, may still leave the user with a peripheral sense of others being there in the real world (outside the walls of the IPT-type system), and therefore diminish the copresence with those inside the VE. The reason for mentioning these immersive systems in the context of online worlds is that this applies in a similar way to desktop systems: users may have a high degree of copresence if, for example, they are fully engaged in a highly absorbing spatial task or participating in an online religious service—both of which involve a common focus of attention. However, the sense of presence and copresence can be weakened not only if their engagements with events and avatars in the world are weak, but also if there are others sitting beside them in the real world or by other distracting events in the offline world.

The difference between the frame of social interaction in MUVEs and other frames of offline interaction, which makes the very definition of virtual reality (VR)/VEs in terms of "being there" so important, is that MUVE frames are entirely technologically mediated. However, while frames should be analyzed in terms of technological mediation, the analysis of interaction *within* frames proposed here is much like the analysis of real-world interaction—although it is drastically reduced in complexity (as seen in Chapter 2) compared with the offline world. This makes the analysis of MUVEs quite unlike other theories of new media that focus on "interactivity" or "media effects" and the like. Put differently, this framework does not treat MUVEs differently from real-world interaction except in transposing it to the MUVE setting, which allows for comparisons with other forms of computer-mediated communication (CMC) and with face-to-face interaction—as long as we do not forget to embed online interaction in the larger context of the offline uses of MUVEs and other new media in society.

A key aspect of applying frame analysis to MUVEs is the extent to which people have become used to VEs. As Cheng, Farnham, and Stone (2002) show, for example, regular users navigate less. Perhaps this indicates that they have become more focused on interpersonal relations than on moving around in the environment. Axelsson and I similarly found, when interviewing regular users of AW (Axelsson and Schroeder 2001), that the involvement of these users in the environment depended on how much they have built their own spaces and routinely interacted with others. This also became clear over the course of the ten hour-long collaboration sessions in AW discussed in the previous chapter (Nilsson, Heldal, Schroeder, and Axelsson 2002); during these sessions with their variety of activities—building together, exploring, making presentations, planning, and the like—attention was unevenly divided between the environment, the others, the task, and, peripherally, the real world.

The main question within the frame of VWs is thus to identify where the focus of attention is directed—at copresent others, on the task or interaction, or on the environment (see also Chapter 2). Even if presence and its various facets continue to be a central question for the psychology of VEs, in terms of social interaction, it is only the backdrop for the "focus of attention" in VWs. In online worlds and for this focus, the interaction with others, including how we present ourselves to others and encounter them in small groups, moves into the foreground. With this in mind, communication (which will be discussed in more detail in Chapter 6) becomes the overriding factor in mutual self-presentation in the context of these shared frames or settings of interaction: different types of shared VEs provide different opportunities and constraints for presenting ourselves to others by communicating with them.[6]

Text-based communication in shared VEs differ in form and content from VEs with audio or from face-to-face communication: in text-based VEs, there is much more focus on addressing each other and gathering contextual information, and there are shorter exchanges measured in terms of number of words per turn taken (compared with face-to-face voice conversations; see Chapter 6). The key difference, however, is that in voice-based VWs, voice does not allow the same measure of anonymity as does text-based self-presentation, with important implications for socializing and how people present themselves to each other.

Once we move from encounters between individuals in small groups—where the self is presented to the other(s)—to larger groups, it becomes necessary to look at different roles that are developed vis-à-vis others in different circumstances, which will ultimately add up to the various roles that avatars have in their different networks of relationships. But before we can move on to these roles, it is important to note how our roles in shared VEs relate to focus: focusing our attention on several people in a VE can be burdensome, and it seems that this is often an obstacle to small group formation in shared VEs, especially in comparison with real settings. This is partly because of the restricted field of view and partly because of the absence of social cues in VEs. Put in a different way, it is difficult to experience the "cocktail party" effect in shared VEs whereby, in the real world, we can follow one or more conversations across the room. Yet not being able to cope with many simultaneous complex impressions will also leave scope to focus more closely on other aspects of our interaction with others in VEs, as we have already seen in a number of examples.

At this point it is worth stressing again that people in AW or SL do not role-play but interact as "themselves" (Boellstorff 2008: 119). This sets social spaces apart from online games, where one has a character, but also from immersive or instrumental spaces where the avatar represents one's body directly. In AW and SL and other social spaces, people recognize that they are "playing" a role, but this sense of play is different from game play where the gaming role is the main role that is played. In this way, roles are shaped by the setting. This also explains why in MUVEs for socializing, there is a certain "frisson" for novices who encounter other people in the form of avatars for the first time, as they may experiment with how they present themselves and which rules they can break or follow.

Thus, in an online world such as AW or SL (and also worlds with voice such as OnLive Traveler [OT]), encounters with strangers typically begin—in some ways as a face-to-face encounter with a stranger would begin—by establishing a sense of who the other person is: name, location, occupation, and the like. The difference from face-to-face encounters is that many social cues of appearance are absent, and the only cue about appearance is one's avatar. This means that this initial introduction will be different from a face-to-face introduction in that first-time encounters may focus on avatars and try to infer information from its appearance. Nevertheless, participants will also compensate for the absence of social cues and for well-defined roles by presenting lots of information about themselves—again, name, age, location—and gathering as much information as they can about others. This is a form of interaction to which participants quickly adapt.

Over longer periods, it has been found (Schiano 1999; Schroeder and Axelsson 2001) that participants generally maintain single stable roles (or "identities") vis-à-vis others and that they increasingly develop and keep to norms that they have come to share with others. This finding highlights that "roles" only arise in relation to others—that is, when others in MUVEs expect us to behave in certain ways. Roles are therefore a separate issue from presence and copresence, the latter being simply the experience of someone else being there (not their role, apart from a "generic" human). Also, the mediated role in a VE is different from a role in a face-to-face encounter—but also unlike other mediated roles if we compare MUVEs with a videoconferencing setting, where we would hesitate to say that people have a technologically mediated "role."

As we have seen, in collaborative situations (see Chapter 4), a role differentiation or a "division of labor" can take place "automatically" because of the different technological capabilities of the participants— *even* when they are not aware of the difference between the systems they are using. So, for example, in our Rubik's Cube–type puzzle trial, the person in the immersive VE concentrated on the spatial task while the person on the desktop system stood back and verbally supervised. Something similar can be expected in online worlds, although there are so far few investigations of how this kind of task and role division takes place—although there are studies of how online gamers collaborate by dividing the task among themselves (Nardi and Harris 2006).[7]

The strength or weakness of the role—for example, leadership in a group (Slater, Sadagic, Usoh, and Schroeder 2000)—is not just a product of the particular encounter or situation but also depends on how strongly roles are shaped or defined in the MUVE as a whole—in other words, whether there is a pronounced system of roles or stratification (Axelsson 2002; Schroeder 1997). One illustration of this is the distinction between online social spaces and online games: In the latter, the debate about different roles is shaped by the discussion among players about whether they should be "in character" (talk and appear in the language appropriate, for example, to a "medieval" setting of knights and ladies) or whether this type of role related to the theme is irrelevant and play can be out of character (Taylor 2006).

Once we move beyond frames and roles as they apply to individual and small-scale encounters, one way to analyze online worlds is by means of social network analysis. This type of analysis is particularly suitable for online worlds because all MUVEs involve technological networks that create relationships between people. Recent studies of related phenomena such as social networking sites have therefore focused on the networks between people (Lewis, Kaufman, Gonzalez, Wimmer, and Christakis 2008), and studies of networks among online gamers are also emerging (Williams 2006). When we move from encounters in small groups to larger groups, we might be able to examine phenomena such as the differentiation of roles within groups or the exchange of resources (see Castronova 2005; Jakobsson 2002; Taylor 2002). Yet other studies have examined the social conventions that are followed in different worlds (Becker and Mark 2002; Schroeder and Axelsson 2001; Schroeder, Huxor, and Smith 2001; Schroeder, Heather and Lee 1998). In this case, much depends on how much users have come to know each other and how they have been engaged in the VE, including shaping it and adhering to its norms and helping to build the VE (Schroeder and Axelsson 2001).

Social interaction in online worlds thus extends from individual avatar-to-avatar encounters all the way to the meso- and macro-levels, where there are populations made up of overlapping network memberships. On this level, many studies (Cheng, Farnham, and Stone 2002; Hudson-Smith 2002; Jakobsson 2002) begin to describe interactions in terms of different online "communities." Yet "communities" implies strong and (often) positive ties, and it is not clear to what extent such groups with common or shared interests (which might serve as a minimal definition of *community*) exist in online worlds. A different way to analyze larger groups might be to focus on stratification. This immediately raises the larger question that has been posed in connection to CMC and shared VEs (taken up by Axelsson 2002): Does CMC equalize the status of participants because of the absence of social cues and other status markers? Yet, as Axelsson argues, in relation to shared VEs, the effect can just as often be to amplify stratification in new ways.[8] For example, in online worlds, stratification and hierarchy can depend on the extent to which individuals are able to display their unique status characteristics— such as avatar appearance and property, or typing skills in text-based worlds—so that they are recognizable by other participants. This, in turn, may depend on familiarity with the VE: Taylor (2002) and Axelsson (2002) give a number of examples where these characteristics are recognizable only to certain participants such as experienced users (see also Schroeder 1997; Spante 2009). In short, social markers are mediated by the frame of interaction: How much attention do participants pay to status markers? How much do they trust them to reflect the characteristics of the "real" users? And on the side of the environment, the geography of the VE plays a role: How much access do people have to each other? How do different spaces foster networks by bringing avatars together in a shared VE space, or do they segregate them into different spaces or worlds and thus promote more differentiated or diffuse networks?

Again, it is worth stressing that apart from online worlds for socializing and gaming, there are few examples of worlds with larger numbers of users for purposes apart from this—such as worlds for meetings or education or large-scale conference-type events. These exceptions are interesting, but one point they illustrate is a negative one; namely, that these online gatherings for purposes apart from leisure have not become very widespread, and it can therefore be assumed that they are currently not regarded as useful. So, in online worlds, outside the groups for gaming and leisurely socializing that have become popular, groups that engage in repeated encounters are few and far between. They can be seen as islands of cliques and special interest meetings (again, education can be seen as one such special interest) in a sea of unstructured socializing among strangers. In this sense, online games, where groups are highly organized into guilds and other organizations for achieving game tasks, have more social structure than online social worlds—even if in this case the guilds are associations for a limited purpose and for a limited time period.

A different way to identify persistent groups in online social spaces is to note that there are various subcultures. Religion has been mentioned. Another group that has been studied are the "Goreans," fans of a particular science fiction writer who role-play in accordance with the themes of his "Gorean" books, which is centered around men dominating women (Boellstorff 2008: 162). Interestingly, this group, which has been studied in SL (Boellstorff 2008; Bardzell and Bardzell 2006, 2007; Bardzell and Odom 2008), also existed in AW in the 1990s, where I encountered them. Here we have an example of a subcultural group migrating from one world (AW) to another (SL), and there are bound to be other examples.[9]

When Boellstorff thus argues that SL should not be seen as a mass of undifferentiated users (2008: 183), this is only partly accurate. It is true that formal groups can be created and that informal subcultures exist. However, in SL, like in other online worlds, much social interaction consists of encounters between strangers, and in this sense, these worlds consist of a mass of undifferentiated users more so than in the offline world because encounters between strangers are comparatively rare in the offline world. Hence, too, the assertion by Boellstorff (2008: 180) and others that online worlds create "communities" can be questioned: if by *community* we mean simply a shared interest in an online world, like a shared interest in a hobby or sports club, then SL and other online worlds are communities. Apart from this, however, it is necessary to focus on the sustained groups that interact regularly within the world for certain purposes, and these are few and far between, and they also have certain constraints (a member can simply disappear) that do not pertain in the same way to the offline world.

Second Life

SL must be discussed in the context of MUVEs simply because it has become the largest MUVE for socializing, with users in the hundreds of thousands since it opened in 2002. This online world has also attracted media and business attention unlike any MUVEs had previously. The number of unique registered users has been subject to debate (Spence 2008a), but any figure in the hundreds of thousands will make this the largest online world for socializing, although these pale by comparison with online games like World of Warcraft that have attracted several million users. Still, the number of simultaneous users in SL at any given time is typically in the thousands, and again, this makes SL much larger than previous online worlds like AW, which on most days had a few hundred simultaneous users, or other current rivals such as There.

As mentioned, apart from the large number of registered and simultaneous users, however, there is little that is technically or socially new in SL that sets it apart from its predecessors. One question must therefore be: Why did it take from the mid-1990s, when online worlds first arrived on the scene, until ten years later for online social worlds to become popular? There are several reasons: One is technical—that standard PCs have graphics capabilities (graphics cards) that can handle worlds like SL much more easily. A second reason that is both technical and social is the widespread availability of broadband connections. Third is the growing popularity of online games like World of Warcraft and EverQuest, which have made online graphical worlds highly popular.[10] And finally, the widespread use of the web, which was still in its infancy as a popular medium in the mid-1990s, has undoubtedly contributed because many people now regard the web as a *place* as opposed to primarily as a means for e-mail communication as in the pre-web era of the Internet. In short, there are several reasons why online graphical worlds could become much more popular in the early 2000s.[11]

Apart from open-ended socializing among people who encounter each other for the first time, SL has generated a number of groups with special interests. SL "formally" (in terms of the functionalities provided by the system) allows "friends," "partners," and "groups" as possibilities for groups to identify themselves as such and has a function for keeping in touch and sharing information (Boellstorff 2008: 233). And as in AW, there are premium accounts that allow certain privileges, but otherwise no formal distinctions are made between classes of users. There are also newsletters, users who like to build together, educational spaces (see Figure 5.1, Oxford University in Second Life), playing games within the world, and the like.

It should be noted that apart from the educational and therapeutic uses, which are still in early or pilot phases, the uses of SL (as with other online social worlds) are primarily recreational. Worlds like SL are being

FIGURE 5.1   Oxford University in Second Life. (Image courtesy of Eric Meyer.)

used for socializing online—they are "third places" (Schroeder 1997; Steinkuehler and Williams 2006) like public parks where people can get together. Obviously, many people enjoy this type of socializing, although there are few studies that have systematically investigated the motives of people who come to places like SL (but see Williams, Yee, and Caplan 2008). It can be noted, however, that the relationships in SL and similar places are typically single-stranded; that is, they focus on a particular shared interest that is pursued online, rather than being multistranded or consisting of multiple overlapping ties—as suggested in Toennies' (1957) use of "community"—and unlike our offline relationships. In this context it is worth mentioning that the attempts by Linden Lab (the company that created SL) to engineer a community spirit, such as through popularity ratings for best content creation and best avatar appearance (which included having post boxes for ballots), have been unsuccessful (Au 2008: 58–60; Boellstorff 2008: 228).

Governance, Economies, and Trust in Virtual Worlds

Online worlds can be governed either by the developers of the system or by users. They can, of course, also be governed by other offline forces— that is, regulated by laws or policies in society at large. Yet apart from these outside forces, the developers very much have the upper hand vis-à-vis users with respect to governance because they can dictate the terms of use (games and other commercial software have "end-user license agreements"). Insofar as the governance of VWs is turned over to users, there are various possibilities for governance such as designating some users to enforce the rules and help others. In some ways, however, the relationship between developers and users are bound to be symbiotic as developers would like their VWs to be popular and users want to them to be well-governed.

The balance between developers' governance and governance by the users of social worlds like SL has yet to settle. Boellstorff argues that Linden Lab has engaged only minimally with users and their requests for how SL should be organized (2008: 220), but this could also be seen as a "hands-off" approach on the part of Linden Lab or as signifying that users have a high demand for input into shaping SL. Lastowka (2008) made the interesting proposal, from a legal perspective, that online worlds should be treated like real-world places such as homeowners associations that allow people to determine and enforce their own rules within the bounds of their own communities. This could be a useful approach—as long as it remains within the confines of VWs, and as long as issues within VWs do not spill over into real-world issues (such as copyrights or harming others).

Virtual World Economies

The economics of VWs can be subdivided into two topics; subscriber fees and in-world currencies. Subscriber fees are straightforward: some worlds are completely free to download and use, whereas others charge a (typically monthly) fee for use, although they often have a free "trial" period.[12] A third possibility is to give fee-paying users more privileges than non–fee-paying ones. In AW, for example, non–fee-paying users were called "tourists" and had no choice about their avatar appearance and could not build, whereas fee-paying "citizens" could. A similar stratification of privileges applies to SL.

Castronova has undertaken an extensive analysis of the economies of VWs (2005).[13] He estimated (2005: 13) that the economies of online worlds—mainly for gaming but including only 3D graphical worlds—would be worth $1 billion if the value of online currencies was transformed into real-world dollars. This "transformation," however, can be questioned. Although it may be true that if all online objects would be translated into real-world currencies at one time they could be worth this amount, it is doubtful whether such a complete sell-off could realistically occur. If, for example, it became known that objects were being sold off on a large scale, the value of the remaining objects would surely decrease dramatically! (It is possible to think of similarities with "real-world" events here.) In this respect, it is also necessary to distinguish between online worlds that allow in-world currencies to be exchanged for real-world money (as in SL) and those that can be used only in-world (or exchanged only illegally) (Au 2008: 127). In most online games, the translation of real-world currency into in-world currency and vice versa has been officially illegal because it would introduce all sorts of problems into the gaming environment and for the companies that own them (Castronova 2005).

In-world currencies have generated a lot of objects and property that are valuable to users in the world. What the value consists of—whether it is earned through game play or by means of creating desirable objects or ownership of property—varies in the first instance by whether the world is a gaming world with currencies and the accumulation of objects contributing to the goal of the game, or if it is a social world where property or well-designed clothes have value as a means of gaining a stake or reputation in the world. It should be remembered, however, that apart from the guarantees about the persistence of the world by the developer, this value will disappear if the world disappears.[14]

Regarding the economic value generated by subscriptions, Castronova estimated that subscription-based worlds had more than 10 million users, although he also says that the number could be much higher (2005: 54–55).[15] A widely used source about user numbers and subscriptions to online worlds (http://www.mmogchart.com/) reports that World of Warcraft, by far the most popular world, had more than 6 million users in 2006 (for social worlds, see Spence 2008a). Subscription-based gaming and social worlds can also be seen, however, in terms of the migration of popularity from one world to another. For example, the largest online worlds before the rise of World of Warcraft were the Asia-based Lineage worlds (at more than 1 million users), although perhaps a better comparison would be the international online game EverQuest with around 500,000 users—and the closest in popularity to Lineage before the rise of World of Warcraft for several years. World of Warcraft, however, has overtaken other online games in terms of the number of users. What we can see is that the popularity of different worlds, including social worlds, has been rising and falling, and it remains to be seen what kind of permanence can be achieved among the populations of online worlds.

It is also worth putting the economies of online worlds into a broader perspective: World of Warcraft and similar online worlds are *gaming* worlds. Estimates in the media for SL, the largest social world, have valued this economy in the millions of dollars. But a similar question mark about the "true" offline value of SL could be raised as for gaming worlds (that is, what would happen to this value if assets were sold off rapidly?). Furthermore, for social worlds, arguably the most important economic value does not have to do with the in-world currency (which in SL is called Linden dollars) or the scarcity of property and objects, but rather the "visibility" or popularity of the world as such (or creating a "community," to use the language of developers). In this respect, the economy of social VWs is similar to phenomena such as social networking sites, which need to be highly visible online and draw in as many members as possible.

Put differently, the economics of VWs are to a large extent those of an "attention" economy where many "eyeballs" translate into high profitability. This applies not just to gaining members by means of visibility in the offline world, but also, for example, to property (or more accurately to space) within the world: the spaces where many users congregate are also those that are most valuable. As Boellstorff (2008: 95) points out, "Traffic provided one of the few measures for the social status of a property," linking geography and the "economic" value of space. This applies to property that is owned as well as to unowned property; the more people who are drawn to and use the space, the more valuable are the objects such as buildings or the services offered in those places.[16]

This point is well illustrated by an issue that is increasingly coming to the forefront in VWs, namely, how objects can be transferred into and out of the VW. In the case of SL, for example, the policy has been shifted to allow users to import and export objects from and into the SL world and to provide users with guarantees that objects and property will remain theirs. This shift toward an "open" model (although it remains to be seen how open) aims to maximize the number of users and ensure that SL is open to the rest of the online world, rather than fencing off the world and locking users in to its own proprietary standards (again, there are similarities here with other online phenomena such as Google Maps). It should be noted that this policy also depends on technical standards (How compatible is the software?) and not just on policy per se.[17] In any event, the idea that, in SL, copyright for user-generated content should remain with its creators has been a major influence on how people conceive their rights to intellectual property in SL (Au 2008: 128). This has allowed users to capitalize on the objects they have created in SL, although it has raised the question of whether these objects may be copied and resold (Boellstorff 2008: 214).[18]

Difficulties in the economies of VWs include that there are various ways of "gaming" the system. The example of "bots" in AW that were developed to automatically build on—and thus take possession of—more land has already been mentioned (see Chapter 3). Similarly in online games, the practice whereby players hire others to gain points or objects on their behalf—"farming"—and thus gain "unfair advantage" has been well- documented in the media (Castronova 2005 provides examples, as do Steen, Davies, Tynes, and Greenfield 2006). The economies of online games also have specific game-related economic issues: There must a balance between the ease and difficulty of being able to obtain goods or points to ensure that the game is challenging enough but also not too difficult to motivate players (Ducheneaut, Yee, Nickell, and Moore 2006). The economies of online worlds for socializing, in contrast, are mainly related to the extent to which users can modify and own parts of the world.

Finally, it is worth reemphasizing that to speak of the "economies" of online worlds is somewhat misleading: Apart from the fact (as mentioned earlier) that the transformation of in-world currencies into the real world is fraught with difficulties, it is also difficult to apply the real-world economics of scarce goods to online worlds. Even if, for example, building things or designing objects involves the costs of labor or effort as in real-world production, these are nevertheless recreational worlds with no real value outside of the online space apart from when this value is cashed in for real-world currency. A somewhat different "economic" issue is the extent to which VWs like SL have been used for commercial purposes such as advertising. However, such usage has been disappointing. Au estimated the extent to which commercial sites in SL are visited (Au 2008: 248, 259) and notes that this is very minor compared with the hype that has surrounded economic activity in SL. So far, the main reason for a company to have a presence in SL, as with universities and other organizations in SL, is novelty marketing value. The same goes for a protest that was organized by IBM in SL and attended by 1800 avatars of IBM employees (Au 2008: 250), which is mainly interesting for its novelty and symbolic value. If, on the other hand, the economy is valued by real-world spending by SL users, most spend little or nothing and Au (2008: 243) reports that only 10% spend $40 or more per month.[19] At this point, however, it will be useful from general issues of governance and economies to more specific aspects of relations in VWs.

Trust

One issue that deserves separate treatment because of its obvious importance to online interaction is trust. Trust has been the subject of major debates in social science. Here we can use Misztal's definition of *trust* as consisting of "hold[ing] some expectations about something future or contingent or to have some belief as to how another person will perform on some future occasion. To trust is to believe that the results of somebody's intended action will be appropriate from our point of view" (1996: 24). The reason that trust is an especially important issue for VWs is because it focuses on the types of relationships that people have online and how they compare with offline relationships.[20]

Again, AW is a good place to examine this issue because the world is long-established (since 1995) and it has had a fair-sized population over time. In what follows I will summarize some of the findings from a study of trust (see Axelsson and Schroeder 2001) in which we conducted ten interviews with long-time AW users. The interviewees were recruited by means of the snowballing technique, and semistructured interviews were carried out via text in empty areas of AW, which took between about one and one-half and three hours. The text was saved for analysis.[21]

All our interviewees were "citizens," or users who paid the annual fee of \$19.95 for AW membership and the enjoyment of certain privileges (for example, choosing from a range of avatars) as opposed to "tourists" who used the system for free. We would also describe our interviewees—beyond the distinctions between "citizens" and "tourist" or between "newbies" and "regulars"—as part of a "core" group of users who invested themselves in the AW world by building homes and having a close-knit group of friends there. This will become clear as we describe them further. At this point it suffices to say that all but one interviewee (who spends at least a few minutes each day) said that they used AW for two and five hours per day and had used the system for at least two years, some going back as far as the beginning of the system in 1995. One interviewee said she used the system for more than ten hours a day, and one said she never leaves except to take a bath.

The age range of our interviewees was between 11 and over 60 years, and there were five males and five females. Seven were American, one was European, and two were Australian. This represents the age range and gender balance of "real" users fairly well (more than 82% of users were over the age of 25, and 39% were female), but it does not reflect the balance between American and non-American users, which was evenly divided between Americans and non-Americans at the time.[22] All were familiar with other text-based MUDs or VWs, but they all also indicated that AW was their preferred system, both inasmuch as they preferred the features of the system and they spent most of their time there. Our interview questions covered a number of topics, including identity, how secure they felt in the environment, their social relationships and activities, and how they felt about how the system was governed. These will be presented in turn and allow some conclusions about trust and online relationships.

Identity.   One set of questions we asked was about the users' identity or self-representation and those of others, including their avatars and names. The answers revealed that seven of ten informants never change avatar under circumstances where their favorite avatar is available—in other words, in worlds where there is a limited set of available avatars and their first choice is among them. When their first choice is not available, the informants have a "second favorite" that they use. The remaining three informants, who sometimes changed appearance, reported that they do so for special purposes: one because she creates and sells avatars and therefore has to show customers available avatars, one changes to a nonhuman and repulsive avatar to get rid of pushy people, and the third occasionally changes to try out new and exciting avatars.

When it comes to names, six of ten informants answered that they never change name. The four informants who do change their name do so occasionally and for specific reasons. According to the four, they use a name that is different from the one they are normally known by in order to obtain anonymity or privacy, to be able to work undisturbed on projects without being contacted by friends who see that they are logged on or by newcomers who want building advice and the like, or to appear in a role-playing or themed environment without anyone relating to them in their usual identity.

The reasons why informants do not change avatar are not as obvious as why they stick to their names. Most of the informants just say that they have "gotten used to it" or "feel comfortable with it" or that the avatar is a standard one and is available in most worlds—and therefore is convenient to use. The reasons why informants do not change their name seem to be stronger. In contrast to avatar appearance, the names used by the interviewees are more often individual choices and creations. The chosen name may resemble a real-life name or have a connection to real life experiences, or it contains certain status signs or letters that have particular connotations for initiated users.

In relation to appearance and name, we were also interested in their perception of other users' appearances and names. To do this, we asked: "Are you drawn to certain types of avatars or names?" and "Do you stay away from certain types of avatars or names?" The answers suggest that informants do not seem to pay much attention to the names and appearance of others. Four of ten reported that avatar appearance and name do not affect which people they choose to get acquainted with or avoid. "It's just optics," said one of the informants, which reflects a common viewpoint. Despite this, six informants said that they tend to stay away from users with certain names (names that indicate low age or rude names), but only one of the informants reported that he stays away from certain kinds of avatars (such as nude ones). Only two informants reported that they are drawn to certain avatars or names. One said that she is drawn to "great avatars" and also, more specifically, to avatars that are used in the theme world where the informant is active. The other informant reported no specific attraction to avatars but said that she prefers names "without numbers and odd characters; easy to type." We can conclude that stable identity seems to be important for self-presentation, especially the user's name. Moreover, users seem to be highly aware of issues involving how they and other users present themselves, and they prefer "sociable" identities in the ordinary, face-to-face sense of sociability.

Threats, Experiences with Others, and Security.   Another set of questions concerned how informants experience the interaction with other users, who are mostly strangers. Thus we asked: "Do you ever feel threatened in AW?" All ten informants answered that they do not feel threatened, but three added that they had, on certain occasions, been afraid of other people. To get a better sense of their positive and negative experiences, we then asked them about the best and worst encounters with people. When it came to negative experiences, four of ten informants reported that they had not had any bad encounters; two reported only general (in contrast to personal) experiences, such as bad behavior in public places; and four informants reported on specific incidents. One of these, a woman who taught building to others in AW, had a bad experience when a former student accused her of deleting his property. Another female informant described how a contracted person failed to pay for completed work and then stalked her. Yet another informant described a "peacekeeper" (someone appointed by the AW administrators in this role) who, in order to restore order in a conflict, threatened him. Another described how, after giving his telephone number to a person, he was threatened over the telephone. Yet another person (a woman) reported on a bad experience when a person said that he would rape her.

Now even if many of the informants have apparently had bad experiences interacting with people, no one seems to take it very seriously; rather, they all seem to recognize that the avatars are virtual and that their threats cannot do much "real" harm. This fearlessness is reflected in the extent to which the informants chose to make themselves available to other users, who may be complete strangers. We asked the informants whether they give out their e-mail address or ICQ (an early IM system), and if so, to whom? It turns out that five of ten informants give either their e-mail address or ICQ number to anyone and even put the addresses up on public places for people to contact them. The other five informants said that they are a little more cautious and give out addresses only to people they know as friends or contacts. The reason for *not* giving e-mail addresses or ICQ numbers to just anyone are not that they feel insecure as such but rather that technical and practical experiences tell them to be careful with what they receive and from whom. E-mail and ICQ can be used for sending/receiving files, which, as experienced users know, is a way of spreading computer viruses. Some of the informants also had previous experiences of people overloading them with junk e-mail and useless information via e-mail and ICQ, something that could make you careful about to whom you open your door.

Thus, it seems that our informants generally do not feel threatened in AW. The main exceptions are when activity in AW threatens to spill over into "real-life" harassment or computer problems, which some—but not all—informants worry about.

Social Rules, Participation in Social Activities, and Contacts.   What about the attitudes of the informants toward the social rules in AW? Here we can distinguish between the rules and regulations that are imposed by the developers/owners of the system and the more informal rules that have emerged among the users themselves. Regarding the formal rules, all of our informants regarded some degree of rule enforcement as necessary. This is clearly related to their extensive experience in AW. Among newcomers and even regulars, one will often encounter the opinion that there should be no regulations at all and that the system administrators should get rid of gatekeepers and rules. Our interviewees, in contrast, had come to recognize that complete lawlessness would be detrimental to the functioning of sociability in AW.

There was, however, a full range of opinions among our informants as to whether the rules should be more strict or more relaxed. Those who expressed a preference for stricter enforcement of rules would like more control over "troublemakers," or users who use foul language or harass others. Those who favored a more relaxed regime, on the other hand, would like to go in the other direction, with more "free" speech and less clamping down by the system administrators on perceived "troublemakers."

This also applies to building regulations. All interviewees indicated that some building regulations were necessary, with some expressing the view that the system administrators could be less restrictive about where they allow users to build, that more functionalities would be useful, and the like.

Similar views were expressed about the informal rules of behavior that have emerged in AW. Several interviewees mentioned, for example, that they avoided places that were not to their tastes, especially places known for aggressive behavior, whereas they sought out more congenial places, places with users who are similarly interested in nondisruptive socializing. Six of the interviewees took an active part in "community" services; they were gatekeepers, peacekeepers, or teachers in the building world. Moreover, eight had been building in AW, in some cases extensively—maintaining their own world (two interviewees) or building in several places. This voluntary and building activity indicates a commitment to AW as a social setting and in shaping its future. Building and social activities are also linked: one interviewee said that building was a good way "to base relationships."

Regarding contacts with other people, six interviewees said that they had full contact lists (the total number that one could have on a list was 100 contacts) and that they had also met other AW users in "real life." The remaining four did not have full lists and had not contacted others outside of AW (although one had had two or three telephone conversations with others), but they all had contact lists and had frequently met with other users inside AW with whom they had become acquainted. Several interviewees also mentioned that they tried to be helpful or friendly toward "newcomers," even though they were aware that newcomers could be burdensome (for example, because things need to be explained to them).

Attitudes toward the System, Its Administrators, and Change.   Our informants' greatest concerns were about system breakdown (which occurs occasionally) and harassment. Clearly, they enjoyed AW as a place to socialize and a place where they have social contacts. Thus, they took a negative view of "antisocial" behavior and thought that a part of their social life was missing when AW was unavailable. At the same time, our informants did not like the increasing commercialization of AW. Several complained that the system developers were allowing AW to become too profit-oriented, singling out citizenship fees as an example. Several mentioned that they did not like the divide between tourists and citizens (the introduction of citizenship fees caused a wave of protests when they were first introduced, which subsequently died down). Again, the reason for this seems to be that they thought AW should remain a social, rather than a commerce-oriented, place.

In relation to how they would like to see the system changed, interviewees commonly expressed the view that they would like the system developers to be more responsive to users. They thought that the administrators at Activeworlds.com could provide better services and take user needs more into account. This view was reinforced by a number of specific suggestions for improvements, such as better building tools, more capacious contact lists, and more responsiveness from developers toward users' queries. At the same time, almost all interviewees mentioned a number of features that they thought had improved the system, such as the ability to teleport and the whisper function.

It can be seen that our informants adopted a "considered" view toward the AW administrators and toward AW as a system. That is, they were all aware of issues that are faced by users in AW and that there could be improvements of the system by the administrators. It also needs to be mentioned that although they thought that changes should be made, all were generally positive toward the system.

Trust in CMC and in the World of AW.   These findings can be briefly put in a wider context of trust and social relations in CMC. One of the main findings about other worlds has been that people prefer to maintain a consistent identity and adapt some of the conventions of the "real world" in relation to greetings, intimacy, sanctions, privacy, and group membership to the "virtual world." Becker and Mark's (2002) participant observation study comparing AW, OT (with voice communication), and LambdaMOO (a text-only world), for example, found that in three systems, a variety of conventions (in their case, greeting and acknowledging, leaving, establishing group membership and indicating privacy, verbal and nonverbal expression and conversation flow, social positioning and intimacy, and sanctions on behavior) were being maintained. Similarly, Schiano and White found, in relation to a study of LambdaMOO that used both empirical measures (logging user behavior) and interviews, that the patterns of behavior in this text-based world did not depart radically from those in "real life" (1998). In Schiano and White's case, the behavior investigated consisted of usage patterns, identity or self-representation, sociability, and sense of place. Negatively expressed, the ideas put forward by Turkle (1995) that users adopt multiple identities in MUDs and more widely held views about the contravention of "real-world" norms in VWs, were not supported by this research.

What if we compare virtual graphical environments like AW with text-based communication? As Lea and Spears have pointed out, primarily with reference to social psychological studies, people's first steps toward one another face-to-face are chiefly based on physical appearance, which, they argue, is naturally not the case in CMC. Instead of observing and judging a person's physical appearance and individual features, social features play a more significant role (1995). In the nonvisual and nonaudible text-centered environment, social categories like age, sex, and group adherence play a more important role than do appearance, voice, body language, and the like for attraction and subsequently for trust and friendship. A frightening appearance, an unnatural body language, or an annoying voice consequently do not influence the progress negatively, as it probably would in face-to-face interaction.

These ideas can also be applied to virtual graphical environments like AW, where you see at least graphical representations of other users. Physical appearance can, for example, play a role in the often playful conversations where a lot of remarks relate to the "physical" appearance of the person, the avatar. Common remarks between AW users are: "Nice avatar," "Aren't you cold in that short dress?", "Wow, you must have been into body building, with muscles like that!" and so forth.

People also tend to pay attention to other avatars' movements and positioning in the virtual space, although perhaps less than might be expected. As Becker and Mark noticed (2002), people in AW become provoked if another avatar comes too close and we also noticed that people frequently make a comment if an avatar moves around with great speed or makes unusual gestures. But as Becker and Mark rightly note (2002), body gestures are seldom used in AW, while emotions in general are communicated with text. So, when forming an opinion of a new acquaintance and estimating how trustworthy or reliable a person is, physical appearance is arguably of lesser importance when most AW users presumably know that it has little to do with the person's identity and trustworthiness.

On the other hand, social categories play a more important role in graphical settings like AW when estimating how trustworthy other people are, at least in the first instance. National background is one important factor. There is a tendency for people to get together in national worlds within AW (worlds like "Russia," "Denmark," "England"; see also Chapter 3 on language-themed worlds and Chapter 6 on communication), where fellow-countrymen gather and communicate in their national language, and this indicates that people would rather interact with and trust people from the same background than with people from a different one. And as we have seen, people trust people they know more than those they do not know.

If we move on from first encounters, Holmes and Rempel (1989) discussed stages in the development of establishing closer relations with others, and this is also what occurs in AW where people proceed from a high degree of uncertainty and a small amount of trust in the beginning of a relationship to reduced uncertainty and a larger amount of trust as they disclose more about themselves and become more responsive to each other's needs. This responsiveness is most clearly revealed when they are required to sacrifice their own interests. Responsiveness and especially sacrifice are important components in relationships in virtual environments like AW, where actions are more obvious and effective than offline social cues for showing affection, reliability, and trustworthiness. Spending time with a newcomer showing him or her around, spending time teaching a novice to build, giving out private e-mail addresses or ICQ numbers, inviting another person to your virtual home and thereby risking material vandalism or personal harassment, and sharing building privileges with another person—these are some of the actions that can be commonly observed in AW.

Trust is thus a matter of having a consistent identity and behavior. This applies to online relations as well as to face-to-face relations, even if many people have argued for a different view (as Turkle [1995] does with her ideas about a multiplicity of different selves). People would have severe problems if they did not know if a person was the same from one day to the next or if they would act in an unpredictable way. This does not seem to be the case—at least not in AW. People in AW act as if they expect others to keep their stable identities over time, saying things like:

"I haven't seen you before, are you new here?"
"See you tomorrow then!"
"Come and visit me when I've finished building my house!"

Our interviewees also confirm this observation when they say that they do not change identity except occasionally to obtain a specific goal, like being able to work with some privacy. They also want other users to keep stable identities so that they can put them on their contact list and maintain contact with them. Conversely, as one informant said about occasional users, "I feel they are just people passing through AW and no use getting too friendly with them."

Our interviews suggest that trust in CMC relies to a greater extent on being able to establish close ties than in more transparent face-to-face relations. Throughout AW, we can see that users build up a sense of whom they are interacting with, and that they come to regard experiences with others as positive inasmuch as they know what to expect from them (recall Misztal's definition of *trust* here).[23] Our "core" users are examples of this—except more so than less regular users. The way "core" users have come to recognize their ties with others and with their environment as stable and rewarding, and threats and problems as things that can be coped with, has allowed them to make online socializing a considerable and routine part of their lives. In short, trust is a product of the network of social relationships that long-term users have built up, and we should not be surprised at this (although people who regard online worlds as places of multiple identities and threatening behavior might be).

Some implications for design can already be mentioned in this context:

- Avatars should be designed so that they allow their users to maintain a consistent identity with which they can identify (the possibility of designing one's own avatar, for example, or allowing information to be linked to names, avatars, or groups of people).
- The social rules in MUVEs should be designed so as to allow users to develop a stake in the online social world (for example, allowing

attachment to places and relationships to others to become cemented).

- The VE system should provide consistent support for online socializing, and it should be responsive to the needs of its users (implementing changes that are suggested by experienced or frequent users, for example, or avoiding system breakdowns, or making a variety of avatar types available in all worlds).

Limits of Online Worlds, Limits of Offline Perceptions

At this point, we can return to more general issues in VWs. As mentioned at the outset of this chapter, there is a major shift when we move from trial use of (often) immersive MUVE systems to research about online gaming and socializing. Research on new high-end systems tends to be within the computer science community and be focused on technology development, whereas research on online VWs is largely within the social sciences and concerned with issues such as identity, trust, and norms (although for online games and social spaces, there are also large *commercial* development communities). One of the aims of this chapter and of this book is to bring these two research areas together and to show how the issues are continuous. However, it is just as well to point out that there is unlikely to be a merger between the two research communities in the short term, which is partly because technology development has not yet converged.

There are, however, many signs of overlapping issues (to be discussed further in Chapters 9 and 10) as people have different virtual embodiments in different spaces and with a range of input and output devices. These forms of "being there together" constitute a continuum, and there may come a time when different devices allow a continuous identity to be ported across different spaces via different modalities, which is how people will maintain continuous connections of online relationships across a range of daily activities—although that may be some time away. Yet it behooves us to anticipate this future because our life is migrating online.

To appreciate this point, we can consider what online social spaces are *not*: as mentioned earlier, VWs have so far mainly been used for socializing and gaming. But even if educational and workaday uses are rare in persistent online worlds, work and education, among other activities, are increasingly conducted online *apart from* in MUVEs. Hence it is worth anticipating what will happen when online worlds are integrated with other technologies for "being there together" in everyday life, such as IM, mobile phones, social networking sites, and others. One way to think about this is that all these technologies are used to organize our information and to stay connected, and as these technologies and uses proliferate, one option will be to rationalize our online identities and connect the online worlds used for socializing and working together such that they are seamless, or at least interoperate, perhaps making them part of a single world with our own private spaces. It has already been mentioned that research is bound to move in other directions as well, for example with mixed and augmented reality and ubiquitous computing.

A different way to highlight the differences in technology development and research is in terms of public perceptions: At one extreme, we have completely immersive VEs or where avatars can interact in a realistic manner. At the other extreme, we have large-scale social worlds where populations regularly interact. However, the public perceptions of both are curious: The former are taken seriously and the various applications, although rare, are regarded as having much promise even if they are also seen as somewhat futuristic. The latter are widespread but online games and spaces for socializing are widely seen as being frivolous. This was already true of early VR systems more than a decade ago (see Schroeder 1996), but these perceptions are still commonplace—again, as in sayings that online gamers or people who spend time in SL should "get a real life." What accounts for this perception?

Online worlds are strange to those who have not experienced them extensively, and the social interaction that takes place online is therefore sometimes regarded as "deviant."[24] Moreover, "gaming" or any excessive preoccupation with a particular hobby (unless it is a "worthy" one) is regarded as a waste of time and lacking in seriousness. And as we have seen, there is also the belief that face-to-face interactions are more authentic and should be valued more highly—even though it is overlooked that many of our relationships already take place via different media. These beliefs should be treated as myths because the view that face-to-face relations are more authentic is anachronistic and often inaccurate. The same applies to the view that online gaming and social-izing are particularly antisocial activities, especially as research has found that these are eminently social activities and that people who engage in online gaming have as many, if not more, offline relations with whom they spend time than those who do not engage in online gaming (Williams, Yee, and Caplan 2008).

Nongaming social worlds share with gaming worlds that they are mainly ways to pass time, but again, there are many examples of such activities in the offline world.[25] Socializing for its own sake—as a non-purposive activity—may be regarded as frivolous or a waste of time. Yet spending time in VWs is perhaps derided more because it is new—because there are many other well-established ways of spending time together that are highly regarded. Finally, from a social science perspective, social actors invariably have masks and roles, so this is not unique to VWs, even if the social interaction is mediated in this case.

Ducheneaut and Moore (2004) argue that online games are about more than gaining experience points (the points that are assigned to the character in the game that get them to higher levels). They say gaining points makes it easier to socialize when not doing anything else (that is, not killings monsters and the like) because people can make conversa-tions *around* the game. And they point out that this makes online games easier for socializing than online social spaces, where there is nothing to do. Perhaps this is true for online games, but a different way to make the contrast is simply that from a gamer's perspective, social spaces are boring, and from the perspective of someone who likes online social spaces, games may be uninteresting. Research on online games points to the fact that gamers do a lot of socializing, both related to the game and uncon-nected to it. It is also the case that online social spaces have a playful (game-like) atmosphere and a set of activities that could be regarded as game-like. These include building, avatar fashioning (for example, in AW, SL, There, and OT), economic activities (SL), and in-world recreational activities like chess, racing vehicles and the like.

From a social science perspective, these activities can be described as being attached to online roles: running around in both types of online worlds is removed from the workaday settings of the offline world. This is also what strikes people who have little or no experience of online worlds as faintly ridiculous; why would someone take on the identity of an avatar, and why would they want to interact with others in this way? The non-workaday nature of the activities may also contribute to regarding these as inauthentic ways of interacting with others. This view, however, is inappropriate: in offline life, there are many roles that are ridiculous and inauthentic, and there are many nonwork settings that consist of highly "staged" forms of leisure. Furthermore, mediated communication often involves non-workaday messages and departs from roles in nonmediated relationships.

In short, online roles may be unlike offline roles, but the main difference is not the inauthentic or non-workaday nature of the activities within spaces for gaming and socializing but rather that, stripped of many familiar offline characteristics, peoples' roles and activities are somewhat one-dimensional. This is what makes the design of these spaces a specialized endeavor of research and development: Designing them so as to allow users to develop their roles around certain activities is critical to the success of online interaction. This is also why they are good tools for social science, as there are relatively few parameters and these can be studied and manipulated.

Hence, the point can be made again (see also Chapter 2) that VWs contain very few elements—other people, the environment, social norms, and conventions—to focus on or socialize around. These are what defines people's online roles and social interaction, and it is also why Walther's idea—that the offline world is gradually imported into online relationships—is both a powerful insight that can applied to VEs but also limited. It is appropriate insofar as people will gradually come to know each other's offline background, their offline personality will "shine through," and their background will become known. But the idea of hyperpersonal relationships has limits because the way people come to know each other—not just via words (as in Walther's studies) but in the setting of the VW—is also constrained and enabled by this setting, unless avatars get to know each other offline.[26] And in online worlds, people fashion their identities and relationships to some extent, but the setting also imposes constraints on the kinds of longer-term sociability that can emerge, even if this setting also opens new possibilities for sociability.

The notion of meeting strangers online is bound to contribute to negative perceptions of online VWs, and again, there are bound to be misperceptions here (helping strangers in online worlds, for example, is commonplace, and highly regarded in the offline world).[27] It is true that social encounters in online worlds are often fleeting, yet this is because these worlds are third places. Unlike offline third spaces, however, it is possible to enter and exit these spaces and encounters more easily, and perhaps the novelty of spaces for encounters with strangers contributes to the perception that they are less genuine than offline encounters.[28] Ultimately, however, this novelty will wear off and the constraints of VWs will have become more apparent, but people will also have adapted to and extended the possibilities of spending time with others in VWs.

NOTES

1. Boellstorff (2008: 113) says that, for SL, virtuality is about sociality rather than about sensory immersion. Perhaps if this interpreted as saying that the prime motivation for coming to SL is to socialize, this rings true. Yet there are many offline social activities that have a similar draw as online worlds, so it is not socializing per se but the unique setting of a shared online space that must be the main appeal.

2. See Damer 1998 and Schroeder 1996. There is also a project to archive (or preserve) virtual worlds (http://pvw.illinois.edu/pvw/; last accessed March 28, 2009). The history of AW has been partly covered in Chapter 2. For a fuller timeline of events in AW, see Mauz's history pages (http://mauz.info/awhistory.html; last accessed March 28,2009). Boellstorff (2008: 52) notes that good documentation about SL can be found on the SL history Wiki.

3. There are a number of VWs that are not treated here for reasons of space and because they have quite different dynamics (see Spence 2008a, b). These include worlds that cater to younger children like Habbo Hotel. Like online games, these VWs are also heavily themed and structured.

4. Goffman did not apply his ideas to communications media, although they found their way into the influential analysis of television by Meyrowitz (1985).

5. Benford and colleagues used the notion of "focus" (as well as "aura" and "awareness") in VEs (1992) and included focus on other users as well as spatial orientation toward others.

6. The different modes of communication can be compared experimentally (Sallnas 2002, 2004) or by observing the differences between them (Becker and Mark 2002).

7. Williams, Caplan, and Xiong (2007), discussed in Chapter 6, are an exception in the analysis of how online gamers with voice versus text-only play different strategic roles in teams.

8. Baym discusses "three common and consistent findings in analyses of online groups: they are normatively regulated, hierarchical, and often very supportive" (2002: 70).

9. Boellstorff (2008: 181) argues that there are so many events in SL that a typology would not be useful, but this complicates matters too much: even in the offline world, social scientists must categorize interactions, and there are far fewer types in online worlds.

10. For ethnographic accounts of World of Warcraft, see Nardi (2010) and Bainbridge (2010).

11. The popularity of SL has arguably plateaued since 2007, but it remains to be seen how the popularity of this and other worlds will fare.

12. Castronova (2008: 172) is wrong to suggest that *all* online worlds have economies: worlds that are free to use and do not have any in-world economic activities do not have economies in any meaningful sense.

13. Much of what follows is drawn from this source. Castronova prefers "synthetic worlds" to "virtual reality," but "synthetic worlds" has not been widely used. His argument is that "synthetic" indicates the world, whereas "virtual" means rendered by a computer. Surely, however, virtual worlds are both, and synthetic worlds could also be used for worlds created in artificial intelligence simulations and the like.

14. Castronova (2001: 16–17) argues that economic "scarcity" is what makes online games enjoyable because users can get a sense of achieving something, but this is not "scarcity" in the conventional economic sense but rather scarcity in terms of what participants in the online world treat as scarce.

15. Business models apart from the subscription model have been tried. These include selling advertising, selling clothes (There Inc.), selling avatars, and dividing worlds into open access versus pay only. None apart from subscriptions have become anything more than niche markets, however.

16. Governments, incidentally, may have a different interest in online worlds: taxing them! At the height of the media attention devoted to SL (2007), the author was asked by a group drawn from across the civil service in the United Kingdom about the possibilities of taxing the populations and businesses in SL and similar online worlds, which is unlikely to be feasible because avatars would move into untaxed social worlds (this is obviously more difficult in real physical environments). According to Au, the United States and Australia have weighed taxing income in SL (2008: 226), but this can also be seen as an instance where the distinction between virtual and real, or between in-world and the real world, becomes clear: only when Linden dollars turn into real money could there really be a question of taxation of virtual worlds, and it is difficult to see how this could be implemented.

17. As mentioned in Chapter 3, to import and export objects into and from AW is easier than into and out of SL.

18. Even in this case, the copyright question is difficult: an artist told me that he had difficulties, at the time unresolved, in exhibiting art works in SL that

consisted of photographs taken in World of Warcraft because they infringed the copyright of the developers of the World of Warcraft software.

19. Au (2008: 167) says they are spending 50 to 60 Linden dollars per week, mainly for renting land, and the bulk of this rental income for Linden Lab are individuals rather than companies. Compare with Boellstorff (2008: esp. 212–213).

20. Trust has also been studied in online games. Williams, Caplan, and Xiong (2007) found that voice in World of Warcraft yields more trust among guild members than for text-only gaming. For an experiment comparing trust and social presence in different modalities (text, audio, video, avatar) in a short task for two persons, see Bente, Ruggenberg, Kramer, and Eschenburg (2008). See also the review of trust in online interactions by Riegelsberger, Sasse, and McCarthy (2007).

21. As ever, the interview material needs to be treated with caution because no face-to-face interviewing took place. There is no reason to believe, however, that our interviewees misrepresented themselves.

22. According to an interview by the author with the system administrators at their headquarters in Newburyport on October 18, 1999, and for the age and gender of users, based on a market research firms' analysis that was shared with the author.

23. Boellstorff (2008: 159) similarly notes that people in SL regard friendships as no less authentic than real world ones, and they also believe these relations to be less burdened by real world prejudices.

24. In the press, online worlds like SL are often discussed in terms of bad interpersonal behaviour (known in the online community "griefing"), but as Boellstorff and others have noted, most of the time what is striking in this environment where most people encounter each other as strangers is how helpful avatars are to each other (Boellstorff 2008: 185-6, see also Spante 2009).

25. Virtual worlds are often seen by those who do not know them as a form of escapism (Boellstorff 2008: 26), but virtual worlds and virtual reality technology have been regarded as such but also hyped as many other things in the media since they first emerged (Schroeder 1996: 123-36).

26. It is interesting to think about how online VWs and games bring together people from different walks of life offline. Nardi (2010) argues, for example, that people who would otherwise not have the opportunity to socialize and play together, people from different walks of life, still do so in World of Warcraft. At the same time, it is also the case that people from quite different cultures enjoy online spaces such as World of Warcraft for the same reasons. So, for example, Nardi says that Chinese players of World of Warcraft like the game for similar reasons as North American players, and they enjoy the same things (sociability and the challenge of the game). Indeed, the main difference is that Chinese players are more likely to access the games from internet cafes. In short, online VWs provide a means for social mingling and engagement in

shared pursuits that is unlike the offline world, although the extent to which they do so remains to be established for different VWs.

27. Boellstorff (2008: 167) says that the first wedding took place in AW in 1996, although nowadays, the notion that people meet first online is commonplace, so online avatar togetherness is bound to become mundane too.

28. For example, Williams, Ducheneaut, Li, Zhang, Yee, and Nickell (2006) found that only a third of World of Warcraft guild members knew each other offline before playing together online.

6

Modalities of Communication

It may seem odd to treat the topic of communicating in multiuser virtual environments (MUVEs) separately—because ideally, in a completely realistic VE, communication in MUVEs takes place just as it does in face-to-face (F2F) interaction: via bodily and facial cues and via voice. This chapter can therefore begin by noting how communicating in MUVEs is unlike F2F communication: First, most large-scale online worlds have used and continue to use text, normally via a text-chat window or in a speech bubble above the avatar speaker (and sometimes both). Some online worlds, as we have seen, have begun to add voice, even if voice has been a feature of some online worlds for some time (e.g., OnLive Traveler [OT]). With Internet telephony, it is also becoming increasingly common to use a separate voice channel while using online worlds.[1] Immersive MUVEs have almost invariably featured voice communication.

Text-chat–only worlds are bound to continue, partly because it is simply difficult to have many simultaneously voice speakers in the same space in a world. Part of this chapter will thus be devoted to text-only communication in online worlds even if, again, text falls outside the definition of a VE. But apart from the use of text, a second way in which communication via text or voice in MUVEs differs from F2F communication is that it is difficult to establish common ground in MUVEs. We have already seen in Chapter 4 on collaboration how this applies to the referencing of space and objects in MUVEs. This difficulty is common to both text-only MUVEs and MUVEs with voice, to immersive and desktop-based MUVEs, and not only to space and the objects in it but also to other aspects of interpersonal relations—although in different ways in each case. The reason for this difficulty is the absence of different facial and bodily cues as well as cues from the virtual space. Part of this chapter will therefore discuss how common ground is nevertheless established, and this part of the chapter relates closely to the chapter on collaboration dealing with navigation and spatial tasks.

A third communication issue in MUVEs, and especially in large online worlds, is, How do avatars, shorn of the background that they normally bring to conversation or to communication, and regardless of whether they are strangers, nevertheless manage to communicate their identities to each other? This chapter will examine a special case, whereby people, who are often strangers from many different cultural and linguistic backgrounds, interact. But the question can also be asked in relation to how avatars convey their identity to each other generally, including in immersive VEs with voice.

Finally, there is series of questions regarding what can be communicated by means of different kinds of avatars and by means of avatar gestures and posture, as well as via the various kinds of limited facial cues that avatar faces provide. What kinds of avatar bodies and faces lend themselves to the most effective communication? To what extent is it possible to convey emotions and other subtleties? Here the chapter harks back to Chapter 3 on avatar appearance but relates appearance specifically to interpersonal communication. Against the backdrop of findings about these questions, we can return to comparing communication in MUVEs with F2F generally.

Before we come to interpersonal communication, we can quickly deal with the audio part of MUVEs that is not concerned with human sounds but rather with the sound of the VE itself (this was briefly touched on in Chapter 2). In this respect it is interesting to consider the two end-states again: an audio environment for a VE that reproduces all the environment's real-world sounds does not seem very useful, as with fully reproducing a visual environment that is video-captured. In a videoconferencing system, it may be useful to reproduce the rustling of papers and squeaking of chairs, but in a VE it will be difficult to implement (and may seem unnatural) to implement such sounds. In relation to the second, computer-generated end-state, many VEs play recorded sounds, such as music or atmospheric "muzak" that is commonly used in online worlds, as well as having "iconic" recorded sounds for objects (bumps, creaking doors, zooming vehicles, and the like).

On the technical side, there are solutions for making the auditory environment realistic in the sense of having three-dimensional (3D) audio, although these solutions are technically difficult and labour intensive as well as expensive in terms of having 3D headphones or loudspeakers.

Audio has not played a major part in MUVE development; nor, apart from improving particular aspects of the MUVE (again, "iconic" sounds to let people know that they are bumping into things) does it play a major part in the experience of VEs. The two end-states in this respect are thus easy to summarize: import realistic recorded sounds into the environment where it is useful, or generate an auditory atmosphere with music and attach sounds to certain objects where necessary or desirable.

The audio of the environment will, of course, provide a backdrop to interpersonal communication. But if we bracket this backdrop, it is possible to focus purely on interpersonal communication, and one way to focus the topic still further is to ask: what do (the rather cartoon-like) avatars add to communication in text-chat or voice-enabled MUVEs? In MUVEs with voice, one aspect of this is straightforward; namely, that the voice and avatar must be matched. We can think here, most easily, of gender and voice: "Female voices in male embodiments were thought of as 'weird,'" note Tromp, Steed, Frecon, Bullock, Sadagic, and Slater (1998: 60). Apart from such an obvious mismatch, how do avatars, communication, and identity interrelate?

This chapter will proceed as follows: first, some findings from research will be presented, and the general framework that was presented in Chapter 2 will be applied to understanding communication in MUVEs. Then, findings from a range of studies will be presented, including studies of collaboration in MUVEs, text-chat in Active Worlds (AW), the voice-world OT, and Second Life (SL), which is mainly text but now has voice. Next, the discussion will turn to communication in online worlds, briefly considering OT, an online world with voice, and comparing text and voice modalities in online worlds. The chapter will conclude by comparing MUVEs, videoconferencing, and F2F encounters, including some design implications.

Research on Communication in MUVEs

Short, Williams, and Christie (1976: 76) were among the first to argue that people choose a medium not on the basis of objective features, but to suit their communication needs. According to Short et al., people prefer nonverbally rich media (1976: 115). In MUVEs, as in other media and forms of computer-mediated communication (CMC), social cues are reduced—both if they are text-based or use voice. So far, however, there have been few comparisons between voice and text-based VEs (but see Sallnas 2002).

Apart from the social psychological analysis of communication, we also need a broader account of communication to tackle MUVEs. A simple point to start with is that "people behave more 'socially', that is, politely and with greater restraint, when interacting with a face" (Donath 2001: 374). To this we can add that people behave even more socially when interacting with a face and a body. These commonsense ideas can be combined with Reeves and Nass' (1996) not-so-obvious insight that people also behave "socially" when they are interacting with televisions, computers, and new media when they think that these artefacts are human-like.

There are many ways to design online faces for effective and enjoyable communication, and realism is only one possibility. For different modes of self-presentation, different nonrealistic options may be suitable, and Donath (2001) has argued that faces should be designed to suit different forms of communication. The research by Reeves and Nass (1996) suggests that human-like features can make devices more like interacting with persons. Again, however, research into what different "face" requirements are under different conditions is at an early stage (see Garau 2003). Finn, in her overview of research related to videoconferencing, points out another limitation of research, namely, that "much of the research" has been focused on "communication: How well is human–human communication supported by a system, or how is that communication altered by the use of the system, or how can that communication be characterized?" (1997: 13). Yet this implies a very communication-centric perspective. In the case of MUVEs, we could ask more broadly, for example: what advantages—apart from *richer* communication—do the noncommunication features of MUVEs or other shared media spaces have?

As Finn further points out, most studies of video-mediated communication have been of dyads, although recently there have been more studies of larger groups (1997: 15). On the positive side, these larger groups correspond much more with normal conversations, but the drawback is that larger groups often mean that there are greater problems with the communication ("it becomes less clear who is being addressed, who has the floor, and so forth"; 1997: 15). A number of studies (for example, Bowers, Pycock, and O'Brien 1996) from the early days of MUVEs onward show that the same is true for MUVEs.

Baym (2002: 63), in her summary of research on interpersonal online relations, says that the "cues-filtered-out took the defining features of CMC to be the absence of regulating feedback and reduced status and position cues," resulting in "anonymity and deindividuation." "The task-oriented claims from this approach," she continues, "have held up reasonably well, but the interpersonal implications ... have been roundly criticized." One problem, she points out (referring to a large literature) is that "most of the lab studies brought together unrealistically small, zero-history groups for a median time period of 30 minutes." These, in her view, have largely left out the "socioemotional" content of interpersonal relations.

The socioemotional "richness" that Baym finds in text-based online life also applies, as we have seen, to MUVEs like AW. But we can go further: studies of longer-term uses of MUVEs with audio (see Chapter 4; Becker and Mark 2002; Williams, Caplan, and Xiong 2007) show that there is no reason why these environments should be regarded as particularly socioemotionally "rich" or "poor." True, there are no cues from physical bodies. Yet people "filter in" or "put in" some of what is missing in their encounters or relationships. Against this backdrop, it is difficult to see how the issue of the "impersonality" of MUVEs could be resolved, except by (1) more laboratory experiments, with their obvious limitations, which compare not only different media (as did Short, Williams and Christie 1975) but also a wide range of different "tasks," (2) further long-term studies of MUVEs, and (3) an understanding that puts the issue within the much larger context of the impersonality or otherwise of different media generally (this will be discussed in Chapter 10).

Face-to-Face versus MUVE Encounters

Communication between avatars is different from F2F communication: whether they communicate via text or via voice, avatars need to focus their attention and be aware of their conversation partners in a different way from how they do so in F2F settings. In F2F communication, this focus of attention and mutual awareness is taken for granted. When avatars speak to each other, in contrast, the situation demands a different kind of engagement with conversation partners; maintaining an awareness of others is an ongoing and attention-demanding effort. A steady "holding the other in the visual and auditory field" is required and needs to be maintained, unless, for text or voice communication, the visual appearance of the avatar is regarded as irrelevant. Compare the equivalent F2F situation, where it is rude to ignore looking at another person while speaking to him or her.

If the other(s) are not in one's field of vision, it is necessary to have a way of figuring out if they are copresent by means of an audio signal from them—because avatars do not have the same kind of peripheral awareness that we have of physical bodies in the real world. That is, the signals of copresence for communication need to be more explicit. One reason we know this is because in MUVEs, silences need to be "repaired" lest they should be interpreted as an absence of the other(s) or lead to confusion about where they are or whether they are still there. For example, in the Tromp et al. study, one participant said: "Silence was strange—'no chatter, no white noise'—as would be the case in normal meetings" (1998: 61). This problem of not knowing whether others are copresent does not arise in F2F communication.

Avatars typically follow the convention of facing the person they are talking to, but they have to move self-consciously in MUVEs in order to do this. This applies both to environments with and without audio, although with audio, this convention is followed more: it does not make as much sense to face a voiceless (text-only) person that you are encountering as it does with voice (Becker and Mark 2002).[2] Yet avatars almost always face each other *to some extent* (Bowers, Pycock, and O'Brien 1996). In a MUVE, one may also not know (or be so worried about, or be *more* worried about!) whether another person is "behind" one's avatar. Finally, an obvious difference with F2F communication is that there may be a disconnect with what is happening outside the online world, in front of the screen (or with an immersive environment, if the avatar is temporarily disembodied): How can one be sure that the person one is facing is really there?

Studies of different types of MUVEs (immersive and nonimmersive, text and voice, large and small groups) show that awareness of the other person(s) is among the most common problems in MUVEs (Tromp, Steed, and Wilson 2003). (Because this is a key point, it is worth mentioning that this has been found using both quantitative and qualitative methods [Rittenbruch and McEwan 2007].) Among the reasons for this is that the shift to focusing from one conversation partner to another needs to be more deliberate than in F2F situations, where gaze and other bodily mechanisms to do this are taken for granted. One implication is that more communication is devoted to this awareness or focusing of attention ("Who said that?" "Where do you mean?" "Did you hear that?" and the like).

The focus of attention in communication thus shapes the interpersonal dynamic. In F2F interaction, there is a difference between encounters with a common focus of attention versus unfocused encounters where people monitor each other casually (Collins 2004; Turner 2002). Both are problematic in VEs, unlike in the real world: No matter how realistic and immersive, it is difficult to establish a common focus of attention (in the real world, this can be done with a subtle eye gaze) and monitor the other's state (in the real world, we can sense that someone is behind us). This difference between a common focus of attention and a casual monitoring of the other(s) has implications for common ground and mutual awareness but also for emotional engagement.

At this point, we can turn to a number of studies that illustrate the contrast with F2F communication and extend previous findings to various MUVE settings.

Common Ground in Immersive and Nonimmersive Spaces

The following is based on an analysis of audio recordings of two people collaborating on the Rubik's Cube–type puzzle task (see Chapter 4). The study compared the immersive-immersive, immersive-desktop, and desktop-desktop settings (Axelsson, Abelin, and Schroeder 2003). In all three conditions, there are difficulties in making yourself understood by the other person, but this difficulty must be put in the context that the pairs in the immersive-immersive condition were able to complete the task just as well as in the F2F condition (see Chapter 4). In other words, mutual intelligibility was not an obstacle to doing the task in the setting where both partners were immersed in the VE. Second, as we shall see, despite the problems of communication, people find ways to overcome these.

One difference between the immersive-immersive and the other two conditions is that, when trying to reach a joint understanding about which object is being referred to, only one speaker in the immersive-immersive condition will do this ("the black [side of the cube] has to go on the inside of the cube [i.e., should not be outward facing]"), but in the other two conditions both speaker and listener will do this. In other words, additional clarification is needed in the desktop condition because, unlike when both partners are immersed, there is a lack of common understanding about which object is referred to. Immersive partners use indicative gestures to identify objects, whereas the desktop partners working with immersed partners would refer to the objects being handled by their partners:

> Immersive: Yes, wait a minute; there is one more in the back as well.
> Desktop: Yes, you are getting that one now ...
> Immersive: Yes.

There is also much use of the body as a point of reference. This is not so necessary in F2F situations when our gaze or posture or nods can indicate what we are referring to. But again, there is a difference between immersed and nonimmersed partners here; the nonimmersed partner uses the immersed partner's body as a point of reference:

> Desktop: Yes, because that has the one with red edges or the one farthest out to the right, too.
> Immersive: The one in your ... over here? This one?
> Desktop: No, in the other direction.
> Immersive: Your, mine ... You mean to your right?

Being in a fully immersive VE and having more interactive spatial interaction with objects is thus an advantage for achieving a common ground in communication, although the nonimmersed person has a more "detached" perspective, which can also be an advantage.

Text-Chat in Graphical Worlds

In a study of AW (Allwood and Schroeder 2000), we found, based on observation, that the participants do not make much use of the gestures of their avatar embodiments. For example, avatars in AW have the capability to smile, frown, wave, jump, and the like, but they are mostly immobile while they are having conversations. This was also found for V-Chat, a similar online world (Smith, Farnham, and Drucker 2002). In other words, communication is mainly by means of text. But the main focus of the study was about how people from different cultural and linguistic backgrounds communicate. To do this, we logged almost 6.5 hours from the central place of entry—"ground zero"—in AW (in the central entrance world called AlphaWorld; see Chapter 3) from 185 participants who made more than 3000 contributions (separate entries prefaced by their online names). Only a few of the results will be highlighted here.

One is that the conversation was mostly English speaking (the study was carried out in 1999). This reflects the preponderance of the English language during the early years of the Internet. More than a quarter of all the contributions were greetings or farewells, with greetings more than twice as common as farewells. This is interesting because greetings are a precondition for participating in a conversation, although farewells are only necessary if a successful conversation has been established (or if people leave without saying goodbye). Here we can bring in Becker and Mark's result (2002), which was based on participant observation about three online worlds: text-only LambdaMOO, voice plus graphics OT, and AW, which is text plus graphics: they found that avatars generally follow the conventions of greetings and farewells as in F2F conversations. This is borne out in what we found in AW, except that it seems that greetings and farewells represent a greater *share* of the conversation than in equivalent offline F2F situations and that avatars tend to leave more often without saying farewells (if we assume that in F2F, these are roughly equal). This contrast between online and offline communication reinforces the point that has been made a number of times already: that there are similarities and differences from physical (F2F) settings. In this case, we see that there is either a greater need to establish common ground by means of greeting and farewells, which confirms the idea that more must be "put into" online relations, or, on the other hand, if mutuality has not been established, it is more possible to leave without saying goodbye (which is difficult in F2F encounters!).

The second most common set of topics, apart from greetings and farewells, relate to events, objects, and persons in AW or in the real world. It is hard to compare this with F2F conversations, but clearly a lot of the conversation in AW goes toward establishing a common context of events, objects, and people. This point is reinforced when we look at the most frequent types of utterance and find that questions like, "Does anyone speak X [a certain language]?" or "Where are you from?" are very common. Names are also used frequently because participants need to identify each other by name in a conversation where threads from many conversations may be taking place simultaneously, but also where avatars need to refer to each other without the normal bodily and facial cues. Moreover, turn-taking needs to be explicitly managed, so this is a frequent component of contributions even though explicit feedback (as in F2F conversation, such as "Uh hunnh") is rare because this is easier to do in voice conversation. Finally, emoticons and abbreviations that are familiar in online chat ("U" instead of "you") are commonly used. It should also be noted that the average number of words per contribution is short (4.9 words), and almost all contributions are one liners, as in IM and SMS messages (see Baron 2008).

If we turn to the question of intercultural communication, even though places like AW are dominated by English speakers (although there are also non–English-themed worlds within AW and online worlds that cater specifically to speakers of other languages such as Chinese), AW is nevertheless a cosmopolitan "third place," with an ebb and flow of participants from different countries depending on the time of day. A close real-world analogy might be an international conference (or, again, a cocktail party) where English dominates but where pockets of compatriots gather in enclaves. Still, the ability to write English well can be seen as a form of stratification, similar to the difference between newbies and more experienced users (see Chapter 3).

A final contrast with F2F settings is the amount of effort expended on communication management. This is not surprising as there may be several conversations going on simultaneously, but the absence of social cues that normally comes from facial expressions and from voice inflections also contributes to the difficulty of managing this "free-for-all."

Language Encounters in MUVEs

Another important aspect when strangers encounter each other in online worlds is how they will handle encounters between different languages.

English has been the main language on the Internet (Crystal 2001), especially if the use of English as a second language is included, although the share of non-English languages has been increasing (see http://www.internetworldstats.com/) and there is now also technology for translation (see, for example, http://babelfish.yahoo.com/). In addition, there are also some "in-world" translation services—for example, in SL. In online worlds, unless they are specifically oriented to specific language speakers, English is often used as a lingua franca that allows people to reach out across the many languages that are spoken.

In MUVEs, just as in F2F settings, not being able to speak—or write—in the dominant language is obviously a disadvantage. This disadvantage (or advantage for English speakers) may, however, be even greater in MUVEs for socializing because much of the activity in these MUVEs (as we have seen in Chapters 2 and 3) is self-presentation.[3] The question then is whether this disadvantage is exacerbated or weakened in MUVEs, and this question prompted us to investigate language encounters in MUVEs. There are, of course, a number of skills that may confer an advantage in text-based worlds, such as being able to type well, using humor, or displaying other social skills, but these other skills may be less useful if one has not also mastered the language.

The literature on text-based CMC and language is too extensive to review here (but see Danet and Herring 2007). One finding that is relevant to graphical worlds is that the longer people use online worlds, the less likely they are to use nonverbal communication (Smith, Farnham, and Drucker 2002). This also means that a focus on text is appropriate (the study of language- or culture-specific gestures or body movements in MUVEs remains, to my knowledge, to be investigated).

To investigate language encounters, we undertook participant observation and logged conversations in the central, most populated parts of AW, in language-themed worlds (in AW, there were a number of language-themed worlds: Mundo Hispano, Italia, and the like; in these worlds, the conversation was often dominated by the "native" language)[4] and in worlds with other themes such as education or role-playing worlds, where there might be conventions other than the open-ended "cosmopolitan" conversations in the central parts of the world.

We categorized the language encounters according to the perceived intention of the new language introduction and the response to it (details given in Axelsson, Abelin, and Schroeder 2003). These online communication encounters take place within a number of "nested" frames, including the real-world setting, the online VE setting, and the frame of graphical and textual space in which the conversation takes place. Although these frames are analytically separate, the people or avatars are communicating are operating within them simultaneously. Nevertheless, these frames will need to be borne in mind in what follows—and we need to return to them at the end of this section.

Before giving examples, it can be noted that the most common intentions for introducing a new language can be broken down into three types: one is to find out if there are fellow speakers ("Anyone speak Spanish?"), a second is to start language play or to perform one's language skills to show that one is a member of the "cosmopolitan" community ("Hey The International Community *S* [smiles]"), and a third is to disturb the ongoing conversation of others to draw negative attention from others ("YOU IS BEAUTIFUL" in capital letters, which is regarded as yelling in online worlds). The responses to the introduction of a new language can be classified as acceptance, rejection, neutral, or mixed (both acceptance and rejection), and the consequence can be either that the new language remains or it disappears. Here are some brief examples (more details are provided in Axelsson, Abelin, and Schroeder 2003).

In the following example, a person asks if a language may be introduced:

"Albarn Steel LH":*Darf ich hier auch Duetsch reden?* [May I also speak German (i.e., Deutsch) here?]
German is introduced for a while and spoken by several users—acceptance—before another user tells the language introducers to change into the main language:
"Lady Heartish A": Ok ... english only now please
Another example is where a language introduction—in this case, Finnish—is rejected:
"Benni": *älkääpä pilkatko* [don't tease]
"pOpmAn": stop talking finnish

And here is an example of a mixed response, because "Kango" leaves a few turns after he tells two Swedish speakers who have begun the conversation in Swedish to change to English as follows:

Mikael: *Hej GK ...Allt väl?* [Hi GK, Everything alright?]
Kango: and bye Happy..:)
"GoodCake": *allt är bra* [everything"s fine]
"GoodCake": *du?* [and you?]
Kango: arrrgh speak englihs

Finally, here is an example of a disruptive language introduction because the speaker is made aware that capital letters are considered shouting:

"RAXOR": I LIVE IN [name of a non–English-speaking country]
Dana van Droen: better take your caps off
Dana van Droen: that is considered shouting here ... and my bot will boot you.
"RAXOR": I DON'T UNDERSTAND
Dana van Droen: don't TYPE LIKE THIS
"RAXOR": YOU IS BEAUTIFUL
Dana van Droen: That is yelling.
Dana van Droen: take you capital letters off please.

What emerges from these and other examples (in Axelsson, Abelin, and Schroeder 2003) is that the response to the introduction of a new language depends on several factors: whether the main language is English, non-English, or insider jargon; whether the setting is a cosmopolitan, language-themed, or otherwise-themed world; and the perceived intention of the language-introducing user (establish contact with others, initiate a language play, or disturb the conversation).

One contrast that can be made with F2F settings is that participants in AW are more willing to try out a new language or try out their non-native language skills. This is because the absence of social cues means that poor language skills are not so embarrassing and, as the main purpose is socializing, do not have such serious consequences. This may also make the setting more accepting or tolerant of introducing new languages. The flipside is that in text-chat in VEs, much more weight is put on the text-conversation than on other interactional cues, and so writing skills are more important, and a rejection of a newly introduced language may be more direct.

A mixed response is also possible, for example, because there are often several speakers present and they may have different responses, and, second, because the response can be to maintain silence, which can be a positive response if it allows others to continue the conversation in another language, or a negative one if the language introducer is alone and trying to find someone to chat to.

Overall, non-English speakers are tolerant toward English because they are used to adjusting to the norm (English), whereas English speakers are less accepting toward non-English speakers. However, this tends to be more true of non–language-themed settings than cosmopolitan ones because these more specialized settings are more likely to be frequented by regular users who have adapted more to being in an international setting. The most tolerant attitude is typically toward users who are introducing English as the new language—because that is the most commonly used language. Insider jargon also plays a role, particularly when it conveys emotions (smileys) and how to use the system (brb, or "be right back"), and this jargon is almost always tied to the English language. (Whether speakers are insiders can often be gleaned from the topic of conversation.)

In short, the VE medium amplifies certain aspects of language encounters (exclusion, but also embracing language plurality) and diminishes others (embarrassment, nonverbal communication). This characteristic of communication in the medium of VEs must be put in the context that in places like AW, not much hangs on the outcome of the encounter. At the same time, because language encounters are more frequent than in the real world (unless you are, say, at a gathering of Olympics athletes or in a United Nations forum), how language encounters are shaped matters more than in the real world.

There are design implications to these findings. For example, it is possible to label avatars with information about which languages they speak in the manner of tour guides who have such labels in the real world (but there are drawbacks to this labelling, such that it may also present a distraction or take away from anonymity). We will return to further implications in the conclusion.

OnLive Traveler and Second Life

To highlight how communication in MUVEs or VWs can differ, we can briefly consider two other examples, OnLive Traveler (OT) and Second Life (SL). OT is unusual in having been a VW with voice from the start. OT is an environment that uses "talking heads" (Figure 6.1) or avatars without bodies, even though they have some of the capabilities of avatars as in other worlds, such as navigation—and, in OT, unlike in most online worlds, their lips move when they speak. The first point to notice that unlike in other online worlds where people have avatar bodies (and where there are usually more avatars in the space), in OT, where they do not have bodies, people tend to do little else except stay in one place and talk, except to move to face each other. In other words, they don't move around as much, explore the environment, or interact with or move around to position themselves in relation to others (although of course they also need to use the keyboard to "push-to-talk" and navigate, and so may be too preoccupied to move around very much). This makes OT close to videoconferencing (although in OT, the faces are very cartoon-like).

OT thus highlights, in a backhanded way, that different kinds of virtual worlds (VWs) produce different kinds of activities. We might put VWs on a scale—from only talking to only navigating and manipulating objects and the environment (although *shared* environments where there

FIGURE 6.1   OnLive Traveler.

is no communication and only object manipulation and navigation are rare). Notice too that in an environment with talking heads, it is likely to be the case that people experience a high degree of copresence but less of a sense of presence in the space (although this has not been measured).

The fact that it is necessary to indicate one's continued copresence by making oneself audible is also illustrated well in an environment like OT. This "making oneself audible" needs to be affirmed even in a two-person communicative situation (is the other person still there if they do not speak?). And here, as in other respects, things become more complicated in MUVEs when there is more than one conversation partner: OT is an environment where the main activity is voice communication, and the primary way to be aware of who is speaking (apart from their distinctive voice) is because their lips move when they do so. So the question in this setting is: Are they still there if their lips have not moved for a while? In text-chat environments, of course, where a distinctive voice is missing, the text needs to be identified with a name if the conversation is in a separate text-chat window or by being placed on or near the "speaker's" avatar—and text silences therefore do not indicate absence as easily (we can think here of the difference between a telephone conversation and an IM conversation).

OT highlights another interesting point: unlike text-chat MUVEs, where silences are easily tolerated, in OT, breaks in the conversation or when avatars have nothing to say produce awkwardness. This is partly to do with the fact that turn-taking in conversation needs to be fluid and thus needs to be kept going—and partly because socializing conversations need to be sustained if the conversation is the main focus of attention.

SL is different again, and there are several distinctive features of communication in SL that deserve mention. For example, in SL, an interesting way to indicate who is speaking via text has been implemented, which is that avatars are shown typing on a keyboard (with the sound of typewriter keys clacking) as they are writing in the chat window. This is a feature designed to enable turn-taking in chat communication (Boellstorff 2008: 153), just as having chat in a speech bubble by one's head is designed so that speakers can be identified. Another observation made by Boellstorff (2008: 117) that relates to how avatars and what they say are connected is that there is a "broad understanding that" that IM (use of a text-chat window that is separate from SL) in SL involves less presence than text-chat within visual range.

Recently, Wadley, Gibbs, and Ducheneaut (2009) have begun to investigate why users of SL prefer voice or text (based on interviews, participant observation, and focus groups) and have come up with various factors. The preferences for text include anonymity and the fact that text can be recorded and copied, although some users prefer voice because their typing skills are poor. The advantage for users of voice is mainly (as might be expected) the richness of communication, but a disadvantage is that use of voice can transmit unintended sounds (other voices or noises in the background) or that users do not want to disturb their physical surroundings by noisy talking. Both modalities also allow for doing different types of things simultaneously: voice allows manipulating objects and navigating with the keyboard and mouse, whereas text allows speaking to others who are not in-world. Hence, too, they find that users have strong preferences for one or other modality, and they argue that VWs should allow users flexible control over which communication modality they use.

On a wider level, it is noteworthy that the introduction of voice capability led to a heated debate among users of SL (Boellstorff 2008: 114, 123; Au 2008: 197). However, the audio channel is still used by very few, according to Boellstorff (2008: 13). This can be compared to other settings such as World of Warcraft where voice *is* used, but the main advantage is quick coordination (as we shall see in the next section). To be sure, text-socializing, even if it is more common and lends itself to a more anonymous form of socializing than using voice, will be used on some occasions and in some worlds—and voice in others.

Text versus Voice, Videoconferences versus MUVEs, Face-to-Face versus Online

To compare the various modalities of communication further, we can begin with a very broad view: text-chat in VWs is partly a product of current technology limitations and partly a product of how graphical VEs have been developed. It can be foreseen that these limitations will be overcome as voice via the Internet becomes commonplace. Equally, however, the text-only format will continue to be used for certain forms of interaction, particularly where self-presentation in words has advantages over presenting oneself via voice. But the reason for making this point is to emphasize that text-chat and audio-only communication will not be replaced by MUVEs with audio technology—text-chat (also on mobile phones) and voice-only communication have *both* been growing with Internet and mobile phone use (Baron 2008). At the same time, if we compare the advantages and disadvantages of VWs with text as opposed to audio communication from the point of how MUVE technology is developing, then clearly voice has advantages for spatial tasks, whereas text-chat has advantages for certain interpersonal encounters (here it may be useful to think about the advantages of writing someone an email as opposed to telephoning them). In any event, with text communication, typing takes away from "being there" and being able to interact with the environment.

A second layer of broader considerations is the comparison between print or written culture versus a visually oriented culture and visual language, or comparing print and text to the oral tradition or to spoken communication. These more general patterns in society-at-large will bear on our understanding of MUVEs. In this respect, an important finding relevant to text-chat in MUVEs is that e-mail is like both written and spoken communication (Baron 2008)—and this finding also applies to text-chat in graphical VEs. Baym (2002: 65) has also noted that text-based CMC has been found to be more similar to speech than to writing. But the other comparison that has been made here are the differences between MUVEs and F2F communication: In this regard, as we have seen, as with the other characteristics of MUVEs such avatar embodiments, it seems that people adapt rather easily to the difficulties of communicating in MUVE settings.

Against this backdrop, we can examine several contrasts between the various communication modalities in MUVEs. First, voice versus text: Williams, Caplan, and Xiong (2007) compared text-only players of World of Warcraft with players using voice and text (Voice over Internet Protocol or VoIP technology) by sending voice technology (hardware, software, and VoIP service) to a sample of players. They found, by means of online questionnaires, "significantly higher levels of relationship strength and trust between voice-based guildmates [players organized as teams] when compared to the text condition over time" (2007: 439; the study took place over the course of a month). Adding the social cues of voice, they suggest, produced greater trust and closer relationships. Williams, Caplan, and Xiong also report some of the open-ended comments by players on the questionnaires to the effect that "voice was superior for joint task coordination, problem solving, and dealing collectively with dynamic situations (however fantastical they may have been)" (2007: 444).

Recently, Wadley and colleagues (Wadley, Gibbs, and Benda 2007; Wadley, Gibbs, and Ducheneaut 2009) have also begun to investigate the communication modalities in online games and compare the use of voice with text-only use (and also the use of both at the same time). Among their findings is that communicating by voice can be problematic because players have to cope with background noise (what is going on in the household) that can be distracting. Also, not everyone likes the loss of anonymity that voice entails. Yet voice also frees up the hands that would otherwise be used for typing, so that voice is most useful in raids when quick reactions are required. On the other hand again, some regard the off-topic chat that happens with voice as inappropriate. Voice also does not scale easily in larger groups when several people talk over each other, whereas text is easy to monitor. Finally, there can be a disjunction between, say, a scary character with a meek voice. Thus, they conclude that voice is a mixed blessing.

The voice-versus-text contrast calls to mind Walther's notion of hyperpersonal relationships in CMC that was discussed earlier (see Chapter 2), and we can now revisit it in the context of communication. One way to think about the notion of hyperpersonal relationships (although Walther does not put it this way) is in terms of what we "put into" our communication to "compensate" for the absence of social cues. This goes beyond the notions of media richness and absence of social cues that have been discussed in the literature (Baym 2002). Instead, Walther's idea of hyperpersonal relations suggests that there are different affordances in different modalities of communicating and interacting with others and that people develop new ways of communicating that are suited to these modalities. In the case of MUVEs, this might entail becoming used to "putting our personalities into" text or putting what avatars do not communicate about us into text or voice (we have

seen examples in Chapters 4 and 5). This will make for not only a different type of communication but also a different form of presenting
ourselves.

If we compare communication via videoconferences versus MUVEs,
in a sense they are mirror images of each other (although they can
also converge; see Chapters 1, 9, and 10): In videoconferences, the key is
facial cues, and the rest of the space is to a large extent irrelevant (the
exception is where documents are being shared, or in larger groups
where people may gesture or raise their hand to call the others to attention, and the like). The space in videoconferences is only important in
creating a sense of togetherness or copresence so as to allow the interpersonal communicative cues to work better; in other words, the aim of
the space is to make the setting closer to a F2F interaction. Thus, in the
most advanced videoconferencing systems, all inessential elements of the
room are minimized in order to avoid, for example, depth cues that may
be misleading and distracting. In most MUVEs, on the other hand, the
interpersonal cues (and especially facial cues) are often missing because
faces in VEs tend to be cartoon-like. Moreover, insofar as MUVEs are
used for the purposes they are best suited to—navigation and spatial
interaction, it is the space and the body that are important, not faces. The
exception is where faces in VEs are highly photorealistic, but in this case
MUVEs and videoconferences converge. Put differently, in videoconferences, we look for movements in faces and monitor how others are
responding to us. In MUVEs, in contrast, the experience of spatial
copresence of avatars is important, and the emphasis is on sharing the
same space.

The key problem in MUVEs with voice—less so for videoconferencing—is that turn-taking is difficult. This problem will be familiar to
people who use videoconferencing; the problem is due to the absence of
the facial and bodily cues of copresent others that make this easy in F2F
relations. (Lags in the system are also to blame, but the systems are also
being improved to address this.) In VWs, this problem is even more severe
because most avatars provide even fewer cues than video images of other
peoples' talking heads. But the problem is also different insofar as there
are different possibilities in a computer-generated world to overcome it:
for example, it is possible to have mechanisms to indicate who is speaking,
such as visually (recall the lip movement in OT).

There are other functions of the visual environment in communication. Whittaker and O'Conaill (1997) have described them as follows: Two are related to process coordination (turn-taking cues and availability cues), and three are related to content coordination (reference [what events and objects are talked about]), feedback cues, and interpersonal cues [emotion and the like]). They go on to list the elements involved in these forms of communication—gaze, gesture, facial expression, and posture— but also the environment and the objects and events contained in it. One reason for listing these elements is that it is clear, on the one hand, that gaze, which is perhaps the most important factor in many communication situations, has proved to be very hard to implement technically. Another is that the role of the environment—and the objects and events in it—can play a large role in communication, quite apart from being part of a "shared task." So far, however, there has been little systematic comparison of the balance between more environment-, as opposed to more face-and-body–related forms of interaction in MUVEs (and in video-communication), so that much research remains to be done.

A somewhat different comparison can be made with media spaces (Harrison 2009), which have been developed to enable shared object-related tasks or situations where mutual awareness is a key requirement of the task. Kraut, Gergle, and Fussell note that in shared media spaces, several processes are supported apart from being able to do the task together; namely "maintaining an awareness of the task state," or how far the collaborative task is toward reaching the goal, and "facilitating conversation and grounding," where *grounding* means "that people exchange evidence about things they understand" (2002: 32–33; this is similar to the idea of common ground discussed earlier). They suggest therefore that shared spaces help in "creating efficient messages" and "monitoring comprehension" (2002: 33). These are very instrumental gains that can be measured by task performance, but especially the latter could also contribute to noninstrumental interaction.

Finally, it is useful to compare MUVEs with F2F interaction: Sociologists who focus on bodily communication or on emotions in F2F settings tend to downgrade the affordances of mediated communication. So, for example, Collins asks, "Isn't it possible to carry out a ritual without bodily presence?" (2004: 54). He answers in the negative: for television, for example, he says that "the stronger sense of involvement [in ritual on television], of being pulled into the action, is from the sound" (2004: 55). He points out that we need to share the excitement of television with copresent others and that televised and radio broadcast events have not replaced participating in "live events." Similarly with video- and audio-conferencing: all these operate, according to Collins, at a lower level of intensity than F2F gatherings. Thus he reaches the conclusion that "remote hookups however vivid will always be considered weak substitutes for the solidarity of actual bodily presence," and although he admits that "some degree of intersubjectivity and shared mood can take place by phone, and perhaps by remote video ... this nevertheless seems pale compared to face-to-face, embodied encounters" (2004: 62). E-mail, according to Collins, "settles into bare utilitarian communication ... nor will people have any great desire to substitute electronic communication for bodily presence" (2004: 63). Finally, he predicts that "the more that human social activities are carried out by distance media, at low levels of IR [interaction ritual] intensity, the less solidarity people will feel," with the exception if devices can directly stimulate the brain to attune our nervous systems to those of others (2004: 64).

Similarly, Turner says that "even when visual media, such as video-conferencing provide us a picture of others ... our visual senses still cannot detect all the information that we naturally perceive when inter-acting in face-to-face situations. Just how far technologies will advance in producing sharper images of others is hard to predict, but the very need to develop more refined technologies tells us something about what humans seek. We prefer visual contact with copresent others, especially with those in whom we have socioemotional investments" (2002:1). He also claims that "the more individuals use multiple sense modalities—visual, auditory, and haptic—in self-presentations and in role taking, the greater will be the sense of intersubjectivity and intimacy. Visually based emotional language will communicate more than either auditory or haptic signals that carry emotions. The more interaction is instrumental, the greater will be the reliance on the auditory channel. Conversely, the more an interaction is emotional, the greater will be the reliance on the visual and haptic sense modalitities" (Turner 2002: 81–82).[5]

The reason for presenting these arguments against mediated com-munication by these two sociologists who have produced powerful accounts of F2F interaction (Collins 2004; Turner 2002) is that their bias toward F2F encounters (or against mediated communication) makes them overlook what CMC researchers have found: the importance of emotional content, the way that people adapt to online worlds and "put more of themselves into" communicating with others, and more generally the rich and varied multimodal interactions that people have nowadays. That is, many features of F2F interaction can, in fact, also be found in mediated interaction. Ling (2008), for example, has produced an account of mobile phone uses that explicitly develops the notion that the emotional intensity of ritual is a key feature of form of communication—drawing on Collins' (2004) theory of interaction rituals. All this serves to highlight that there is still a bias among social scientists toward F2F interaction and communication and that much remains to be done to tease out how emotions and other interpersonal relations are conveyed in MUVEs.

Questions of Communication Design

Communication in VWs does not just follow certain norms but it is shaped by sociotechnical capabilities: For example, with text or voice chat, either everyone within a certain spatial vicinity can hear or read the conversation (as in the real world), or everyone within the world can read or hear it regardless of whether they are close to the speakers, or only certain selected avatars can read or hear it. Combinations of these options are also possible (although they are awkward: in SL, for example, when some speak via voice and others via text, the mix can be confusing as it is not clear how the two groups overlap or if they are separate). These design options are technical as well as social; the options need to be implemented with certain forms of social interaction in mind, and obviously the options chosen will strongly shape the interaction between avatars.

For example, unlike in large groups, where our interest might be in language encounters or in the length of turns, in small groups we might also be interested who dominates verbally, such as in carrying out a spatial task that requires a lot of communication and where participants are using different systems. Some of these patterns in relation to using different systems and performing different tasks have been described in

Chapter 4, and we have seen, for example, that the immersed person will concentrate more on the spatial task, while the nonimmersed person will be more preoccupied with giving verbal instructions.[6]

Text is more flexible regarding the options than voice: voice conditions need to approximate real-world voice conditions, as in OT, because with voice, if there are too many users speaking within earshot of each other, the conversation will become an inaudible babble. A second reason that voice is difficult applies to both online VEs and to videoconferencing; namely that turn-taking is difficult in a space where the absence of bodily proximity and weaker facial cues do not allow the same kind of easy turn-taking that we take for granted in the real world.

Different implementations of communication also create different atmospheres in online words. The "talking heads" in OT create an atmosphere that is different from worlds with full avatar bodies. And there is a difference between worlds with avatars that have speech bubbles above their heads, as in the VW There (Brown and Bell 2006), and worlds like AW where the text is also displayed in a separate space below the world. But whatever the atmosphere created by the interface, the difference is important to communicative interaction: If a speech bubble is only above the avatar's head, this means that the user's visual attention will be focused there rather than on the text in the separate space, with implications for how people talk about where they are and how they address each other.

In the context of the focus of attention in communication, it can be mentioned that presence could also be regarded—not as "being there" but rather in the sense of presence as when it is said that a speaker has a certain "presence." This is a useful notion for online worlds and video-conferencing in view of the absence of other cues about the presence of speakers in the sense that we can ask how much attention does a speaker "command," or how much attention do we devote to one speaker as opposed to others?

For MUVEs that support audio communication, one finding that has emerged again and again (see Chapters 4 and 9) is that the quality of the audio communication is a major obstacle. Again, it can be anticipated that as a technical problem, this will be overcome with better audio quality—although the problems of communication in the absence of social cues such a realistic gaze or nods will remain. However, one design implication for shared VEs can be mentioned immediately: There is little point in developing a technologically sophisticated or visually complex shared VE *unless* the audio communication works well because this is critical for effective or enjoyable interaction.

Consider, in this context of audio communication, the following statement: "Despite the multimodal nature of face-to-face-communication, the most pervasive and successful technology for communicating at a distance is the telephone, which relies solely on the voice modality" (Whittaker and O'Conaill 1997: 24). There are two implications that could be drawn from this. The first is that the telephone has been perfectly adequate for communication, and therefore it is pointless to try to develop more multimodal communication tools. A different implication might be that we do not really need much of the richness of F2F communication to communicate in an effective or enjoyable manner. Both of these ways of thinking have implications for MUVEs.

Much of the work on videoconferencing and shared media space systems has been aimed at office or professional users at work. An interesting point here is that it is not clear whether these professional work uses will lead the way in videoconferencing uses or if domestic uses will do so—and whether different systems are required by these settings. Shared media spaces, for example, are more likely to be relevant for the work context, although this depends on what is included in shared media spaces: If the term is used in the narrow sense of sharing documents or design objects and the like, domestic users are less likely to need spaces, but if the term includes sharing a web space to browse family photographs together or communication via a social networking site, then this obviously applies to domestic users. It is difficult to forecast which applications will lead the way, as illustrated by the miscalculations of how telephones would be used when they were first introduced (Fischer 1992).

One design implication that relates the topic of communication to previous chapters is that because we know that mutual awareness and turn-taking in MUVEs is difficult, and because the two other major activities in MUVE are navigation and object-related tasks (or focusing on the spatial environment and the objects in it), perhaps environments and systems should be designed to facilitate communication *more* than in F2F settings (for example, with tools for indicating who is speaking, or who wants to speak or take control of an object, and the like), and the environments should otherwise be designed to make navigation and object-related tasks as undemanding as possible so that more attention (or more of the cognitive load) can be devoted to communication.

In keeping with the overall argument of this book that we can already foresee the (two) end-states of "being there together," we can now apply this argument to communication and to the auditory part of MUVEs. With human communication, the two end-states collapse into one: Apart from the artificial voices of bots (or agents) and the nonverbal communication of *generated* bodily movement (and, in a sense, text communication), all communication is "real" or captured; in other words, at the videoconferencing end of the scale of the two end-states. It is difficult to think of why it should be otherwise, unless people want to "hide" their voices with voice modulators to anonymize themselves. The auditory end-state will thus be a mix of real voices—and, in relation to the auditory part that is not related to human communication mentioned earlier, an environment consisting of specific sounds that enhance the environment (including the "iconic" sounds such as of objects snapping together or doors closing). This said, text-chat MUVEs are bound to continue alongside this end-state. Text-chat is also useful in accompanying videoconferences and MUVEs to, for example, overcome the technical and social difficulties encountered with these systems ("Are you still there?" or whispering so that copresent others cannot "hear").[7]

NOTES

1. The difference in this case is that the audio is not spatial; that is, it is not attached to the avatar. Also, the voice conversation is only between the avatars that have this feature enabled—not among all avatars in the world.

2. Becker and Mark (2002) suggest that people follow conventions more in OT than in AW because voice increases social presence. But it may also be that the audio quality is better if people face each other (obviously this does not matter in a text-only environment). Whether social presence or the practicalities of the audio are more important for how people face each other would be interesting to investigate.

3. In online gaming, there is a somewhat different dynamic since experienced players often use a highly developed jargon; see, for example, Nardi and Harris (2006). For text-based MUDs, see Cherny (1999).

4. See also Boellstorff (2008: 155) for places with languages other than English in SL.

5. Compare Fischer's (1992) account of the use of the telephone for emotional support rather than instrumental messages.

6. Group size is among the key differences for how different tasks can be done in audio versus text. For example, Löber, Schwabe, and Grimm (2007) have shown that for certain tasks, audio may be preferable for up to four people, but for larger groups (in the case of their experiments, seven or more), text communication is preferable. They also compared groups of four for productivity in the task, and found that audio can be faster, but if the task involves "rehearsability" and "reprocessability" and where a tight work schedule can be agreed, text communication is better (Löber, Grimm, and Schwabe 2006).

7. As Boellstorff notes (2008: 153), there is no analogue in the real world to being able to whisper to someone at same time as talking to a group.

7

Research Uses of Multiuser Virtual Environments

We have seen that social interaction in virtual environments (VEs) is different from real-world interaction in many respects. This means that multiuser VEs (MUVEs) have a number of advantages for research: Research participants and researchers do not need to be co-located, interaction is possible in VEs that is not possible in the real world for practical or ethical reasons, all aspects of the interaction can be captured accurately and in real time and analyzed later, and the parameters of the interactions can be manipulated in different ways. Here as elsewhere in the book, it will not be possible to give a complete account of MUVEs and research.[1] The main point is rather to give some examples to indicate the range of possibilities and to link the uses of MUVEs in the study social of interaction to the wider social aspects of the technology that are the focus of the book.

To this end, the chapter will describe some of the research methods that are used, which include experimental designs and gathering observations from "naturalistic" settings. The chapter will also discuss some of the disciplines involved, since the disciplinarity of research in this area itself raises some interesting questions. And, finally, we will review some of the main findings from research using MUVEs that, as argued throughout the book, divide into studies of small-group encounters and large-scale dynamics of online populations. To this can be added immediately that different systems permit different types of research: immersive systems allow the user's body to be tracked, and so allow investigation, for example, of how body posture affects interaction. Or again, in immersive systems, there are much more life-like encounters because persons are represented with full-size avatar bodies. Desktop systems and heavily populated online worlds, on the other hand, will lend themselves more to analyzing the aggregated behavior of large numbers of users rather than the behavior of individual avatars. Finally, the second part of the chapter will illustrate some of the variety of how MUVEs can be used to study interaction, contrasting qualitative and quantitative approaches to the fine-grained analysis of how avatars interact.

The Varieties of Social Research in Virtual Environments

It is useful to distinguish between several different *aims* to which social research in VEs can be put; namely, to:

- Improve the design of VEs and other communication systems
- Advance our knowledge of mediated social behavior (and, if the behavior studied online transfers back offline, to advance knowledge of offline behavior)
- Conduct research that would not otherwise be possible

Put differently, the aim of research may be to help us build better communication tools, to understand the world in which people interact with one another in digital media, or to use VEs to put people into situations that they cannot be put into in the physical world or in face-to-face encounters. Roughly speaking, the first tends to be research *into* VE systems themselves, the second *uses* VEs to study mediated interaction, and the third cuts across both of them. In any case, examples of all three will be given below.

If we categorize the social science uses of MUVEs by type of research method, we see that these fall into a few types (Table 7.1).

The most common method of research so far has been to put participants into experimental situations with the aim of seeing how they react to certain situations in the VE. A second method is systematically to observe the "naturalistic" behavior of users. This is often a qualitative approach, consisting of participant observation or ethnography and trying to obtain a fine-grained understanding of social interaction in online VEs, perhaps using interviews.[2] Third, there is a quantitative approach that might include tracking the movement of populations in online VEs or recording avatar encounters. It is also possible to manipulate ongoing or "naturalistic" settings by introducing some experimental variables into them, as Williams did when he studied online gamers after

TABLE 7.1   Types of research methods used in multiuser virtual environment research and their main characteristics.

Type of Research Method (and Main Disciplines)	Aim	Example	Advantage	Disadvantage
Experiment (social psychology)	Generalization about online behavior, factors influencing behavior in MUVEs	Using VR as a tool to measure the effect of eye gaze in social interaction (Bailenson et al. 2005)	Allows inferences about causality due to highly controlled studies	Behavior is not naturalistic in laboratory settings
Participant observation/ ethnography (sociology)	Understanding motives and implications of interaction in MUVEs	Compare different conventions in interpersonal interactions in MUVEs such as greetings (Becker and Mark 2000)	Allows for detailed and in-depth analysis of patterns of interaction	Labor intensive, need to conduct interviews one-by-one, difficult to generalize
Quantitative analysis/capture/ logging of online populations	Establishing patterns of social interaction in MUVEs	Correlating height and attractiveness with success in an online world (Yee et al. 2007)	Captures large amounts of data from thousands of people and/ or details of small-group encounters	Data interpretation may be difficult because complex behaviors cannot always be "read" from data, or the context and significance of interactions may be overlooked
Experiments introduced into "naturalistic" settings	To see how virtual experiences cultivate real-world attitudes	Examining how game play affects notions of real-world violence (Williams 2007)	Examines users who gain virtual experiences in everyday life	Lack of experimental control

providing them with them the tools for audio communication against others who only used text-communication.

This leads to another way to break down the research field—which is by discipline. The main ones apart from computer science are social psychology, communication studies, and sociology. But as we have seen, there are others, including political science, economics (see, for example, Castronova 2005), geography (Schroeder, Huxor, and Smith 2001), anthropology (Boellstorff 2008), media studies, and others. It is worth mentioning that the line between computer science and the social sciences has sometimes been hard to draw in MUVE research, and that there are a number of subdisciplines in computer science that overlap with social sciences here (human–computer interaction and computer-supported cooperative work). And we have seen (in Chapter 4) that VEs can be used to study distributed collaboration, which is often analyzed by measuring task performance. Finally, we need to remember the contrast with research on video-recorded interaction here (see Fielding and Macintyre 2006), especially because there are different constraints and possibilities in terms of research ethics and methods. Because video-recording captures real people, it may not be ethical, for example, to capture certain encounters because of their sensitive nature or because research participants may want to remain anonymous. In VEs, this concern may not apply because the participants can take the anonymous appearance of avatars—in fact, in MUVEs, different types and levels of anonymization are possible.[3] The advantage of encounters in videoconferencing settings, on the other hand, is that these encounters are more realistic or true to life.

Apart from the different ethics of the two types of research, a fundamental difference between them is that research on videoconferencing is typically aimed at improving "photo-realistic" "talking heads"–type communication, whereas MUVE research is aimed at enhancing interaction in three-dimensional (3D) spaces with computer-generated avatars (although, again, the line between the two is perhaps becoming blurred, and all sorts of combinations of the two can be envisioned: for example, computer-generated faces set among photo-realistic spaces, or the opposite). Finally, a videoconferencing scenario limits research to capturing realistic interaction, whereas in a MUVE, the scenario of how people interact can be manipulated in various ways (again, recall the discussion of the two end-states in Chapter 1).

Finally, it can be mentioned that one field that has so far been underrepresented in research with and on MUVEs is communication studies or media psychology. This is partly because communications research has to a large extent had a different agenda (*mass* media), and partly because the study of interpersonal communication has, in the areas closest to computer science, often been focused on text-based communication. The research on social presence, initiated by Short, Williams, and Christie in the 1970s (1976), is an exception, and we have seen that this tradition of research has continued with work on social cues and media richness. But as I have argued, VEs and other media will become increasingly intertwined in the future, and so will social research that relates to both.

Research on Small Group Interaction

A major focus of research has been on how realistic avatars need to be for certain forms of interaction. As we have seen, a key finding has been that behavioral fidelity is more important than representational fidelity; put differently, it is more important that avatars act in a human-like way (for example, in terms of nonverbal communication) rather than that they have a photo-realistic appearance (Garau 2006). This strand of research tends to be related to the aim of improving MUVEs as communication systems, but it is also possible to regard it as a more fundamental issue in social science: What kind of signals do people need in order to communicate with each other in interpersonal interaction?

One way to investigate this is to see what minimal life-likeness an avatar needs for a person to respond to this avatar as an emotional being. For example, in a study with Bailenson, Yee, Merget, and Schroeder (2006), we found that even what is essentially a box with colors representing human emotions can elicit responses in a VE as if the box was human-like. This line of research follows on from earlier work of Reeves and Nass (1996), who showed that people treat computers like people. But it also illustrates how work on avatar realism can come from both directions: What is the minimum life-likeness needed for interaction in terms of behavior at one end of the scale, and how realistic should avatars be at the other end?

In relation to examining interaction between avatars, Blascovich and colleagues (Blascovich 2002; Blascovich, Loomis, Beall, Swinth, Hoyt, and Bailenson 2002) proposed a model of social influence in VEs. According to the model, there is a tradeoff between realism (the degree to which human representations look and behave as they would in the physical world) and perceived agency (the extent to which interactants think they are interacting with another actual human being). The higher the realism, particularly communicative realism (e.g., facial expressions), the less is the perceived agency needed to achieve social influence, and vice versa. Hence, according to the model, social influence is likely to occur when either realism or agency or both are high.

Realism and agency are two important aspects of avatar interaction, but VEs can be used as an experimental tool for the study of many different kinds of behaviors: do we behave differently toward people of different shapes and sizes? What is the effect of different types of appearance? Different types of facial expression or forms of emotional expressions? An almost limitless number of permutations can be imagined here, especially if we add that the characteristics of one or both avatars can be altered, that the size of the group can be increased beyond two, and that the environment in which they interact can be altered in many ways. Findings in VEs that allow precisely controlled conditions and more easily captured results can shed light on what we know about face-to-face interaction, although precisely *how* these experiments will shed light on face-to-face interaction—such as discrimination, or leadership, or the role of emotions in encounters—remains to be seen.

Another question in relation to social interaction in VEs (which is more often posed for videogames) is about aggression or violence. Persky and Blascovich (2006) compared four conditions: playing an aggressive game (shooting a gun at an opponent, in this case an image of a person) versus a nonviolent game (shooting paint at an abstract painting), and using an immersive head-mounted display (HMD) versus a nonimmersive (desktop) display.[4] The findings were that only the immersive setting intensified the aggressive outcomes—in this case, self-report of aggression and a behavioral measure of aggression (here, "punishing" poor performers with blasts of noise). And although this was only a single-user design, the implications for MUVEs are clear: the more powerful the technology, the more the aggression there is (although there have been quite mixed results in the research on videogames and online games generally; see the review by Lee and Peng 2006).

The study by Slater, Sadagic, Usoh, and Schroeder (2000) that was discussed in Chapter 4 examined leadership and different types of technology or systems. The study examined three people performing a task, with two people on desktop systems and one using an immersive (HMD) system. The task was to solve a word puzzle in an office environment, a task in which people had to collaborate by moving around the room looking at different words on pieces of paper stuck on the wall and asking each other how words fit together to make a saying (See Figure 4.9). The study then compared this same group performing the task in an equivalent real-world setting. The interesting finding here was that the person who used the immersive system was regarded as the leader in the group even when no one was regarded as the leader in the equivalent real-world setting—and even though the participants did not know what type of system the others were using.[5] In other words, technology can make a difference without people being aware of this.

The Rubik's Cube–type puzzle study showing that people collaborate just as well at a distance as face-to-face has already been described (see Chapter 4), and distributed collaboration is typically studied separately from interpersonal influence. But it is easy to see that the various areas of research are interconnected: Is it possible to separate, for example, the parts of peoples' interaction that are interpersonal (facial expressions, bodily movements) from those that are collaborative in relation to an object-centered task (manipulating the cubes)? They will often be linked, but VEs allow precisely this kind of disaggregation of different parts of interaction. For example, a study by Vinayagamoorthy (2006) compared peoples' interaction with and without a mask in an immersive MUVE—in other words, factoring out their facial expressions and thus concentrating on the impact of their posture on interaction.

VEs can thus be easily manipulated. Bailenson and colleagues call this type of research about behavior in small mediated groups "transformed social interaction," which involves somehow altering the behavior or appearance of an avatar from the behavior or appearance of a person's physical self (Bailenson and Beall 2006). In other words, this research program takes advantage of the fact that, unlike in telephone conversations and videoconferences, the physical appearance and behavioral actions of avatars can be altered in VEs. These changed characteristics will, for example, have an impact on the ability of interactants to persuade or instruct others (Bailenson, Beall, Loomis, Blascovich, and Turk, 2004; Bailenson and Beall 2006). Another possibility that can be taken advantage of here is that every user perceives their own digital rendering of the world, and thus these renderings need not be the same (or congruent). For example, in a three-person interaction, one person could see the appearance of a second person in one way (i.e., tall), while to the third person, this second person appears small.

Much work is currently ongoing to explore these possibilities. For example, Bailenson (2006) has presented findings that show that if the face of someone with whom one is interacting is altered to appear more like one's own face, then this person will be regarded as more persuasive. Or, again, Pan (2009) has shown how immersive VEs can be used in psychotherapy to help address shyness and anxiety, such as when a man meets a life-like woman and interacts with her. This type of research opens many possibilities for learning about what kinds of appearances work in VEs, with potential repercussions for understanding how appearance influences interpersonal interaction in face-to-face situations in the real world. A powerful use of single-user VEs (although one reason for mentioning these is that they are at the borderline between single- and multi-user VEs) is to test self-perception theory in various conditions, such the "mirror experiments" carried out at the Virtual Human Interaction Lab. These experiments allow users to encounter themselves as they might appear with different body shapes, and how this affects their perception of themselves (Fox, Arena and Bailenson 2009).

Research on Large Group Interaction

Research on larger groups has been far less extensive than work on small groups. We have already encountered some findings about how people interact in VEs, but it will be useful to consider these in terms of what they offer social research. The early study by Becker and Mark (2002), for example, which was based on participant observation, compared three environments: visual plus text, visual plus voice, and text-only (which is not a VE on the definition used here).[6] In the visual environment (Active Worlds [AW]), people were represented as human-like avatars and used text to communicate; in the voice-based environment (OnLive Traveler [OT]), they were represented as talking heads; and in the text-only environment (LambdaMOO), they described themselves and the environment in words. Becker and Mark studied greeting and leaving behaviors, interpersonal distance, and other social conventions. These findings have been discussed in Chapters 5 and 6. What deserves highlighting here is that this is one of the few studies that made comparisons between different kinds of social environments. Furthermore, the findings based on participant observation by Becker and Mark can be compared with those of experimental studies, such as Blascovich (2002), who also examined interpersonal distance but with an immersive (HMD) system and found that people kept a greater distance with more life-like avatars.

Becker and Mark also discussed general social norms, but it is also possible to focus on a particular aspect of social organization: how do people engage in behavior such as religion or in creating the built environment online? One question here is bound to be, Do people behave similarly in online social institutions as in real-world ones? So, for example, can the conditions of a real-world religious service such as common emotions toward a sacred object be re-created in an online religious service? Schroeder, Heather, and Lee (1998) argued that they can, although the atmosphere is also more likely to be disturbed by inappropriate behaviors (flying around, insulting comments) that are impossible or unlikely in a real-world church. Or take the question of the built environment (see Chapter 3): Clearly it is possible to build extensively in a virtual world (VW) without the constraints of a shortage of space that apply to real-world settings. And yet, as virtual places have to be built up, it is still necessary to cluster them in such a way that people will be drawn to them and to central hubs or points of interest—lest they become virtual "ghost towns" (Schroeder, Huxor, and Smith 2001). As discussed in Chapter 5, these online VWs are "third places" (Steinkuehler and Williams 2006), spaces for socializing that are neither home nor work, so that social research in this case can focus on the types of interaction that occur in these "public" situations.

Boellstorff's strategy (2008: 5) to study VWs only in terms of within-world interaction because "the vast majority interact only in the virtual world" is appropriate for the purpose of analyzing in-world social dynamics. However, his "conceit" (2008: 61) of not taking the real-world context of VWs (in his case, SL) into account has a shortcoming: Surely we must take into account what kind of environment SL is in terms of its real-world context—that is, as a space or world for leisure activities or for socializing. One way to illustrate this shortcoming of his method is by reference to a specific argument he makes about the relation between online and offline (2008: 63): namely, that if people from different countries behave differently in VWs, then this difference will show up in SL. In other words, people's real-life social context will shape their SL behavior (although he also argues [2008: 64] that this does not exclude analyzing how the real-world impinges on interaction in VWs). Yet these two points are surely inconsistent, and the answer must be that neither is correct: Yes, it is always necessary to take the real-world context into account, yet if in-world dynamics have a life of their own, this dynamic will often be such that the difference between people from different countries will *not* show up in SL.[7] Hence, too, complete studies of interaction in MUVEs will also include data about offline users, even if these data are inferred by comparing online and offline populations (Williams, Yee, and Caplan 2008).

Still, much can be done by logging activities in online worlds. So, for example, the early study by Smith, Farnham, and Drucker (2002) used quantitative methods to capture avatar movements in an online VE and found, among other things, that the more frequently (and thus longer) avatars have used the environment, the fewer gestures they use (2002: 210–212). This finding could be an indication that gestures are not regarded as useful in a graphical environment or that the technology that is used to express gestures is not good enough. It is interesting to consider that this could be empirically tested, for example by giving gestures only to some avatars only or by giving enhanced gesture capabilities to some part of the population. Another finding in this study related, again, to interpersonal distance and found that avatars maintain interpersonal space in relation to those with whom they are interacting (2002: 213–214).

Quantitative data capturing user behavior were also used in the study by Penamurthy and Boerner (2006), who studied how people move around in a large social space—what points of interest they stop at, how often they talk to each other, and generally how they move around within the space in relation to each other and the features of the environment. This type of social research is much more difficult in the real physical world because it would require capturing many people in complex 3D spaces. (There are precedents for this type of social observation in studies about physical social spaces such as those pioneered by Whyte [1971], but these observations were extremely labor-intensive.) Note also that this type of research raises questions of research ethics: under what conditions should such a complete recording of peoples' movements and interactions be allowed (see Chapter 8)?[8] The equivalent situation would be the recording of all of a person's doings in a reality television show, without any scope for privacy. Still, the point of this type of research is that it can tell us about how people interact online, or it may be possible to simulate online what places of interest people are most prone to visit, in order to transfer this knowledge to a similar real-world environment.

Online social spaces open one avenue for social research; online games present another. Yee, for example, has used a variety of methodological approaches to explore the demographics, motivations, and social dynamics of players in online games. His online survey research showed that online games appeal to a broad age range—with an average age of 26 years and no correlation between age and weekly use (Yee 2006a). Yee's work on player motivations provides some explanations for why these online games are appealing to such a broad demographic. Using a factor-analytic approach based on a number of converging statistical analyses, Yee articulated a set of motivational components of online game-play (Yee 2007), showing that online games are appealing to a variety of players.

In other work, Yee explored the social dynamics of online games at the individual and organizational levels. For example, in a study using longitudinal data collected directly from an online game (Ducheneaut, Yee, Nickell, and Moore, 2006), Yee and colleagues used social network analysis to argue that online gamers may be far less social than previously assumed. Yee (2006b) has also shown, in terms of the broader social implications of these online worlds, that there is a blurring of work and play whereby people who play games are actually laboring for over a dozen hours per week within the game. Moreover, there is a distinct perseverance of physical nonverbal behaviors in online games such that nonverbal norms like eye gaze and personal space continue digitally even though there is no functional reason for them (Yee, Bailenson, Urbanek, Chang, and Merget 2007). In short, in online games, it is possible to examine the similarities and differences between online and offline behaviors and the relation between the two (offline motivations for engaging in online worlds and how behaviors in online worlds transfer to real-world settings).

A different way to think about these different types of research (apart from small groups versus large populations) is to distinguish between those situations when it is more effective to create a new social situation, such as a new graphical environment, and to see how different patterns of social interactions develop, compared with those situations when it is more useful to study "ready-made" interaction in an environment that has been ongoing for some time, to study "life online" or naturalistic interaction in VEs. Both have advantages and drawbacks: the former is labor-intensive in setting up the conditions, but it allows the researcher to "design" some of the parameters of the social environment (and, if the aim is observation, to be a part of the environment from the start). The latter requires less effort in starting up, but the study of the "given" features of the environment will require becoming familiar with patterns of social interaction that have a history, and thus require, strange as it may sound for VEs, historical research on the part of the researcher, or at least ethnographic immersion.[9] Whichever research strategy is adopted, VEs have certain advantages over the study of face-to-face social behavior in the physical world, whether these consist of experimental settings or ongoing life online.

VEs can thus be seen as laboratories in which there are many new possibilities for social research—although it is also important that research ethics and other considerations may impose limits on what can be done (see Chapter 8). There is also a more long-term perspective on these possibilities, which is that social sciences become more robust as they use research technologies that can record and manipulate different conditions (Collins 1994). For Collins, sciences advance rapidly when research instruments can build on previous results and move on to new territory. Previous examples in the social sciences include video- and audio-recording of social interaction and the computer-supported analysis of quantitative datasets. This may seem a distant prospect for VEs as much of the research that has been described can be seen as "blue sky." However, this research field will change as more and more social interaction takes place via multiple modalities in variety of online environments. And it should be remembered that new technologies often open up unforeseen new research directions.

Analysing Interaction in MUVEs

At this point it will be useful to give some concrete illustrations of the kinds of analyses that can be performed in MUVEs, focusing on small-group interaction. As we have seen, it is equally possible to analyze large groups or whole populations of avatars. But if we are interested in the details of encounters in small groups, MUVEs lend themselves to fine-grained analysis of this type of interaction, both for immersive and non-immersive desktop systems. A key question in regard to small groups is, what is the best method to do this? Given that every detail of the interaction can be completely captured, what forms of analysis should be used, particularly if, say, the goal is to improve how the systems support collaboration? (Both studies presented here, incidentally, were focused on collaboration; hence, the term CVEs [collaborative virtual environments] will sometimes be used, but the arguments could equally apply to social interaction per se, or MUVEs.) The main divide here is between quantitative and qualitative analyses, and both can be described here to highlight their respective strengths and weaknesses, especially in terms of generalizability and the lessons we can derive from them.[10]

The two methods are, first, one whereby quantitative data are captured, interaction is categorized into a number of activities, and statistical analysis is performed on frequencies and sequences of events. The second is based on the transcription of individual fragments of interaction (the trial on which this is based has been described briefly in Chapter 4), which are analyzed in terms of their key dynamics (Table 7.2).

Despite the fact that both methods allow researchers to see precisely what is going wrong—and what is going right—in these interactions, there are few studies that have so far carried out these kinds of in-depth analysis. The reason is partly that the technology is still not in widespread use, and these analyses have therefore mainly been for trial uses and users.

As we shall see, both types of analysis typically involve a large amount of effort, so it is useful to think about which level of effort is warranted and how it will be possible to generalize from a particular MUVE to other settings (or to find patterns of interaction in MUVEs that are common or exemplary). In what follows, the focus will be on method rather than on analyzing interaction or drawing out lessons for usability.

TABLE 7.2   Main features of the Strangers & Friends and COVEN trials.

	COVEN	Strangers & Friends
Length of sessions	2–4 hours weekly or fortnightly over 3–6 months and over 4 years	3+ hours in the course of one day
No. and type of participants	4–16 Novices and experienced users	6 pairs Novices and experienced users
System	High-end desktop computers, DIVE and dVS software	Two IPTs (five- sided and four-sided), DIVE software
Applications and tasks	Demonstration worlds, WhoDo game, London travel demonstrator	WhoDo game, Rubik's Cube, Poster puzzle, exploring Landscape, building together in a Modelling World
Method of study	Recording sessions, questionnaires, interviews	Recording sessions, questionnaires, interviews
Method of analysis presented here	Quantitative analysis of sequences	Analysis of interaction fragments

One point that is worth making is that the studies presented here were neither experimental studies (conditions were not controlled) nor field studies of in situ workplaces but rather hybrid trials with both experienced users and novices, and for longer periods of use, which approximate a realistic scenario for the use of the technology. Fraser calls this "the collection of 'naturalistic data' within 'experimental' situations [which] is employed to circumvent the lack of everyday use of CVEs" (2000: 5). In other words, they are quasi-experiments.

Method 1: Quantitative Analysis of Sequences

The quantitative analysis of sequences was developed by Tromp (2001) to address the need for a method to analyze small-group interaction VE experiments during the COVEN (COllaborative Virtual ENvironments) project, which had regular meetings between a small number of users on desktop systems (although the software has also been used for immersive systems). The first step in this method was to create categories for scoring the observed behaviors. The methodology is based on Bales' Interaction Process Analysis (1951) for the analysis of social interaction in small groups. The method provides instructions on how to develop protocols for a complete microscopic analysis of interaction, down to the smallest unit of observable behavior. With this method as a starting point, the next steps were to, first, observe a video recording of representative interactions, noting all identifiable single acts or behaviors. With Bales as a guide, this yielded twenty-six categories.

Then a focus group consisting of six social scientists from different disciplines tested these categories on another representative recording of an interaction session, and based on this test, the categories where further reduced to eight basic categories: communicate (C), external (E) (i.e., person relates to an event in the world outside the VE), gesture (G), manipulate (M), navigate (N), position (P), scan (S), and verify (V), and again tested with a focus group of six CVE developers. Next, these were broken down into subcategories that categorized differences within these categories, which yielded subcategories such as communicate about task at hand (C1), communicating about problems with the CVE (C2), and the like. This allowed the identification of some of the most common subcategories, and also which of these would require singling out for more detailed analysis.

Next, an analysis was performed on a small set of the data to see how best to combine the categories with each other—for example, communicate to verify (CV), position to scan (PS). All this meant that it could be determined which categories occurred frequently and which occurred much less frequently or not at all. For instance, pure "verification" acts (V) were not observed during analysis of the final dataset, although "communications to verify [that the CVE was working]" (CV) were observed frequently. These various categories will be different from those for other settings, but the same methodology can be followed.

At this point an example can be given: in Table 7.3, each row is the record for one observed act. The observer records the acts, the time the act starts and ends, who performs the act, to whom and for what act the response was made, and at whom the act was aimed. There are three types of actors: Actor A—the person whose act is being recorded; Actor B—the person at whom Actor A aimed this act (if anybody); and Actor C—the person whose act (that took place previous to the observed act

TABLE 7.3   The WhoDo Experiment 15:09:00–15:09:17.

Time 1: Start of Observed Act	Actor A: The Acting Person	Category: The Observed Act	Time 2: End of Observed Act	Actor B: Person to Whom the Act Was Aimed (0 = All)	Actor C: Person Who Triggered the Act	Time 3: The Time the Triggering Act Occurred
15:09:09	P2	C	15:09:10	0	.	.
15:09:11	P2	C	15:09:14	0	.	.
15:09:11	P3	S	15:09:12	0	.	.
15:09:13	P3	S	15:09:14	0	.	.
15:09:14	P2	C	15:09:16	.	.	.
15:09:14	P3	C	15:09:18	0	P2	15:09:09
15:09:15	P1	E	15:09:28	.	P3	15:09:14
15:09:16	P3	S	15:09:17	0	.	.
15:09:17	P3	S	15:09:18	0	P3	15:09:16

of Actor A) seemed to have triggered Actor A's act. In this example there are three participants—labeled P1, P2, and P3—in a sequence lasting seventeen seconds (in an environment that has been described in Chapter 4; see also Figure 4.8). Time 1 is when the observed act starts, Time 2 is when it finishes, and, if this act was triggered by a previous act, the time at which the triggering act started is recorded in column Time 3 (so that it is possible to exactly identify the triggering act).

In Table 7.3, participant 2 at 15:09:09 (Time 1) becomes the first person to act in this sequence and is therefore placed into the column Actor A. Participant 2 is addressing everyone ("everyone" = 0 in column Actor B) with a communication act C, which finishes at 15:09:10 (column Time 2), a communication act that therefore lasts one second. A number of other acts of various durations follow under Time 1 (another communication by P2, two scans by P3, another communication act by P2), until at 15:09:14, participant 3 communicates in reaction to (column Actor C) something participant 2 did at Time 3 (15:09:09). Participant 3's communication lasts until 15:09:18 or four seconds, and from this information it can be deduced that the time elapsed between meaningfully connected utterances of participant 2 and participant 3 is five seconds.

This method allows the observer to follow sequences of interaction in a microscopic manner, with the unit of analysis the smallest discernible segment of verbal or nonverbal behavior. Apart from analyzing the sequences in detail, this method also allows a breakdown of the types of acts that occur over a particular period. One example are data collected from four trials ("WhoDo," which we have encountered in Chapter 4, and a business game application of COVEN) with between three and nine simultaneous participants and lasting a total of thirty-two minutes and one second yielded a total of 705 individual acts. If these acts are added up, Tromp (2001) found, for example, that communication acts account for almost half (48.1%) of the total observed acts. Interestingly, if communication (C) is broken down into general communication (CC, 20.4%) and communication to verify the correct functioning of the VE and the equipment (CV, 27%)—with the remaining communication being to announce something external to the environment (CE 0.3%) or a communication with the external environment (EC 1.1%) making up the rest—it becomes obvious that obtaining feedback (CV) is something that occupies a lot of participants' time!

Another possibility is to compare different types of users (novices versus experts), different types of applications (WhoDo game versus business game), and different periods of the session (beginning, middle, and end). For the sequences mentioned and the 705 acts identified, and with several subcategories in addition to those just mentioned (the subcategory NP, which is to navigate into position in order to act upon an object, perceive acts of others, or move others' awareness, and subcategory SS, which is to scan the space [GG, gesture; MM, manipulate; and NN, navigation, are still the main categories]), we get the breakdown shown in Figure 7.1.

Figure 7.1 shows, for example, that novices communicate more than experts, although experts scan the environment more. Or, for example, participants communicate more at the end of the session and navigate less at the end of the session. And they communicate generally (CC) more in the WhoDo application than the business application, but they communicate more to verify (CV) in the business application than the WhoDo application.

Another possibility is look at patterns of how activities are conjoined. If we assume that acts occur randomly, cross-tabulation allows us to say

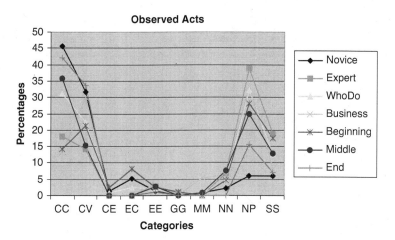

FIGURE 7.1   Frequencies of Observed Acts for various Categories.

how much more likely one activity is likely to follow another. For example, scanning is not often followed by other scans but is interleaved with other activities; many acts are preceded and followed by a scan, which shows that scanning is a very necessary part of way-finding (and could be a candidate for automating; that is, finding a way to make this scanning automatic). A further possibility is to look at how much time particular activities take. For example, it turns out that in this sample, navigation acts mostly take between one and two seconds (slightly longer for navigating backward), and communication acts seem to vary most in their duration.

A number of usability recommendations could be made on the basis of this kind of data—for example, regularly recurring tasks that could in the future be partly or fully automated, or there could be better mechanisms for providing feedback to others or navigating into position (some of these are discussed in Tromp 2001; Tromp, Steed, and Wilson 2003).

The advantages of this type of quantitative analysis of sequences are therefore that sequences can be identified closely and dissected in detail for different kinds of analysis: who engages with whom? For how long, with what frequency, and with what consequences for later interaction? In addition, conjunctions between activities can be identified, which allows for analysis of what users are trying to achieve. The disadvantages are threefold: one is that this type of analysis is very time-consuming (although commercial software for annotating video recordings of human behavior can make this simpler and faster). Another is generalizability— How valid will the analysis of these sessions be for analyzing other kinds of CVE sessions? And, finally, what are the limits of quantitative analysis: That is, the qualitative information about the user experience is lost through reducing the data to quantitative information (although this can be avoided to some certain extent by being very specific in providing the definitions for the categories). Finally, a point that applies to all methods is that the quantitative or other information still has to be "translated" into design guidance.

Method 2: Analysis of Interaction Fragments

This brings us to a second method. The main aim with this method (developed by Heldal 2004) is to identify fragments that support or disturb the flow of collaboration (some examples have already been discussed in Chapter 4). The analysis in this case was done for a trial with two networked immersive projection technology systems (IPTs), one in London and one in Gothenburg, and partly used the same software as in the trial described in the previous section and also used one of the same environments (the WhoDo murder mystery game application). The results are described in detail elsewhere (Steed, Spante, Heldal, Axelsson, and Schroeder 2003); here, the focus, again, is on the method of analyzing interaction.

The trial used video- and audio-recordings, as well as questionnaires, interviews, and observation. These recordings could be analyzed, and a method can now be described briefly for how interaction fragments can be transcribed to examine problems and successes among the participants. The following notations are used (see also Chapter 4):

LxGx The x'th couple ($x = 1 \ldots 6$), where one partner, Lx, is working in the IPT system in London and Gx is in the IPT system in Gothenburg.

LxGx Taskq yy:zz The x'th couple working in Task q has worked already for yy minutes and zz seconds with the tasks. For example,

L2G2 Puzzle 10:30 means that L2G2 has worked already for ten minutes and thirty seconds (approximately) with the Rubik's Cube–type puzzle.

Lx : blabla Lx saying "blabla"

Lx => Wait Lx interrupts Gx by saying "Wait," or says very quickly, "Wait"

A person navigating straight ahead is shown with an arrow and her or his face and the 3D glasses are shown in the direction of the small line (the 3D glasses) on the circle (their body). A person navigating backward is shown with the small line pointing away in the opposite direction to the arrow.

Now we can look at some examples. The first is from the WhoDo application, where one participant is trying to turn into a corridor (Figure 7.2).

This example shows how difficult it is to follow a path without colliding with walls.

Another navigation and orientation example can be given from the Poster World application, where participants had to put together certain words into a sentence from different posters on a wall. In Figure 7.3, the rectangular boxes on the top wall represent three posters:

In the Poster World application, instead of turning somewhat and navigating sideways (or stepping sideways like in an art gallery), almost all participants zigzagged back and forth.

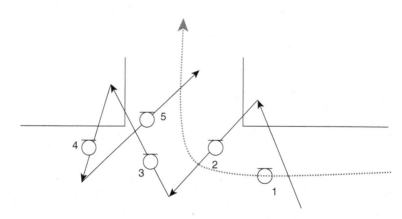

Figure 7.2   L1G1 Whodo 10:30.

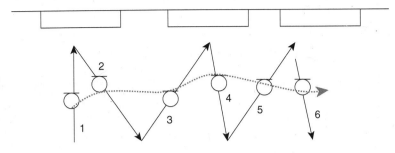

FIGURE 7.3   Zigzags in front of a wall.

What we can see in these examples is that participants have different kinds of problems navigating and orienting themselves in different settings. These problems can be identified by visual depictions of movements combined with transcribed conversations and can be supplemented by checking with interviews and questionnaire responses of the participants.

Another kind of example deals with how users cope with objects in the environment. The figure in Chapter 4 (Figure 4.8) shows the WhoDo application, where the task is to look for a hidden murder weapon. What we can see if we analyze images of this trial and this task is that, for example, the participant sometimes goes through objects as if they did not pose an obstacle (i.e. if he is standing in the middle of the table) and at other times treats them like a real object as when he kneels to look under the table. In other words, objects are sometimes treated like they do not have physical properties and at other times as if they do.

Among the advantages of analyzing recorded interaction fragments is that we can see where people's focus of attention is directed and how, for example, they cope with the environment and the objects in it (including each other's avatars). A second advantage is that fragments can be analyzed in great detail, including making sense of the whole scene and the dynamic within it. And finally, the recordings can be made available for reanalysis, which can reduce the errors of one researcher's transcription and interpretation of the data.

The disadvantages, as with the method described in the previous section, are that it is very demanding, and it is hard to generalize or to know whether these usability issues will transfer to other settings. Unlike the quantitative analysis of sequences, there is the further problem that the fragments may not be representative of overall patterns—but the flipside is that the researcher can readily observe what kind of significance the events have for the participants within the overall scene, even if this is of course the observer's own interpretation. A final comparison is that the quantitative analysis of sequences puts a great burden on the researcher in terms of "making sense" of how the interactions are transcribed (Table 7.2), even if on the plus side the data can then be aggregated and certain patterns can readily be discerned in these data. The method of analyzing interaction fragments, on the other hand, will often make "more sense" to researchers, but it will not be clear how representative the fragments are.

The Two Methods

The two methods are not mutually exclusive but could be combined in a complementary way. But it is possible to compare them from a broader perspective: Both methods share the problem of generalizability and transferability to other settings. The combination of the two methods, however, can overcome the problem of identifying common or exemplary forms of interaction: The aggregated data from the quantitative analysis of sequences can identify events and sequences that are common or frequent, and the analysis of interaction fragments can identify patterns that are typical or critical to the interaction. The combination of the two methods will therefore provide a robust—if very demanding—way to advance our understanding of interaction in MUVEs and thus provide a basis for improving usability. It can be added that the problem of generalizability and context-dependence also applies to face-to-face interaction, although sociologists of micro-interaction have also attempted to arrive at generalizations about micro-interactions in everyday settings (see Turner 2002).

At this point it can be noted again (a point made in Chapter 2) that interaction in MUVEs is not as complex and varied as it may first appear. In fact, once we reduce the activities and elements of interaction in current systems to the ones that are most common—interaction mostly on spatial tasks between avatars and with an audio link—then this type of interaction is not very complex in comparison with the immense variety of face-to-face interactions in the physical world. In other words, as discussed in Chapter 2, interaction in MUVEs consists of a comparatively narrow range of phenomena. This also has implications for usability design: Perhaps an exhaustive attempt to address usability may not be the best way forward, whereas concentrating on a few of the most common or typical problems *may be*—especially as in practice only a few usability redesign iterations can take place during the development cycle of a MUVE development project.

It can also be mentioned that in both these trials, users for the most part enjoyed and were impressed by their collaboration: Tromp et al. say for COVEN that "participants ... usually successfully performed their tasks" (2003: 257), although they also state that there was a considerable amount of frustration with not knowing other users' intentions. And Steed et al. (2003: 54) say for the Strangers and Friends trial that, apart from one pair that "got off on the wrong foot," most pairs did not report any problems with their collaboration, were successful in their tasks, and enjoyed the experience.

Finally, it is worth noting that the links between various processes of interaction and the successes and failures in these processes are something that *outside observers* can (often, but not always, easily; see Bowman, Gabbard, and Hix 2002) become aware of through analysis. In these same processes, however, the *participants* are not necessarily aware of the successes or failures in their interactions—as has been seen in the examples when the participants successfully cope with the various "unnatural" aspects of this setting, and when they fail to overcome problems that they could easily avoid if they made themselves more aware of their situation in this setting.

What the analysis in these trials typically shows is that the *nontechnical* aspects of how users interact with each other are more important than technical ones (Heldal 2004). Thus the problem with both methods, the difficulty of generalizing to other settings, may also be less important than identifying common and typical patterns of interaction between users, which is a strength of both methods. How to combine them will thus be an important starting point for analyzing interaction, for usability, and for social science analysis.

NOTES

1. This essay draws on an overview of the topic co-authored with Jeremy Bailenson (Schroeder and Bailenson 2008). See now also the overview by Fox, Arena, and Bailenson (2009).

2. The line between capturing behavior and observing it may, of course, not run between quantitative and qualitative studies; both could be either.

3. A point that can be made here in passing is that for both videoconferencing and MUVE research, the appearance of the user can be altered or "blurred" so as to anonymize the interaction. It is also possible to alter voice communication so that it is not possible to recognize the user, again, allowing for anonymity. This anonymization brings advantages from the point of view of research ethics, although there may be a tradeoff if these forms of anonymization make the analysis of the interaction less realistic and so less valuable. Interactions in *text-based* VEs are least problematic from this point of view because the names of people who make the text utterances can be given pseudonyms. Some would argue, however, that even these text-based encounters are not unproblematic: Even if they take place in publicly accessible spaces, they should not be recorded or revealed for research purposes as they may reveal the identities of those who made the utterances and/or disturb the confidentiality of the setting. Finally, in MUVEs, the possibilities for surveillance and capturing data about people are much more powerful than with other technologies and media, which calls for research guidelines that address these capabilities (see Chapter 9 for these issues and Eynon, Fry, and Schroeder 2008).

4. This setting, with only one real person inside the environment, again falls outside our definition of a *multi*-user VE, although it clearly has implications for MUVEs with two or more people.

5. The measures used were questionnaires with questions such as, "Who did you think contributed most to this task?" using Likert-type scales, and this was corroborated by means of observation. One of the reasons for the person with the HMD being regarded as the leader is that this person was able to move around—navigate—in the VE more easily and so could also do the task and communicate it more often.

6. It is interesting to note that one of the earliest studies of text-only environments, Turkle's *Life on the Screen* (1995), which could also be relevant for MUVEs in the sense used here, claimed that people would play with multiple representations of themselves in LambdaMOO. This was disproved in a study by Schiano and White (1998), who showed that people tended to maintain stable identities, and more so, the longer time they spend online.

7. Boellstorff (2008: 61) argues that is not necessary to seek out individual real-world users. Yet the question of whether to do research that connects avatars with the people they represent is separate from the question of whether the real-world context of VWs should be acknowledged in research. Both will provide a

more accurate understanding of VWs and should be pursued where possible, although seeking out individual users offline entails methodological issues and issues of research ethics. See on this point also Nardi (2010).

8. Another interesting possibility for carrying out social research in VWs is to use "bots" (programmed agent avatars). This is a technique that was used by Friedman, Steed, and Slater (2007), who programmed a bot to engage in encounters in Second Life to investigate, among other things, interpersonal distance. One advantage of this method is that it is not necessary for the researcher to engage in time-intensive field research—the bot runs around to do this—and another is that the responses of avatars to the bot can be captured (or "logged") automatically. A number of studies, as we have seen, have used agents in experiments in immersive VEs (Blascovich 2002; Slater et al. 2006) and small groups, where the advantage is that the experiment can be designed such that the agent always responds in the same way. In online VWs, the main additional advantage is that this kind of research can be scaled up to examine large populations. A potential limitation of this type of research is that even if it receives research ethics approval, it runs the risk of being annoying to online populations (imagine the real-world equivalent of robots pretending to be humans carrying out large-scale social science surveys or marketing research in public places).

9. Harris, Bailenson, Nielsen, and Yee (2009) took another approach: They examined SL by sending a group of students into SL, collecting data from their avatars, and asking them fill in online questionnaires on a regular basis over a six-week period. In this way, they could monitor the expanding networks of friends they made and the way they explore the various regions of the world (and found that they do this less over time). They were also able to code the activities their student participants recorded, finding a balance between learning activities (such as building classes) and recreational activities (parties). These kinds of studies, combining quantitative and qualitative data about avatars, will be a useful complement to ethnographic or participant observation studies (such as Boellstorff 2008).

10. The following is based on Schroeder, Tromp, and Heldal (2006), and more details of the studies can be found in Tromp, Steed, and Wilson (2003), Steed, Spante, Heldal, Axelsson, and Schroeder (2003), and Heldal (2004).

8

Ethical and Social Issues in Multiuser Virtual Environments

Research Ethics

As we have seen in the previous chapter, multiuser virtual environments (MUVEs) present many new opportunities for social science researchers, but they also present new dilemmas.[1] In this chapter, we can focus on three areas where researchers commonly confront ethical issues: experiments in interpersonal behavior, large-scale data capture, and participant observation.

Experimental Research

A number of researchers have begun to undertake experiments with VEs because they provide conditions that are otherwise not possible or are difficult in face-to-face environments. So, for example, it can be tested what happens when people interact with someone whose appearance has been changed. Or people can be made to interact in ways that can be measured more accurately. One experiment, for example, sought to find out to what extent people maintain interpersonal distance under different conditions depending on the appearance of another person's avatar (Blascovich 2002). And another set of trials examined people with a fear of public speaking and how they coped with an audience in an immersive VE (Slater and Steed 2002).

Many more scenarios can be envisaged. Multiuser environments provide an endless array of new possibilities for this type of social research. The question is, What are the limits to this type of research? There are, of course, a number of limits to the usefulness of the research, such as whether the results from experimentation in virtual settings can be transferred to face-to-face behaviors.[2] The key question that concerns us here, however, concerns whether there are any limits imposed by research ethics on this type of research. For example, should research participants be put into "dangerous" situations in VEs? Or, in view of the fact that avatars may not entirely resemble the research participants, where should the line be drawn in terms of how closely the avatars need to resemble the participants whom they represent in terms of ensuring anonymity (in cases where, in similar video-recorded experiments, people's faces, for example, would need to be blurred to ensure anonymity)?

One experiment that illustrates these limits is the virtual Milgram experiment. This experiment is particularly useful because it focuses on a central issue—namely, the ethics of interactions between people and avatars. The original, non-virtual experiment was intended to reproduce the famous experiments carried out in the 1960s by the psychologist Stanley Milgram to test the extent to which people obey authority—in this case, the authority of the experimenter. The experiment involved research participants being told to administer ever higher doses of electrical shocks to a person at the behest of the experimenter in response to whether the person correctly answered certain questions. As the shocks become more severe when the person gets the answers wrong, the person to whom the shocks are administered begins to scream with pain. Unknown to the research participant, the person to whom the shocks were administered was an actor. Nevertheless, Milgram found that people obey to an extent that sheds a troubling light on human obedience to authority. For a number of reasons, including the distress caused to research participants, these experiments were deemed to contravene research ethics and could no longer be carried out in their original form.[3]

This experiment was replicated by Slater and colleagues (2006) and a number of steps were taken to address the ethical concerns identified in the original study. But the main innovation was that the experiment was carried out in an immersive CAVE-type VE and the "actor" on whom the shock was administered was a life-size and realistic avatar. Slater et al.'s results were similar to those of Milgram in terms of the stress levels of participants, although there was "lesser intensity" of the responses, an important replication because doing this experiment with "real" recipients of pain, as mentioned, is no longer acceptable (2006: e39). Participants felt increasingly uncomfortable about the experiment and responded to the virtual character as if it were highly real. In fact, some participants stopped administering the "painful shocks" and approximately half the participants said afterward that they had wanted to stop the experiment.

The key difference in terms of causing distress to research participants is that they would have been aware, on a conscious level, that they were only administering shocks to an avatar, so that no actual physical harm could be done to the avatar (and they had been told by the experimenters that they were interacting with an avatar). However, the whole point of immersive environments is that one is supposed to experience the situation as if one is interacting with a real person. So that while research participants may be able to bring to mind that they are interacting with a graphical avatar to whom no physical harm is being done, they are experiencing the situation as if they are inflicting physical pain on a real person.

How realistic avatars need to be for people to perceive that they are interacting with a real person is a long-standing question within the VEs research community (as we saw in Chapter 3). Research on this question is likely to continue in various directions. In any event, however realistic the avatar or the level of immersiveness of the VE, if participants experience the avatar as if they are encountering another person, two pieces of ethical guidance can be suggested: one is that certain experiments should be allowed that could not be allowed in the equivalent face-to-face setting. One example is experimenting with the "bystander effect" (whereby people are less likely to intervene in an emergency when there are others than when they are alone) in which, for example, the reactions to a crime could be taken much further than in a face-to-face experimental enactment (in relation to witnessing a crime perpetrated on a virtual victim with virtual others, for example).[4] Slater and Steed also carried out experiments on the fear of public speaking in front of a virtual audience (2002: 164–168). This, again, is a good illustration of beneficial research because although it may cause some participants considerable anxiety during the experiment, it may also help them to overcome or alleviate this anxiety in real-world circumstances.

Second, however, there will be limits to what kind of experimentation can be done with avatar encounters; for example, participants should not be able to abuse each other's avatars. This should apply even if research participants will know, on a conscious level, that the avatar cannot experience pain. Or again, it is clearly unacceptable to conduct an experiment that is aimed at seeing how far a research participant is willing to go in killing a virtual human. Put the other way around, people should not be put in position whereby they treat virtual others as beyond ethical boundaries, even when the research participant will be aware that an avatar is not the same as a physical person. (Interestingly, this would also apply to the avatar as an artificial agent, if the research participant could not tell that whether the avatar represented a real person or was merely an agent.) Slater et al.'s "virtual Milgram" thus points to some limits of this type of research: Some extreme social situations should be studied because the distress to participants is not great and the value of the experiment *is*. Some extreme social situations should not be studied because the distress to participants is too great and is not justified by the benefits of the study. So even if virtual humans are not real, this does not mean that interacting with them cannot cause undue distress to the real participants interacting with them—even if they know that this cannot be the case. The "virtual Milgram" pushed this boundary: arguably, the benefits of new insights in this case outweighed the costs of the distress to participants, but this argument (as in other similar cases) has strict limits.

Put briefly: just because it is virtual does not mean that any type of research can be done with human participants, and even if the virtual humans are not real, that does not mean that "anything goes." VEs are useful because certain experiments can be done that cannot be done in the physical world and with people interacting face-to-face. Others cannot be done because they will, for example, be too realistic. Where to draw the line will be an ongoing debate in the years to come.

Data Capture of Large-Scale Online Populations

Research on large-scale populations of avatars also holds great promise for studying how people interact online. The difference between the virtual and the physical is that in online worlds, whole scenes or even worlds can be recorded and later reproduced for research purposes. In the physical world, too, of course, people can be covertly recorded (as with closed circuit television cameras), but in online worlds, the possibilities of recording, reproducing, and analyzing interactions, especially covertly, are more powerful. In quantitative anonymized studies of online environments for gaming, collaborating, and socializing, just as in the offline world, population data for the most part do not raise ethical concerns. An important difference, however, is that in an online virtual world, *all* interactions between the avatars can be captured.

This consideration can be related to a wider question: in online worlds, even if one's behavior is public and can be observed and captured, is it nevertheless always allowable for researchers to use data from these worlds? Take the equivalent real-world scenario: there are still ongoing debates about the extent to which the state or private firms should be able to engage in video (e.g., closed circuit television) surveillance, especially without those who are under surveillance and recorded being made aware of this. In VEs, however, people could be made to feel as if they are constantly under surveillance! In other words, this type of research may be the equivalent of being constantly under surveillance, as in George Orwell's novel *1984* or in "reality" television programs where participants are permanently under the gaze of the camera. This raises novel ethical issues because people using the environments do not necessarily expect to have all their behavior recorded.

At the same time, online worlds, unlike physical encounters, have novel possibilities for presenting research findings in anonymous ways. It is possible, for example, to blur the names of avatars that are next to their text bubbles (see, for an example, Brown and Bell 2006: 229). Or again, it is possible to record and reproduce the gestures of an avatar and yet anonymize their identity by changing parts of their appearance with which they could be identified. The range of choices that researchers have thus also differ from those in the physical world.

Research in online worlds has a further problematic aspect: the data collected, even if it is anomymized, might nevertheless be traced back to a person because the data are so complete. Say, for example, that one wants to analyze conversations in Second Life, which, like other online worlds, has text conversations. Now we can imagine that part of a text conversation has been logged and is presented in a publication in the following anonymized form:

Y says: Hello!
X says: Hello there, Y, I would like to be friends with you.

Now even if the names in this text excerpt have been anonymized, it may nevertheless be that the person who said, "I would like to be friends with you," once the text has been published, can be traced back to X and X's name and behavior are revealed on the basis of linking this text snippet back to the context in which it occurred (if the text has been recorded, say, by logs that were undertaken, not by the researcher, but by the online worlds system, and a search is done by means of text- or data-mining). This situation is akin to being able to track searches back to those who initiated them or tracing text in the Enron corpus (a large corpus of e-mail text that was made available in the wake of a scandal involving the firm Enron) back to those who sent the e-mails (Eynon, Fry, and Schroeder 2008).

Another case where not individuals but whole populations *could* have a sense that their privacy and anonymity were compromised can be illustrated with Williams, Yee, and Caplans's (2008) study of 7000 players of the online game EverQuest2. This is based on access to data from the company Sony, the owners of the game. Insofar as the data are anonymized and the study asks innocuous questions, it avoids ethical dilemmas. What if, however, the research went beyond the analysis of large-scale networks, to enquire, for example, into which groups behaved in the most unpleasant way? In this case, even though no individual player is identified, disclosing details of identifiable groups that certain players are part of and frequent could be seen as an intrusion into the privacy of their environment.

It is thus not so much that the boundary between online and offline should be abandoned, as some have argued (Taylor 2006: 153). Rather, here, as in relation to the other issues discussed in this section, researchers will need to weigh the same ethical considerations as they always do in dealing with human research participants and to adapt these to the novel technological possibilities and constraints of online virtual worlds. They will continue to face the choice alluded to earlier, between Kantian duty-based or "deontological" ethics with their absolute respect for the individual's aims and the calculation of consequentialist or utilitarian ethics, which weigh the balance of harms and benefits. In the case of online worlds, can researchers violate the privacy of people's online behavior? Do the benefits of disseminating research results about online populations outweigh the harms of disclosure? Should researchers seek consent from those they observe and report on? In this respect, there are issues that overlap with those that arise in participant observation, to which we can now turn.

Participant Observation

Participant observation in online worlds, which might be used as part of an ethnographic methodology, has a number of advantages over using this method in the offline world, including ease of access and the possibility for unobtrusive observation ("lurking"). One question faced by participant observers in online worlds is thus about how they should inform those whom they are observing about their research activity. One way to do this is for researchers to identify themselves as such, for example via their "profile" in Second Life, which is attached to their avatar and which can have a link to a web page with information about the type of research they are doing. This solution has been adopted by many researchers.

Thus there is a balance to be struck between revealing that you are a researcher and engaging in unobtrusive observation. Clearly, it will often be good practice—beyond legal or institutional requirements—to identify yourself as a researcher in the case of ethnographic or participant observation in a VE. Yet there may be a tradeoff in this case between the advantages of covert observation that does not disturb the environment and revealing one's identity as a researcher, which ensures transparency but may also lead to changed behavior on the part of the participants.[5] Anecdotally, there have been a number of cases when many researchers descended on an online environment and there was resentment against their presence. The well-established rule in anthropology to leave the field so that future researchers are not disadvantaged must be an important consideration.

As discussed earlier (especially Chapter 5), online settings are perhaps most often akin to "third places" (public parks, coffee shops, street corners, and the like), places that are neither public nor private but "in between," as in Oldenburg's (1989) work. Against this background, online social spaces clearly exemplify an imperative to be sensitive to the values and aims of people in different online settings (Eynon et al., 2008). This sensitivity to context will involve treating different virtual worlds in different ways—for example, whether they are small private encounters or the movements of large-scale populations. Or again, there may be occasions or whole worlds in which people interacting online are behaving in a public way, as in a public meeting or in a virtual world that is open to all for, say, commercial or educational purposes. It may also be, however, that certain spaces within a virtual world such as an online church, although formally public, include interactions that should be treated as private, such as when personal details are revealed (see, for examples, Schroeder, Heather, and Lee 1998), or if a whole online world is expressly designed to provide a private forum for interaction among a group that would be difficult in an offline setting (or in another virtual setting).

Research ethics then requires treating online interactions in virtual worlds with the same sensitivity that other—offline—social settings are treated. For participant observation or fieldwork, there have been extensive debates in anthropology about the role of the observer—and these will provide some guidance. And in special cases, it may also be that online virtual worlds need to be treated as sensitive fieldwork—for example, where vulnerable groups such as children are involved (Lee 1993).

These points can be taken further (if we recall the discussion in the previous section about data capture): As we have seen, one view that might be taken in relation both to participant observation and to data capture is simply that all online behavior is public. Thus, one could say that users of online worlds should be aware that their behavior can constantly be watched and captured and put on display in, say, a research presentation. The opposite argument could equally be made, however, that avatars should not feel that they are constantly under surveillance or subject to being research "guinea pigs." Somewhere in between these two extremes lies a standpoint that researchers and users of online worlds will both be comfortable with: on the one hand, that researchers should not assume that everything in online worlds is fair game for research and that they treat the environment as if it deserved similar considerations of privacy and anonymity as in an offline social space. This will allow those who use online worlds to experience them as having a modicum of privacy, not just regarding their personal details and doings but also in terms of the environment as a whole not being a zone for a research-intensive free-for-all. This middle ground will enable participant researchers to carry out fieldwork as long as they do not assume that all online behavior is public and that people who interact as avatars will have their interactions with others openly broadcast to the wider world. This stance requires sensitivity to context on the part of the researcher and applies to the fieldwork of participant observers as well as to data capture about populations.

The wider context is that even if the online world is formally a public space, researchers will nevertheless want to maintain the trust of those whose online behavior they are studying. This includes not disregarding the sense of privacy that, for example, people's avatar representations may have in the settings of particular online worlds—even if this may involve guessing what may be intentions and values of the person "behind" the avatar.

This brings us to a final issue, which is that those who research online virtual worlds may want to contact people offline, to find out, for example, how their online avatar persona relates to their offline persona. One question that arises, therefore, is, Under what circumstances can—and should—the researcher contact the subject outside the virtual setting? In this case it is useful to ask why such a move from studying the subject online to offline is deemed to be necessary. There can be three main reasons for this: One reason is to validate the information that has been obtained online, the second is to embed the subject's online behavior in the context of their real-world social setting, and the third to obtain more in-depth knowledge of the subject, such as their motivations or the significance they attach to certain events. As to the first of these, the question can then be raised of why face-to-face questioning might provide more valid answers (as Walther [2002] points out). In the second case, it may be awkward to engage with people offline if one has only dealt with them online (for example, Taylor 2006: 1–19). This also applies to the third case, although it may be, for example, that the subject can be contacted not offline but by other means such as the telephone or e-mail. One dilemma in all these cases is similar to contacting people offline who have previously been encountered or contacted by other means: What kind of burden may be imposed on the research subject?[6]

Ethical and Social Issues in MUVEs

Effects of Shared Virtual Environments on Real Behavior

Apart from research ethics, what kind of ethical and social questions do MUVEs raise? One question that has been raised particularly about leisure uses concerns the longer-term effects of MUVEs: Do violent online multiplayer MUVEs, for example, cause violent offline behavior among users? Perhaps MUVEs are more compelling because they are more interactive than other online games or spaces, so that more time is spent in them. Yet apart from interactivity, online VEs are not very different from other forms of online leisure, and it is therefore unlikely that better progress will be made about this question in relation to MUVEs than has been made in relation to video or computer games— or, for that matter, television. It will be easier to measure specific effects of MUVEs—Do they enhance sensorimotor skills or the ability to find one's way in a real environment after finding one's way in a virtual model of that environment?—than to provide answers to complex issues with many variables, such as the effect of media on violence. If we consider the leisure uses of MUVEs more broadly, and although MUVEs may be more "realistic" than other leisure media, the question of their effects is perhaps best seen in the context of the use of new interactive entertainment generally (especially bearing in mind that the game *content* that specifies the users' roles and activities is not specifically related to VEs).

Somewhat different considerations apply to training, such as for the military, where the aim is to prepare for the battlefield. A recent example is America's Army (Zyda, Mayberry, Wardynski, Shilling, and Davis 2003), a massively multiplayer battlefield simulation for U.S. Army recruitment and training. Here an important question will be, Does prolonged training in this MUVE potentially desensitize users when they confront real battlefield situations? Or is it possible that it will make users *more* sensitive to the difficult situations they may encounter? In this case, there is a direct coupling between the purpose of the MUVEs (training) and their effect (the ability to confront challenging life-or-death situations)— unlike for the gaming/socializing uses of MUVEs—so there should be an obligation on the part of those who develop and promote the use of these systems to investigate and identify their likely effects. The same applies to the use of MUVEs for other training, therapy, and instrumental purposes: There should be reliable knowledge about the effectiveness and impact of the transfer from the VE to real-life settings because this, after all, is the specific purpose of these systems. It can be added on this point that the training and other instrumental purposes may not be for transfer to real-life settings but for carrying out tasks or other purposes within VEs themselves. In this case, the same considerations nevertheless apply: If the purpose of the system is for critical training and the like within MUVEs, then reliable information about effectiveness will be essential.

Different Capabilities in MUVEs

The technological system has a direct bearing on the ethical and social issues because the type of system, including the context of its use, shapes the interaction between users. Axelsson (2002) has argued, for example, that in a MUVE with mainly text communication, the type of system affects communication, with disadvantages for those with inferior network connections or with lesser technical abilities. Another example is how the type of system—desktop or immersive—affects collaboration on tasks. Slater, Sadagic, Usoh, and Schroeder (2000), as we saw in Chapter 4, have shown that in a three-person task where users do not know what type of system their collaborators are using, they will tend to ascribe leadership to the person using the more immersive system. In this case, the evidence is compelling that this leadership ascription is due to the differences in the systems rather than other factors because we have comparisons with doing the same task in a real face-to-face situation, where users do not single out any particular person as the leader. It can also be pointed out that users may become aware of their different capabilities only over the course of time. Roberts, Wolff, Otto, and Steed (2003) have shown for a collaborative task—building a gazebo, with several users using different systems—that desktop and immersive users have different possibilities and constraints. But whereas initially desktop users were not aware that they were using a different system from their collaborators who were using an immersive projection technology (IPT)–type system, they gradually became more aware of the difference depending on their stage of the task.

One reply to these imbalances or inequalities caused by the systems is that there are technological solutions for this, for example, by attaching to avatars information about what kind of capabilities they have. Axelsson (2002) suggests, for example, that the various "powers" of avatars and their systems should be made transparent to users (this could be done, by attaching labels—like name tags—to avatars). But we can note here, first, that it is not clear how feasible this is. To appreciate this point, we can imagine the complexity of a situation in which users have access to all the information about all the capabilities and constraints of all other users or avatars (and, of course, these can change dynamically). In this case, it is difficult to envisage how users could keep track of all this information about, to name only a few things, bandwidth, fidelity of input/output devices, the avatar's ability to manipulate objects and to navigate, the changeability of their appearance, the "physics" of their avatar (Is it possible to walk through them or not?), and many more. In other words, this transparency may be useful, but it may also be difficult to implement and cope with. Second, even if complete transparency in this regard is feasible, how desirable is it? We can think here of visible status markers in the real world, such as ethnicity or gender: Should similar differences in avatars or in technological systems be highlighted— or downplayed—to facilitate an "even-handed" and fluid interaction among users? Surely this will depend on the context in which the MUVE is used.

The implication is that there should be, at the very least, an awareness among users, and especially among developers of MUVE systems, of the "inequality" that is created with different systems and an ongoing dialogue about the possibilities and appropriateness of overcoming this inequality, even though it may be difficult or undesirable to eliminate it. It can be stressed that this issue is different for MUVEs than for other technologies: it will be obvious in the case of other technologies that people who use different technologies will have different capabilities (the quality of their television sets or the power of their cars). In the case of MUVEs, however, the issue is more urgent because MUVE technology is still fluid, and users are not aware of the differences because they may not be apparent.

This issue can be put into the wider context of computer-mediated communication and the much-discussed "digital divide" in Internet access and use (see DiMaggio, Hargittai, Neuman, and Robinson 2001). This could be said to concern not only the gap between those with and without Internet access (the information "have's" and "have-not's") but, in the case of MUVEs, it could also relate to the type of bandwidth or devices to which users have access.

Appearance and Identity

Appearance or embodiment in MUVEs is about how users appear to each other (and to themselves) and what capabilities their avatars have (manipulation, navigation, and the like). Identity is about the relation between the avatar and the real person whom the avatar represents (all this is discussed earlier, especially in Chapter 2). Sometimes the issue of agents is raised in the context of encounters between avatars, but this is actually a separate issue to do with the life-likeness of intelligent agents powered by artificial intelligence—although this may overlap with questions of identity if the user cannot tell the avatars of agents apart from the avatars of real users.

Howsoever the question of optimal avatar appearance for interaction and communication in particular MUVEs becomes resolved technically, the fidelity and capabilities of different avatar embodiments will—like the type of system—influence how people treat each other in MUVEs. Avatar appearance and capabilities are highly related to the various contexts that have been described. Compare two cases: one, a task in a highly immersive MUVE such as an IPT where two users are collaborating on a spatial task, and the other, a desktop MUVE where users have cartoon-like figures and the purpose is to socialize. In the former, avatar appearance may be of negligible importance because the users are almost exclusively focused on the objects and the task, whereas in the latter the users may be searching for clues about the other users' identity in their avatar appearance because the features of the avatar, even if they are very basic, may be an important part of how the users choose to express their identity (Taylor 2002). It is different for the *capabilities* of the avatar embodiment—how they can manipulate objects and how their bodies are tracked—which may be highly important to the object-focused task and of minor importance for the purpose of socializing. The point here (as argued in Chapter 3) is that we cannot assume that greater "accuracy" of avatar representation or greater capabilities of the avatar body will be appropriate in all cases, and hence that they necessarily go hand-in-hand with particular ethical and social norms and conventions.

As for identity, the issue that has received most discussion is identity play or deception, a topic that has been extensively studied for online communication in general (Baym 2002). It has been shown, however, that the longer the users spend in MUVEs, the more likely they are to maintain a single consistent identity (see Schiano 2002 for a text-based environment; see Schroeder and Axelsson 2001 for a graphical MUVE; also see Chapter 5). Further, the point that is often overlooked in speculations about multiple identities or deception with identities is that it is simply hard to appear in different guises to people over the course of time. Indeed, with the regular uses of MUVEs, it may become more important to find mechanisms to ensure that users can identify each other easily in encounters across different systems and sessions (such as contact lists) and to find consistent and easy-to-use means of doing this.

There are also many preconceptions in connection to identity about interpersonal relationships in MUVEs. One is that MUVEs do not allow users to establish "real" interpersonal relationships with other users. However, the findings from the studies of both short-term (Blascovich 2002; Slater and Steed 2002) and long-term (Hudson-Smith 2002; Jakobsson 2002) dynamics among users point to the fact that users treat these interpersonal encounters as having the same depth as face-to-face relationships and they develop strong attachments to other users even where they have not met in real life. This point is directly relevant to the ethical and social aspects of MUVEs: MUVEs aim at "being there together" with other users, and an ethical and social guideline that follows is that the relationships in the VE ought to be treated on a par with face-to-face relationships insofar as they succeed in this aim.

There is, finally, a continuum of how online relationships map onto face-to-face or real-life relationships: some users will know each other only through MUVEs, and others will be familiar with each other in real life. How online and offline relationships relate to each other will be critical for the users' relationships, and here it is possible to speculate that different norms will emerge in relation to the two situations (or the many in-between cases). Further, in the light of what was said earlier about not downplaying the significance of purely online relationships and about how norms in new technology emerge slowly, it is not clear what rules should and will govern these various relationships.

Shaping the Environment, Ownership, and Persistence

For regular uses of MUVEs for leisure purposes, several important inter-related issues are the extent to which users can shape the environment, the persistence and ownership of the environment, and the compatibility of the environment with other environments.[7] A number of studies have shown that users who spend a long time in MUVEs take great interest in being able to modify it to suit their own needs (Schroeder and Axelsson 2001; Schroeder, Smith and Huxor 2001). At the same time, MUVEs are volatile places insofar as they can be destroyed by a single mouse-click. Further, even if developers or users were assigned the rights to the objects (including their avatar representations) that they created, there would still be the question of how these would be maintained over the longer term and also how compatible they are with other VEs—either subsequent versions of the same VE or other VEs that are part of another system. For example, if a system like Second Life or Active Worlds produces a new version of its software or if some developers or users break away from the existing virtual world and create a separate new one with the same system, and if users want to take their creations (or indeed their avatars, or the milieu and the relationships they are familiar with) and migrate into the new environment—what constraints and possibilities do they face?

These issues, even if they seem remote and of minor importance today because they arise in the context of leisure, will take on increasing importance as users identify with the MUVEs they use and as these MUVEs become used for purposes that are ever more important to users. Further, they *do* also arise in relation to short experimental or pro-totype uses: We can think here, for example, of a scenario in which two users collaborate to manipulate objects together—if one user has grasped an object, should the other be allowed to take it from him or her or not? If a MUVE is used for collaborating on a task, how persistent does it need to be for collaboration to continue successfully? In this context, finally, it is worth mentioning again the possibilities of surveillance in MUVEs, which pose issues not just in research ethics but also in terms of the privacy of users in leisure and other uses of MUVEs—although here we enter the domain of legal questions that are, to a large extent, so far untested (unlike those of virtual property). In the end, from an ethical and social point of view, these and other questions may add up to how inhabitable—or how enjoyable and engaging and useful—MUVEs are.

Summary

For instrumental uses where the effectiveness of MUVEs is critical to the application, it is necessary to have an accurate assessment of the effectiveness of the MUVE sessions. For leisure uses, there are various ethical and social issues about the nature of MUVEs that need to be taken into consideration, but the key here is to enable a rich and rewarding experience for individual users and for the community of users. MUVEs must also be put into the context of other new technologies and media because much can be learned from these other tools, and they also provide a larger context into which MUVEs fit among other visualization, communication, and related technologies. But it is also useful to think about this the other way around: MUVEs are potentially the furthest possible extension of tools that allow the user to share a computer-generated space with other users *and* to interact with the space, and so they enable us to think about the future of other technologies, and how they will merge with and complement MUVEs.

There are, of course, many other issues relating to MUVEs, and the issues touched on here could be discussed in much greater detail.[8] One guideline that emerges from this overview that should govern the development of MUVEs is that MUVEs should broaden—rather than narrowing—the possibilities that users have with these new tools. Following on from this, it is worth reiterating that the key to usability and the inhabitability of MUVEs may not so much be "realism" but the degree to which the user can shape and make flexible use of the environment. And, as mentioned earlier, the issues for instrumental and leisure uses that have been treated separately (following the discussion in Chapter 2) may in the future become more intertwined. So, for leisure uses, usability and effectiveness issues will move into the foreground, just as for instrumental uses the issue of inhabitability and modalities of interpersonal relations will become increasingly important. While the two sides currently fall into two separate clusters, they are likely to converge with more widespread and routine uses of a variety of systems.

Finally, we can therefore ask, not only what do MUVEs do now, but what will they look like in the future? Here we need to recall that many of the early predictions about the shape and uses of new technologies—say, the computer or the mobile telephone—were spectacularly wrong, especially in forecasting the speed, extent of diffusion, and realm of application. Thus we cannot rule out scenarios of very life-like (even if not very "realistic") worlds being used regularly for a wide range of purposes. More likely in the medium term, and perhaps more important, is that people will spend increasing amounts of time with a variety of systems that provide the experiences of mainly visual and auditory environments (as argued in Chapter 2). And it can be safely predicted that the technology will continue to improve, mainly in better displays and network connections, even if we cannot foresee their ultimate shape or uses.

If we look beyond current systems then (this will be done extensively in the next two chapters—here the point is to concentrate on ethical and social issues), on one side, PC-based graphics and audio communication over networks are becoming more powerful, and on the other, expensive IPT systems are being complemented by inexpensive projection displays (Jacobsen 2003) of various shapes, sizes, and degrees of immersiveness. Yet it should be remembered that although MUVEs offer many possibilities—virtual objects can easily be manipulated by users for instrumental tasks in VEs, for example, or additional space can easily be created if a heavily populated VE becomes too crowded—there are nevertheless ultimately some inherent limits for the devices, the features of the environment, and the ability of sensory apparatus to handle them.

We can therefore imagine a variety of more and less immersive systems and a variety of more and less complex and interconnected virtual worlds in which we spend a great deal of time. One way to put social issues into perspective, however, and make it more manageable is to ask, How much time will we want to spend there? Even if the environments are in some respects much more malleable or flexible than the real world, there are also limits on the extent to which virtual worlds will be useful for users. For example, how many encounters with people, and how much space for being there together, would we like to have—and how many and how much can we cope with? Or, what kinds of appearance and identity are most suitable to these encounters, and what kinds of manipulability improve the spaces that we share with each other? The question of how much time we spend "being there together" will depend crucially on a better awareness of ethical and social issues, which will enhance the usability and inhabitability of MUVEs—and vice versa.

NOTES

1. For research and prototype uses, the questions surrounding experiments with research participants (human subjects) will be governed by guidelines developed by professional groups, including the American Psychological Association (www.apa.org/ethics), the American Sociological Association (www.asanet.org/members/ecoderev.html), and, for the study of the Internet, the Association for Internet Researchers (www.aoir.org/reports/ethics.pdf).

2. One issue that relates specifically to immersive VR systems is that some research institutions require periods after experiments before participants are allowed to drive, for example, because they may continue to be disoriented after having been in a VE.

3. For criticisms of the Milgram experiments, see Bridgstock, Burch, Forge, Laurent, and Lowe (1998: 66–69) and Willer and Walker (2007: 44–47).

4. The "bystander effect" is a research topic that Slater and colleagues are currently pursuing.

5. For a particularly striking example, where the researcher became "stalked," among other things, see Hudson-Smith (2002).

6. Some of the issues arising in this case have been dealt with in Eynon, Fry, and Schroeder (2008: 25–30).

7. The legal issues are not specifically covered here for lack of space and expertise, although what are arguably the main legal questions, concerning identity and property, are at the same time social issues (see Lastowka and Hunter 2003). There was also a special issue of the journal *Presence: Teleoperators and Virtual Environments* (volume 14, number 6) devoted to "Legal, ethical, and policy issues associated with Virtual Environments and Computer Mediated Reality."

8. A comprehensive mapping and discussion of the issues has been undertaken by the author together with Malte Ziewitz and Eric Meyer as part of the Presence Research in Action (PEACH) project. The report can be found at http://www.peachbit.org/

9

Multiuser Virtual Environments and Other Technologies for Being There Together

In Chapter 1, it was argued that there are two technological end-states, fully immersive computer-generated virtual environments (VEs) and immersive three-dimensional (3D) video-captured environments. It was also discussed, in Chapter 2, that existing multiuser VEs (MUVEs) fall into a limited number of types, and these are as yet far from these end-states. A different way to think about MUVEs and these end-states is, Are there nevertheless technologies that approximate the end-state of MUVEs and that are used in everyday life? To address this, we need to relax the definition of "being there together" as based on sensory perception and broaden it to include a wider set of experiences of "being there together." In that sense, "being there" does not need to be "immersive" if this could simply mean having a *sense* (in the nonsensory meaning of the term) of being in another place. Similarly, "being there together" may then only require that people that have a *sense* that others are there with them. This relaxation makes it possible to discuss some everyday uses of communication technologies that do not meet the strict definition but where, as we shall see in a moment, researchers have nevertheless used the concept of "presence."

Before we do so, it is worth noting again that research on MUVEs has been done in a very technology-specific way. It has also been confined to narrow topics within certain disciplines, especially computer science and psychology, with little interaction with the rest of the social sciences such as media studies and sociology or with wider topics such as videoconferencing, online gaming, mobile phones, instant messaging (IM), and social networking technologies. Perhaps a narrow focus is appropriate for studies of single-user VEs that are oriented to psychological effects or human factors, but single-user VEs are increasingly being eclipsed by MUVEs. And the technologies for "being there together" are bound to become ever more complexly interrelated as they proliferate. As this happens, it will become increasingly important to draw together the insights from various disciplines and about various forms of online interaction in virtual spaces.

We have seen throughout this book that some MUVE technologies are more oriented toward engagement with persons (copresence), whereas others are focused more on interactions with objects and the environment (presence). When we now relate MUVEs to other forms of mediated relationships and spaces, it makes sense to note, first, that certain forms of interactions are much closer to copresence (IM, videoconferencing, and mobile phones), whereas others (online games, social networking sites, or shared workspaces) are closer to presence. Second, it is worth spelling out how these other technologies depart somewhat from the definition of MUVEs:

- Videoconferencing achieves the sensory perception of other(s) being there together by means of high-fidelity video capture of participants (that is, the technology is not a computer-*generated* environment).
- Online social spaces and games provide the experience of being there together by means of avatar embodiment, which the user experiences with a first-person point of view (although sometimes it is a third person or bird's-eye point of view, which again does not fit the definition), and although a space is shared with other users, communication is often via text (again, a departure from "being there together").
- Online awareness tools such as IM or social networking technologies allow users to identify whether other users are there, whether they are available online, and/or whether they are represented symbolically or in the form of images of themselves. This is closer to awareness of others than being there together.

With these points in mind, we can now examine some of the major findings about non-VE technology and then relate this back to social interaction in VEs.

Other Technologies for Being There Together

Videoconferencing

Videoconferencing of the "talking heads" type has recently *technically* achieved a very high standard such that users in some cases no longer perceive *technology-specific* problems to be an issue. There are now several systems that feature a conferencing room where the quality of "being there together" is such that it is very difficult to detect shortcomings in the audio or video quality—for example, in terms of lag (Figure 9.1).[1]

Moreover, the space is designed to create a strong sense of being there together in the same place by having identical rooms at each distributed site, combined with high-quality lighting and spatial audio, which achieves the effect of sharing the same room with the other participants. At the same time, this type of system highlights the main current limitations of videoconferencing, which are cost and access: Systems like these are still very expensive and there are few sites where they are available, although arguably this is a matter of time. Once such systems become ubiquitous and inexpensive, the other reason why people prefer face-to-face meetings will move into the foreground—namely, physical bodily copresence.

It is difficult to convey the experience of a high-end videoconferencing system to someone who has not experienced it (the same applies, of course, to immersive VEs). A high-end videoconferencing system really does produce a sense of being there together, and this does not come across from images of the system. It is possible, however, to describe the highly realistic nature of these systems in words: First, a telling difference

FIGURE 9.1   High-end videoconferencing system.

between high-end or immersive videoconferencing systems and less "immersive" or less "telepresent" systems like desktop videoconferencing is that even the *co*-located interaction between meeting participants is incorporated in a natural way since users are seated around a table as if around a real table. Thus it is possible, for example, to have two groups, with two persons at each site, with each co-located pair carrying out a separate conversation but monitoring the conversation at the other end peripherally. This is easy to do if everyone is sitting around the same table in a physical room, but it is almost impossible in a videoconferencing system where "talking heads" are arranged on a wall-type display (so-called Access Grids, to be discussed in a moment): in the latter case, there is a constant worry about what the "other side" can and cannot overhear of the co-located conversation, and whether the non–co-located side wishes to "break" into this conversation.

The smoothness of the interaction is also evident in turn-taking, which is difficult in standard videoconferences but proceeds smoothly in high-end videoconferencing. Stops and starts in replying to each other are an important part of conversational turn-taking, and this has long been identified as a key problem in videoconferencing systems. Turn-taking is also difficult in Skype audio and video conversations where there is a lag of some milliseconds and the cues for turn-taking are missing. Still, even in poor-quality videoconferencing in two-person mode, people can become habituated to this lag. In a high-end videoconferencing system, however, this problem has become almost unnoticeable and more than two people can take turns fluidly.

The main reason why turn-taking is smooth in high-end videoconferencing technology is not so much video quality but rather that the audio quality is much higher than in conventional videoconferencing, and spatial 3D audio also gives everyone a sense of who is speaking. The visual side of these systems is also important—producing the effect of a shared room space by means of the same room furnishings in the different locations, the distances between participants, and eye level of speakers—all these enhance the sense of being there together (and this is also why lower-quality systems are so poor in this respect). The fluidity of the interaction, however, is mainly due to audio quality.

High-end videoconferencing technology is currently used only by early adopters and there is little research into their uses. Even so, these systems illustrate that, at least in terms of meetings between talking heads, a technological endpoint is being reached even if adoption is lagging behind (one indication that a point of technological saturation is approaching is that high visual and audio fidelity of these systems almost makes participants seem "hyperreal"). Thus we can expect an increasing use of these systems and more and more videoconferencing experiences of being there together, even if there are many social reasons why video-conferencing will not become widespread or take the form of high-end or immersive systems. It is worth mentioning that these types of system are typically used for meetings that are one or two hours long and they connect a small number of sites (up to four or six locations) with up to some two dozen or so people attending meetings.

As already mentioned in relation to MUVEs, there is a maximum number of people that can participate effectively in "being there together" for a meeting, and this is to do (in high-end conferencing setting just as in an MUVE setting) with the fact that it is difficult to pay attention to or keep track of many people simultaneously. A further similarity is that larger meetings are much more difficult to manage, just as tasks or meetings (such as classes in desktop virtual worlds) are difficult to manage in MUVEs. Visually and socially, there is an upper limit in the number of people (perhaps between five and ten) who can actively participate (as opposed to being a passive audience) in a meeting, and high-end videoconferencing and MUVE meetings are both limited to this number. It should be noted that this is not a technical limit—there is no technical reason why dozens or hundreds or more people should not be displayed in a videoconference or MUVE settings; the limits are rather those of visual and social attention that can be paid to others in a mediated as opposed to face-to-face setting.

MUVEs, however, have the advantage that this limit of attention can be expanded by means of giving them "artificial" features to allow people to focus attention on them (such as highlighting who is speaking, or arranging avatars so they are easily overviewable). Now it is true that there is no such limit to equivalent large-scale offline meetings, such as lecturing to a large group where there can still be two-way interaction. This recalls the point made by Bailenson (see Chapter 8) that in a virtual setting (although not in a video setting), it is possible to make it *seem* as although there is a one-to-many way paying of attention. Yet again, recall that this possibility has limitations, since a single person cannot pay attention interactively to others unless he or she can "steer" their avatar to pay attention to several others simultaneously (effectively multitasking, for which there are limits—a single person would find it hard to multi-task to pay attention to several others. This raises the possibility of finding a technical means to do this: for example, a mechanism whereby a single speaker could pay attention to a large audience—by programming the speaker to look at, or respond directly to, each audience member). Another limitation is that there is no physical bodily copresence, which is required for certain events like live music performances and where the physical copresence of performers and audience is part of the experience.

A popular videoconferencing technology that addresses the problem of many simultaneous users are Access Grids, which allow a number of head-and-shoulders video images (or images of several people in a room) to be arranged on a wall (Fielding and Macintyre 2006). Unlike in videoconferencing, there is no attempt to create the space of a conference room where people face each other, but all participants are visible to each other in close-to-life size format. Webcams can be seen as a lesser version of Access Grids where participants are displayed in small windows and not all participants may be visible to each other. What is interesting in the case of Access Grids is that a stratification of attention occurs: unlike in a room-type videoconferencing setting where attention is allocated as in the equivalent real-life setting, in Access Grids, how much attention participants devote to each other depends on the layout of faces on the wall and their prominence in relation to one's own position. Second (again), there is stratification by technology and modality, with those participants using inferior systems or perhaps participating via voice-only being relegated to lesser participation. Participants therefore sometimes liken Access Grids to watching television; that is, being rather passive (perhaps this could also sometimes be said for online gaming and social spaces). Finally, Access Grids and webcams, like videoconferencing, often entail confusion about what is going on at other sites (How many sites or faces are supposed to be participating? Are others supposed to have joined the meeting but cannot due to technical difficulties?) and what is going in the background outside the field of view. And as mentioned, especially as the number of participants increases, management of meetings becomes difficult. Interestingly, an advantage of shared online spaces that is overlooked is that this confusion can be avoided in principle, because participants can always check the spaces around the other participants by wandering around in the space to check if the avatar is moving or related activities are ongoing. Anecdotally, the experience of Access Grid–type videoconferences is that the sense of "being there together" can be highly variable, so that on occasion, these distributed meetings can be experienced as being very impersonal and disengaging, and on other occasions they can seem lifelike and intensely engaging.

People use videoconferencing not just for work meetings, but also for video-mediated communication (VMC) for nonwork purposes. As Kirk, Sellen, and Cao (2010) point out, with inexpensive tools like webcams and Internet-based video telephony (such as Skype), VMC is poised to take off. They studied seventeen participants in twelve households who used VMC regularly (at least three video calls per month) and found a variety of motivations for this mode of communication. Examples include grandparents seeing grandchildren and couples who live far apart from each other. Interestingly, in the former group, video quality hardly matters, and in the latter group, sometimes the audio is switched off—it is the sense of visual togetherness that is most important. The authors conclude that "propinquity" is the key motivation for this mode of communication, and this seems close to the sense of "being there together" that has been elaborated here. Note too that the authors find (as Licoppe does for his mobile phone users and "connected presence" [2004]) that the expressive or intimate aspects of communication are as important, if not more so, than the instrumental ones.

Apart from a few studies, there is nevertheless an absence of systematic research on videoconferences, unlike with immersive MUVEs. But despite being unable to make comparisons between MUVEs and videoconferencing that are based on research findings, clearly there will be many overlaps in how the two types of systems afford "being there together." Still, the "as good as sitting in the same room together" form of "being there together" in these systems also highlights a key characteristic of MUVEs: Videoconferences, not MUVEs, which reduce the need for travel and yet approximate face-to-face meetings, will be by far the most widespread *workaday* use of "being there together" technologies. Yet unless MUVEs provide realistic capture of people's facial expressions in a setting in which these expressions can be conveyed adequately,

MUVEs will not succeed in replacing face-to-face meetings (although curiously, there are few studies that directly compare videoconferencing with VEs [but see Garau 2003; Sallnas 2004]). This point can be put the other way around: The other technologies for being there together (VEs without realistic "cartoon-like" facial expressions, online spaces, awareness and social networking technologies) will be used where facial expressions are *not* critical and other features—interactions with other bodies and spaces in VEs, interacting with large numbers of people, having a sense of other people's online availability, and self-presentation—are more important.

A major drawback of videoconferencing is the absence of some social cues (or social presence; Short, Williams, and Christie 1976), which is mainly due to two factors: one is that videoconferences are typically talking heads (or torsos), and the second is that they are typically used for social interaction that is intensely interpersonal—needing to "read" the other person's intentions and being able to get them to "read" yours in meetings are of the utmost importance.[2] This "mutual reading" is something that co-located people can do easily. Further, it is something that we are used to achieving with other forms of mediated communication like telephones when no visual channels are involved. A second major shortcoming of videoconferencing, already mentioned, is poor audio quality. This is important to social interaction because it makes for awkward interaction (poor turn-taking and associating voices with the person's location from which they are coming). Only expensive high-end videoconferencing systems have overcome this problem to such an extent that it is not noticeable. Poor audio is also a shortcoming in MUVEs, although it is perhaps less noticeable in these unrealistic settings. Moreover, since both (or all) avatars are equally disadvantaged, this absence may not be perceived as a disturbing one, even if it is much more difficult to communicate facial social cues in MUVEs than in videoconferencing.

In MUVEs, the major shortcoming is that facial expressions are often static, missing, or unrealistic.[3] This can be put in perspective by noting that social cues (or the absence thereof) are in a sense overrated: After all, we use e-mail and telephones on a daily basis and make up for the absence of facial expressions. Again, the bias in our perception of communications media toward regarding face-to-face communication or interaction as the gold standard prevents us from recognizing the extent to which we do this.

There are also two contradictory trends that affect videoconferencing and that are extraneous to the affordance of the medium: the first, which mitigates against uptake or diffusion, is that people must go to specially equipped rooms to make use of high-end equipment (Hirsh, Sellen, and Brokopp 2005). The second, which is pushing more people to make use of videoconferencing, is the cheap and ready availability of videoconferencing equipment on consumer PCs in the form of webcams, combining these with internet telephony (such as Skype), and similar technologies. There are obvious parallels here between the high- versus low-end videoconferencing options and high-end (immersive) versus low-end (desktop) MUVEs used for conferencing.

Note, incidentally, that there is bound to be stratification in videoconferencing with different types of equipment, but again, thinking that face-to-face is the gold standard is misleading: It is not necessarily the case, for example, that those who can attend a meeting or a lecture in person have the highest status. Someone who can "only" participate via videoconference may be doing so because their time or ability to travel to a meeting where others are assembled face-to-face is most precious, whereas the time resources of those that attend the same meeting face-to-face are less precious. Going even further, someone attending a meeting where others participate via videoconference and who can only attend via voice, perhaps because they are on a mobile phone while traveling on important business, may be putting themselves out of the reach of the more powerful technology because they can afford to do so.

At this point it is useful to return to the point that videoconferencing is constrained by the number of active participants. Thus, one of several things happens as the number of participants in videoconferencing increases:

- It becomes a one-way "broadcast."
- In larger videoconferencing meetings, it is not possible to focus attention on more than a small number of persons at any one time (Vertegaal 1998).
- Some participants may have access via "lesser" technologies (voice conference only) and awareness of these persons and engagement with them is weaker (or peripheral).

All these phenomena also occur in larger-scale meetings in MUVEs, as anyone who has experienced large-scale meetings in VEs can attest.

There are two directions in videoconferencing: high-end videoconferencing for formal meetings, and ad hoc videoconferencing for informal purposes in the home.[4] The former are structured and need to get something accomplished (hence the frustration when the meetings are poorly structured after much effort was made to set up, go to, and attend such a videoconference, which is not the case with a face-to-face meeting). The latter are suited for people who know each other well, for flexible encounters, and where the quality may not matter since the point is more a kind of visual togetherness or connected presence.

It is interesting to note why certain technology combinations do not work, such as video heads on cartoon bodies, for example, which is a low-tech solution that is easy to implement but has a lack of reciprocity or of a disconnect between heads and bodies (it will be hard to interact with a head that seems not to belong to its body). So although this solution will be implemented where this disconnect does not matter (it is easy to envisage certain scenarios for co-design or co-inspection of a space), this combination will not suit scenarios where heads, bodies, and spaces need to be connected in a natural way. A point that goes in the opposite direction is that technologists typically want to make videoconferencing like face-to-face, but this may not the best way forward since, for example, people might want to know what they appear like: having a window with your own appearance in a videoconference ("picture in picture") or MUVE is highly unlike face-to-face interaction (how often do people talk to others while needing a mirror of their own appearance!), but it is understandably an important support for "being there together" in a MUVE or videoconference.

One reason why videoconferencing has not been more successful is that reciprocity breaks down—or it cannot be established or maintained. We have seen that this also happens in MUVEs (recall the "bad pair" in the long-term immersive collaboration in Chapter 4, or the situations with poor interactions in Chapter 5). But in MUVEs, there is not the same kind of expectation of face-to-face-like reciprocity. Still, with *high-end* videoconferencing systems, reciprocity may not break down. In any event, it is difficult to measure the differences—between different types of videoconferencing systems and between a videoconferencing system and face-to-face interaction—quantitatively. Yet what people say about these meetings is revealing: they are typically awestruck at the quality of the systems and clearly enjoy their use, yet insist that nothing is as cosy as face-to-face.[5] It will be different for low-end systems (such as video Skype) for casual get-togethers, interviews, and the like. Finally, people will get used to these various systems and adapt them to suit their purposes.

It is worth stressing again that technical issues or better quality is not the main issue for videoconferencing, even though technologists insist that they are. Instead, making the systems fit for the purpose, which may involve less technology or lower quality or non-naturalistic or nonrealistic technologies and environments—are more important. It is also worth noting again that there is, to my knowledge, no up-to-date and reliable published research on the uptake and everyday uses of videoconferencing (apart from the studies mentioned). Yet there is considerable anecdotal evidence that this uptake is increasing. Further, there is bound to be a stratified order of these uses, as it seems that high-end videoconferencing technology is mainly used among those whose time is valuable (professionals in a few sectors) and by access to the equipment. The consequences of these uses are also (anecdotally) obvious: They save time, and they are used despite the continuing problems (turn-taking, the need to go to special rooms, the requirement to manage meetings well). At the same time, there are also less obvious consequences: the loss of serendipitous "meetings in the hallway," the absence of informality, and the loss of physical copresence. Even more generally, the use of these technologies affects the frontstages and backstages of meetings and interpersonal encounters (see Chapter 2), how people interact in mediated settings, the modalities of communication, and the appearance of people and of the environment. In any event, there are similarities between low-end (i.e., Skype video) and desktop VEs, and immersive VEs and high-end (immersive) videoconferences, and these will be worth bearing in mind when we discuss the various types of being there together.

Instant Messaging and Mobile Phones

Nardi, Whitaker, and Bradner's (2000) analysis of IM has interesting parallels to MUVEs. This study shows how IM is not primarily used for information exchange or for individual communication acts. Instead, IM is used for what the authors call *outeraction,* which is defined as "communicative processes ... in which people *reach out* to others in patently social ways" (2000: 79). Nardi et al. examined IM in two work organizations (a telecommunications company and an Internet company) and found that "intermittent instant messages were thought to be more immersive and to give more of a sense of a shared space than ... email exchanges" (2000: 84). This made IM "similar to the 'virtual shared office'" (2000: 84) that has been demonstrated with open videoconferencing links. IM is used expressively in this setting in the sense that it creates what they call *awareness moments,* whereby people feel that the other person shares the same space. They note that IM is typically used in conjunction with other communication technologies and with face-to-face meetings, such that one can speak of different "communication zones" that "delimit a virtual 'space'" (2000: 86), or rather several such spaces that people step into and out of (to use their terminology).

IM thus supports different relationships and, despite limited awareness, provides a better link between users than e-mail because users have the option to use it or not to use it in conjunction with other modes of communication and because it affords symmetrical opportunities to all users (unlike, say, a telephone or face-to-face conversation in which the addressee *must* respond if they are available or an e-mail exchange in which the sender cannot be sure if the addressee is present for reply). Put differently, IM allows users more control inasmuch as both parties have the possibility to make themselves unavailable. For videoconferencing, in contrast, it has been argued that one reason why this technology has not been as popular as expected is that people either have to take themselves at a set time to a particular videoconferencing room, or if the equipment is in their office or home, they *have* to be available for a visual engagement. (Moreover, on a practical level, videoconferencing often has technical problems, whereas IM is a comparatively robust technology.)

Licoppe has found shared spaces and availability in the quite different context of mobile phones. Licoppe says mobile phones are used for "'connected' presence ... in which the (physically) absent party renders himself or herself present by multiplying mediated communication gestures up to the point where [physically] copresent interactions and mediated communication seem woven into a seamless web" (2004: 135). His research, unlike that of Nardi and colleagues, focuses on the private or nonwork use of communication technologies, and it is based on user logs and interviews. He contrasts the "connected management of relationships" or "connected presence" via mobile phones and texting with the "conversational mode" of communication via stationary telephones: Conversations via stationary telephones are typically longer conversations that take the form of a routine ritual with distant others to affirm a bond. Mobile phone use (including texting), by contrast is typically short, and, further, the content does not matter as much as the fact that one affirms one's availability to the other or that one is thinking about the other. Licoppe describes this as a "connected" or also a "phatic" (conveying general sociability as opposed to specific meaning) mode of communication. This mode may be irregular, but it continuously affirms the relationship and becomes part of managing one's relationship with a few close people over a set of proliferating media. And again, as in the case of IM, mobile phone messages often lead to interactions via other media or face-to-face.

In other words, in both cases, the technology is used expressively as opposed to instrumentally and to indicate a state of mutual availability or awareness.[6] If we are interested in "being there together" in everyday life, then, the emphasis shifts from the experience of individual encounters to the maintenance of relationships. What Nardi and colleagues and Licoppe nevertheless find, interestingly, is that the subjects themselves talk about the experience of these relationships in terms of presence and copresence, describing it as a sensory experience. What we can therefore see in the cases of IM and mobile phones/texting are media with little "media richness" and little immersiveness or ability to interact in a powerfully immersive way—yet these media nevertheless yield a powerful sense of "being there together," perhaps more so than stationary telephony, videoconferencing, shared virtual spaces, or face-to-face meetings. The reason in both cases is that participants have more control (including over "where" they are), more flexibility (possibility to switch media, multiple modes at the same time), more permanence (the channel can be kept open), and more awareness (one can have several users in one's field of vision in IM).

Clearly from the point of view of the human senses, completely immersive and all-surrounding environments with full representations of oneself and other users provide the richest possible medium (although in the two quite different end-state varieties—immersive videoconferencing and immersive computer-generated environments). Yet it is also possible to envisage mixed modes apart from the extremes of "rich" and "poor" modes. For example, there may be socially "rich" but sensorially "poor" modes, and vice versa. Or it is possible that different modalities could be used in combination at different times to maintain different states of "being there together."

In the case of IM and mobile phones/texting, the sense of presence may be quite low, but the technologies will rate highly in providing a sense of togetherness and being used for extensive periods of time to maintain multiple contacts. Presence here is not so much "being in another place" per se but continuously letting the other know your whereabouts and keeping updated about theirs. This continual awareness therefore shades into copresence but also has elements of co-location or "presence." And if this form of copresence applies to IM and mobile phones, it could also apply to a panoply of other new technologies for mediation, such as social networking sites or devices that disclose one's state or location to others or mobile phones with location sensing.

If we compare these two technologies for "being there together" with MUVEs, we can note that in IM there is a symbolic "avatar" presence, whereas mobile phones maintain availability without avatars (although this is changing with the increasing availability of images on mobile phones in addition to voice and text). On the other hand, IM maintains this connection only with a small list of users, whereas mobile phones allow connectedness with a larger group—at least in theory. In practice, as Licoppe shows, regular mobile/texting contact is with a small group, and IM lists can be long but probably also have a small core of connected groups. IM thus has "more" copresence than mobiles and more constancy, and it is less interruptive, whereas mobile phones/texting are more accessible and flexible and voice (to adapt a point made by Sallnas (2004) in her comparison of text-only and voice MUVEs) presents a copresence "reality check." Finally, both can convey a sense of "presence" if the location or place of the sender or receiver is disclosed via background sound in mobile phones, images for IM, and location if the mobile device has geospatial sensing capabilities (Licoppe and Inada 2006).

Online Spaces for Gaming and Socializing

Online spaces for gaming and socializing have been discussed in Chapter 5. Here we can compare them to other forms of "being there together." Note, first, that they often depart from the definition of MUVEs that has been used here but also come in several varieties. The main distinction (made in Chapter 5) is between online spaces for gaming that require adopting a game-defined character and pursuing game-defined objectives, and online spaces for socializing that involve open-ended interaction in the manner of a "third place" (Steinkuehler and Williams 2006). In both, the emphasis is on the interaction between avatar bodies and less on the experience of interaction with other people's facial expressions. The main difference between online socializing as against online gaming is function: Socializing involves "free" interaction, interacting for a various purposes (conversation, building together, exploring places, and the like), whereas gaming entails adopting a particular character and pursuing the game (collecting points, undertaking certain tasks, coordinating with others in the pursuit of quests, and the like). The two are not mutually exclusive; indeed one study has shown that game players engage in more social activity as they become longer-term users (Axelsson and Regan 2006).

People spend a lot of time in games (Ducheneaut, Yee, Nickell, and Moore 2006; Yee 2006). Yet online gaming interaction is also constrained by its rules and highly structured environments—for example, in socializing according to guilds and quest groups, partitions of the environment into different worlds (player versus player, player versus environment, regional, and the like), the definition of characters by roles, and the tasks for achieving levels. Indeed, the environment is designed to shape activity in a behaviorist way—Duchenaut et al. (2006) call it "Skinnerian" in the design of stimulus and response. In short, these are systems that operate according to "experience design."

It is also difficult to draw a hard line between online gaming and socializing as against other MUVEs since the former can also be used for collaboration. In practice, however, online games and social spaces tend to entail desktop systems and large populations, whereas what are conventionally considered MUVEs tend to be small groups and immersive or high-end systems. There are nevertheless systems and uses that defy this distinction, as when people play online games in networked IPT systems or use games for small-group therapy.

Still, online gaming and socializing involve a number of contrasts with videoconferencing and MUVEs:

- Interaction in online spaces is typically via text, whereas MUVEs and video-conferencing use voice.
- In online spaces, the emphasis is on conveying identity via avatar appearance without regard to realism, whereas for videoconferencing (and in some MUVEs), the focus is on facial expressions, shared interpersonal attention, and the conversational task.
- Online spaces involve large populations, although these are "partitioned" in practice into small groups for the purpose of interaction (and into populations in different worlds), whereas videoconferencing and immersive MUVEs involve an upper limit of a small number of people who can pay attention to each other and carry on a purposeful conversations and task in the same space.
- In online spaces, the environments (buildings, landscape) provide a context, whereas in videoconferencing the environment plays little role—and can be a distraction.

Apart from interpersonal interaction, a major aspect of online spaces is object-focused interaction. Here, as discussed in Chapter 4, the main drawback of desktop systems is the limited field of view and lack of reference points for interaction (Hindmarsh, Fraser, Heath, and Benford 2002). This shortcoming, as we have seen, is overcome in immersive IPT systems where object-focused collaborative tasks can be carried out "as good as being there together" (Schroeder et al. 2001). This advantage of immersive VEs does not rule out that desktop systems are used for carrying out spatial tasks in dyads (Sallnas 2004) and small groups (Nilsson, Heldal, Schroeder, and Axelsson 2002).

It is not just interaction with objects that is important in online spaces, however. Equally important is interaction with the environment, which includes the landscape, buildings, and other features that put the interaction in context and facilitates it (Brown and Bell 2006). And as we have seen (see Chapters 3 and 5), the environment also shapes the norms of interaction and communication in different ways depending on the environment. Some environments, such as the Sims Online, have been shown not to be compelling in supporting interaction, and so have failed (Steen, Davies, Tynes, and Greenfield 2006), whereas other environments that do this well can be highly successful (Ducheneaut, Yee, Nickell, and Moore 2006). At the level of how environments support populations, MUVEs need successful economies, forms of governance, interaction in large groups—and content, which engages users. Online spaces thus focus on engagement with the social and built environment rather than fostering copresence as such.

Technologies for Awareness and Social Networking

If we expand the notion of "being there together" still further, there are a number of technologies that do not provide a sense of being there in the same virtual space but nevertheless create a sense of being together online. Social networking tools and other forms of awareness technologies involve the user's "presence" if the word is used in a broader sense. One example is the use of mobile e-mail among Japanese teenagers, which Ito and Okabe (2005) describe as providing "ambient virtual co-presence." Lenhart and Madden (2007) similarly describe how teenagers use social networking sites such as MySpace and Facebook to create online identities and stay connected with their friends. Collectively, these can be regarded as technologies for maintaining awareness of each other online, with online identities providing the means for sustaining a network of relationships. And although people interact with each other via these technologies, the interaction is sometimes synchronous, asynchronous, or alternates between the two. With more awareness technologies becoming added, it will become difficult to distinguish between awareness technologies on the one hand, and "always on" (Baron 2008) or being "tethered" to each other (Schroeder 2010) on the other.

All these systems seem remote from, say, immersive VEs and high-end videoconferencing systems. But where should one draw the line, for example, between a webcam on a social networking site or a video blog when they are used to interact with other people—and a videoconference? Or between a life-size cartoon-like avatar in an immersive VE system and a more realistic avatar representation in an IM window?

There are several reasons why these technologies are increasingly becoming a means for being there together: One is that the various modalities for communication are often used in "always on" mode such that these devices keep people more permanently connected. A second is that there is a degree of interoperability or continuity between these devices, such that one's availability or self-presentation can be expressed across several devices (an IM icon on a PC or a mobile phone, a webcam on a social networking site or used for Internet telephony). Finally, the mechanisms whereby one's identity is represented—whether by means of an avatar body, a photograph, a geo-location indicator, or simply having the device switched on to signal availability—can be transferred across devices and thus make up a single representation. Social networking sites, for example, which involve a user's profile, including an image of the user, can express availability online, just as IM may contain a profile of the user's identity. And voice, text, and video- or computer-generated representations and spaces may travel with the user rather than being fixed to the physical location of the device.

The various technologies are thus not mutually exclusive but provide a continuous representation of the user's online presence: a social networking site may be combined with IM, or a mobile phone may provide the user's virtual and real location. Further, social networking tools, IM, or other technologies may include functionalities for community creation and finding people by interest or community membership, which may be bounded in virtual spaces. The line between the various forms of awareness and always-on and technologies for online togetherness is thus hard to draw since they all support signaling one's availability online, representing oneself to others, and group membership.

From the user's point of view, the differences involve function: IM and mobile phones in this context are about awareness and availability, whereas social networking sites are about establishing an identity that can be recognized by others and to coordinate activities in small and larger groups. But again, these functions are not mutually exclusive. And all these tools function as communication devices, yet in such a way that they widen the notion of communication (not only one to one or one to many), but unlike virtual- and videoconferencing, this communication does not primarily entail that people encounter each other directly in the same space.

Multiple Modalities, Multiple Networks

As we increasingly move online, there will be increasing engagement with video-captured persons and with avatars. And as the spaces that include these representations of others become more common, they will provide a familiar and popular context for interacting with others. In this sense, the shift to "being there together" via a variety of online representations is becoming a preferred "media-rich" mode of communication. At the same time, in certain circumstances users may prefer a mode of "communication" (in the broader sense just mentioned) without online representations or via media that are less rich. Here we need to bear in mind that fewer social cues or less media richness does not necessarily mean that people do not have a rich sense of the other person. As Walther (1996) has argued (in an argument that we have encountered in previous chapters), in computer-mediated communication where social cues are minimal, such as text-only collaboration, people make more of an effort to represent themselves in words; they put more into constructing or controlling their identities and may, in fact, reveal more about themselves in this way. This may take longer than in richer media, but it can also mean that people get to know each better than in face-to-face interaction or in rich-media interaction since they establish "hyperpersonal" relationships.

The need for richer media arises in specific circumstances. One of the major requirements for fidelity of expression and awareness in small groups is to support turn-taking. In small groups, the expressiveness of avatar faces and bodies (nonverbal communication) has been a major research agenda within videoconferencing and MUVE research (Garau 2003; Vinayagamoorthy 2006). And apart from facial expressions in virtual- and videoconferencing, this research also includes shared objects or task support for meetings. However, whether our appearance or how we present ourselves is crucial sometimes depends on if we already know people offline. And for object-focused tasks, it may not matter if the medium includes facial expressions or if the collaboration is between "strangers" or "friends" (Steed, Spante, Heldal, Axelsson, and Schroeder 2003).

In small groups, a common focus of attention needs to be maintained, the flow of the interaction needs to be kept going, and the absence of attention of any one participant is noticed (if we consider that active participants are annoyed and distracted if other participants' attention is noticeably preoccupied elsewhere). In larger groups, participants still congregate to face each other—so they form small clusters and we can treat these like small-group conferencing. Yet as we move away from smaller groups to larger ones, the requirements shift from supporting turn-taking and a common focus of attention to the rules and conventions governing social behavior that apply to the populations of large online spaces.

In these larger online spaces, there are different requirements for online representations. In some cases, symbolic representations of availability and awareness of others may be sufficient. There may also be a requirement for consistent self-representation (where avatars need to recognize each other by appearance, or if one needs to find the same person via a profile on a social networking site). In other situations where one is known offline to others, such as social networking sites or a personal web page, a continual modification of one's self-representation may be the appropriate norm to keep others interested or engaged (Lenhart and Madden 2007).

In the larger online world, consistency may also have a broader significance, not just in terms of a consistent representation of oneself, but being consistently represented as being available or aware of others in the same space: The online world, like virtual spaces for socializing and gaming, is very large—but unlike online spaces for gaming and socializing, it is not one space or world but many. Thus, it may be important to know which online space the other person is available in, or whether they are available in several. The same applies to availability generally: where are others available? And again, are they available in multiple online spaces? Online populations must be distributed in a consistent way across different worlds or spaces so that people and groups know where and when they can find each other (and people will, of course, want to be unavailable in some spaces and worlds).[7] On the other hand, despite being vast, our engagement with others or with our networks only consists of a few people in terms of routine interaction and engagement.

Finally, as we have seen, the different functionalities of the various technologies discussed here, in small groups or large, and with a greater or lesser focus on objects and the environment, can be seen as distinct or they can be seen as overlapping. They are distinct in that virtual- and videoconferencing are mainly a modality for meetings and small group tasks, whereas online spaces and gaming are a means for informal inter-action and collaboration in the pursuit of game tasks and socializing. Social networking technologies and other technologies for being online together provide a means to maintain a constant yet changing online identity vis-à-vis others, while IM and mobile phones provide a means to maintaining day-to-day availability and awareness. Thus we can make comparisons between these technologies on a number of dimensions (Table 9.1). But again, the contrasts may be drawn too sharply; in reality, many of their characteristics overlap, and the figure only captures some ideal typical characteristics.

On the other hand, these functionalities can also be regarded as a continuum varying on a single dimension, whether they are more inten-sive or more extensive in terms of interpersonal engagement (although in the varieties of the two end-states, virtual- or video-mediated). Online environments for being there together have two peaks with the highest level of interpersonal engagement (Figure 9.2)—immersive videocon-ferencing and immersive VEs. These two typically also afford the greatest copresence (or engagement), and in dyads and small groups, these two peaks allow the most powerful interaction. And although the two peaks are currently separate, we have seen that there are technologies that blur them.[8]

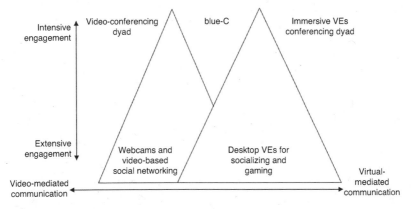

FIGURE 9.2   Level of engagement in four technologies for "being there together."

TABLE 9.1   Comparison of four technologies for 'being there together'.

	Virtual Environment	Videoconferencing	Online Spaces for Gaming and Socializing	Social Networking and Awareness Tools
Appearance	Face with limited expressiveness, body	Head and torso	Avatar	Iconic representation, photo
Environment	Room and larger spaces	Small space within room	World	Spaces consisting of pages and windows
Realism	High	High	Low	Low
Object and environment interaction	High	Very limited	High (but restricted by field of view)	High (but restricted)
Facial Expressiveness	Low	High	Low	Low
Group Size	Small	Small	Large	Large
Communication and Interaction	Synchronous, brief	Synchronous, brief	Synchronous, extensive sessions	Synchronous and asynchronous, constant
Communication modality	Voice	Voice	Text, sometimes voice	Text, sometimes voice
Key Disadvantage	Expense, poor facial expressiveness	Expense, poor audio and bodily cues	Poor facial expressiveness	Lack of social cues
Key advantage	Object interaction	Facial expressiveness	Engaging setting for interaction	Awareness, availability, and self-presentation can be managed

From these peaks, there is a descending order of intensity as groups get larger and the extent of interaction and ability to communicate constantly and synchronously with each other are diminished—and as we move toward desktop systems with more limited capabilities. However, this is not a straightforward descent: online chat (as opposed to immersion) can have a high degree of engagement, and crowds can be highly engaged if there is common focus of attention.

On the other hand, we could start at the base of these peaks (which indicates popularity of uses) where most people are online with each other for a variety of purposes for large parts of the day via online awareness technologies—this is the most extensive form of interpersonal online engagement. Broadband, mobile phones, and other devices are used as always-on technologies at work and in the home, with people drifting in and out of the awareness and engagement in smaller and larger groups online and whereby many are almost constantly connected with each other. Some of these technologies will have video-based representations of people, others will have avatars, and still others have geospatial location or in-world location, and with the two types (video and virtual) merging to some extent as representations of people take mixed forms. Regardless of form, this is a much more common way of being there together for most people and consists of far greater spaces and worlds than immersive VEs and high-end videoconferencing—even if, as mentioned earlier, the way people interact with others on a routine basis is in smaller groups. Still, in comparison with these much larger groupings that are used on a day-to-day basis, immersive VEs and high-end videoconferencing are marginal to most people most of the time.

What can we conclude? I have compared various technologies for being there together, mainly for communication but also for a variety of other purposes. But a number of other related technologies and practices could also have been discussed that are used for being there together: for example, shared virtual or video spaces for interacting not primarily with people but with objects and environments. This includes shared visualizations, workspaces, and augmented and mixed reality systems that often enhance the real environment with a virtual space. Other forms of mobile computing and tools for online collaboration could also be included. And if we go beyond digital technologies, letters and other technologies could be included (Licoppe and Smoreda 2006).

There is a range of interaction here—with more spatial collaboration at one end and more interpersonal communication at the other. Still, the technologies discussed here are the main ones for computer-mediated-communication, and even if they will continue to exist side-by-side with each other, a number of factors will lead to their convergence:

- The current problems of audio or voice and video/graphics quality will be overcome.
- Users will not be forced to use a particular modality of representing themselves or communicating because of technology constraints or tradeoffs. Instead, using text as opposed to voice, or a realistic or constructed avatar representation, or engaging with a small or large number of simultaneous users—will become a matter of choice, convenience, and the suitability (or constraints, depending on one's social science perspective) of different means of communicating and interacting online for different circumstances.
- Communication via videoconferencing, which has been a separate technology, will increasingly merge with digital telephony and with 3D spatial virtual environments.

As these technologies converge, both in technological terms and in terms of uses, a number of questions arise that have already been discussed in passing and that go beyond current research agendas, especially in presence research. For example, so far, presence and copresence have been studied either in terms of particular applications or as a measurable psychological state (and often both), and mostly for individual users. If, however, there is a shift toward a variety of technologies and uses that overlap and that are used for similar purposes, there will need to be a shift in research agendas to include: how is the self presented and how are others perceived in various online modalities? How (intensively or extensively) engaging are the various representations of users; and how various modalities support interpersonal communication and spatial interaction. The range of issues raised by "being there together," apart from presence and copresence, could thus be broadened to address a number of other questions:

- What kind of appearance is conducive to interacting in situations of online copresence?
- What kind of environment or space, small or large, is appropriate for different copresent encounters and for developing appropriate social norms to govern copresence?
- When is a more realist, and when a more artificially constructed, self-representation conducive to copresence?

- What kind of technological system, with what affordances (Hutchby 2001), is suitable for mutual availability and awareness in situations of regular online copresence?
- How should online spaces and worlds be designed to support maintaining awareness of others and signaling availability (or being away), especially across a range of spaces and places?
- What type of engagement, extensive or intensive, video- or virtual-mediated communication, is best suited for people to interact and communicate throughout the day?
- How to combine technologies and uses such that they provide the most useful and enjoyable experience of being connected to others in online spaces and worlds?
- What is the upper limit of the number of people who can experience copresence and share a focus of attention in the same space, and when is such an experience and shared focus unnecessary?

People will increasingly traverse online networks with different online self-representations and make use of online spaces to engage with others. As our interaction with others moves online, we need to present ourselves and make ourselves available to others, just as we depend on the representations of others and awareness of where they are online. As online connections and spaces become ever denser and more multiple, the lessons that can be drawn across them will become ever more important. There are signs that videoconferencing of different kinds—high-end and low-end—is finally turning into more than just a rare occurrence, even if it remains confined to certain niches. Yet the differences between high-end videoconferencing and immersive VEs, online worlds, and other always on technologies will become increasingly eroded. Research on MUVEs will benefit from engaging with this larger changing landscape of technologies for being there together.

NOTES

1. "Lag" is in fact composed of several elements, including delays in the network (latency) and the rendering of images. For our purposes, the non-technical term "lag" to encompass all delays will do. There is ongoing research about how these systems are still not perfect, such as with awkward overlaps in

turn-taking, which can cause nonsmooth interaction. This research and refinement of the system will doubtless continue, but it is unlikely to be a major issue for users.

2. An interesting study of video-mediated interaction was done by van der Kleij, Paashuis, and Schraagen (2005), who compared the paper-folding task of making an origami shape for groups of three who did not know each other before in a high-end (life-size people around a table) videoconferencing system with face-to-face interaction over the course of four one-hour sessions at two-week intervals. They found that after the first session, when the face-to-face team performed better, there was no significant difference between the two conditions in the subsequent three sessions, and groups in both conditions improved over the remaining sessions. What was unexpected was that cohesion did not increase in both conditions over time, although satisfaction increased over time as team members became more familiar with each other. Surprisingly, mental effort was higher for face-to-face teams in comparison with video-mediated teams, and this difference remained even as groups in both conditions gained experience. It seems that laboratory experiments like these turn up unexpected findings about video-mediated tasks, although more such experiments that approximate the situations in which people work together over a series of meetings are needed to enable us to gauge how well "being there together" in videoconferencing settings work over time.

3. Static eyes are a key problem in VEs. But Steptoe, Steed, Rovira, and Rae (2010) showed that avatar-mediated communication compares well with video-mediated communication (videoconferencing) if the avatar's eyes blink, dilate, and mimic the user's gaze. In their experiment, they found that people are better at detecting deception (lying) for avatars with eyes that have these kinds of animations than those without eye animations, and that avatars with eye animations compare well in supporting communication with high-definition video-mediated communication.

4. I have benefited from an extended discussion with Abigail Sellen (on February 12, 2009) of Microsoft Research Cambridge on this topic.

5. This sentence is based on my conversations with those who demonstrate videoconferencing systems, those who use them briefly, and various people who have used other such systems. I am not aware of (publicly available) research on this matter, apart from what has been cited here.

6. For another example of mobile email users, see Ito and Okabe (2005: esp. 264–266).

7. For online self-representations and availability, the implications here shade into the problems of having a single true identity for the purposes of security and legal identity.

8. For example, technologies that merge video and 3D computer-generated environments like the blue-C system (Gross et al. 2003), which allows video-captured 3D images of users' faces and bodies to be represented in immersive 3D computer-generated spaces.

10

The Future of Being There Together

This book has examined various forms of "being there together" in virtual environments (VEs). In this final chapter, we shall need to put the various findings that have been discussed in a broader context: How does "being there together" fit into the wider landscape of our uses of information and communication technologies? This will mean widening beyond the concept of copresence, which is central to multiuser VEs (MUVEs) and includes concepts (discussed in Chapter 9) that are used for other media, such as mutual awareness, connected presence, and engagement. It will also mean discussing online relationships more broadly than in terms of social interaction inside MUVEs. I shall argue that it is useful to think about the various modalities of "being there together" as a continuum—with MUVEs in which people are fully immersed as an end-state and various other modalities approaching this end-state. This argument has been sketched in the introductory chapter, and now is the time to flesh it out.

Multiuser Virtual Environments as an End-State

The end-state of MUVEs consists of a purely mediated relationship in which the users of this technology experience "being there together" with others in a fully immersive environment. As argued in Chapter 1, there are actually two—and only two!—versions of this end-state: computer-generated VEs and fully immersive videoconferencing. Despite current technical limitations, these immersive displays represent an end-state in the sense that, barring direct sensory input into the brain (in the manner of science fiction novels such as William Gibson's *Neuromancer* and Neal Stephenson's *Snow Crash*), synthetic environments for "being there together" that are displayed to the users' senses cannot be developed further than fully immersive MUVEs or videoconferencing environments. Nevertheless, even if these fully immersive environments are fully developed technically, they will have certain possibilities and constraints for their users, just like other media. The point of specifying these two end-states is that they have and will continue to have quite *different* possibilities and constraints.

MUVEs and other new media can be seen as varying on three dimensions: presence (being there), copresence (being there together), and the *degree* of being there together. This third dimension captures a number of different elements, but the main reason to introduce this dimension is that we not only want to know about "being there together" in abstract terms (the experiential state of the user at a particular point in time) but also about the actual *extent* to which our relationships are mediated in this way. This yields a cube of three "being there together" dimensions (Figure 10.1).

On all three dimensions, we can take the individual's presence in a real physical environment and a face-to-face encounter as our starting point (0,0,0). On the first dimension, being in the physical world is at one end of the *y*-axis and having a sense of being there (alone) in a purely media-generated place or space is at the other end (0,1,0). On this dimension, highly immersive environments such as CAVE-type environments (Cruz-Neira, Sandin, and DeFanti, 1993) are at the top end of the *y*-axis (0,1,0), but simulators and IMAX screens also provide the user with the experience of "being there"—although with limited possibilities for interacting with the environment.

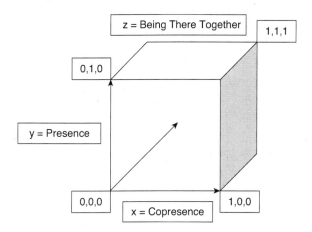

FIGURE 10.1   Three dimensions of being there together.

On the second dimension, again with face-to-face encounters in the physical world as our point of departure at one end, the other end consists of mediated relations with persons whom we encounter only virtually (1,0,0). Telephones minimally provide us with this sense, although they lack the spatial component (not entirely, as shown, for example, by the use of mobile phones for location awareness, which will be discussed shortly), and instant messaging (IM) also provides some degree of spatial copresence. So these two technologies can be placed somewhere along the continuum of copresence, with the telephone providing some experience of copresence ($<1,0,0$) and IM providing a somewhat spatial experience of copresence ($<1,<1,0$).

"*Completely*" mediated relationships then constitute a third dimension (the z-axis). This is the *extent* to which one's relationships are mediated through environments for "being there together." This third dimension has several aspects: first, the "affordances" or "constraints" of the mediation; second, the extent to which one's relationships with others are *exclusively* mediated in this way; and, third, the time spent in these mediated encounters compared with one's face-to-face relationships. Together these constitute the extent to which "being there together" is mediated. Once we add this third dimension, some everyday technologies like the telephone will receive a much higher value for this third dimension than MUVE systems because people typically spend a lot of time with many others on the telephone and little time in MUVEs.[1] The end-state in this case would thus be one in which in which people live entirely inside immersive virtual worlds (1,1,1).

For reasons that will become apparent, I argue that it is important to think about—or imagine—what it would be like to conduct all our social interaction in a fully immersed and mediated way. But to preview this argument briefly: The main reason why it is important to think about living entirely in MUVEs is that we already spend much of our time in mediated relationships that approach the end-states of being there together. And as long as we think of these mediated forms of togetherness as a kind of aberration from face-to-face interaction or from a natural state of togetherness, there will continue to be impediments to clarity in thinking about these technologies. But to return to the three dimensions: these allow us to plot all experiences of "being there together" as approximations toward this end-state (Figure 10.2).

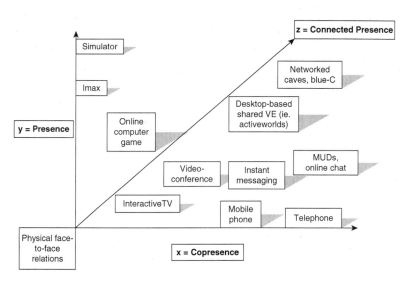

FIGURE 10.2   Presence, copresence, and being there together in different media.

Before this end-state and Figure 10.2 can be elaborated further, three points need to be made: First, of course it is true that all forms of mediated environments only complement—and do not replace—physical, face-to-face environments and relationships. However, Figure 10.2 focuses on *mediated* relationships. Second, any plotting exercise like this is highly imperfect: the extent to which people experience a sense of being there with others in, say, telephone conversations, online chat rooms, and different types of virtual reality systems will vary considerably according to context. Still, this is a problem of research approaches and what they yield—and techniques for researching "being there together" so as to capture people's different experiences are bound to improve over time.

A final and related problem is that it is visually difficult to represent the three subcomponents of "being there together" in any precise or quantitative way. This is especially true of the extent of time spent in these environments, although one solution would be to plot volumes with various sizes for each individual and situate the different media properly in relation to each other in the three-dimensional (3D) space of the cube. In other words, it might be possible to make a proper 3D image in which the media were located in relation to each other in three dimensions rather than in two dimensions, as here, and the shadows behind the boxes in Figure 10.2 could represent the three subcomponents (affordances, exclusively mediated relations, and time spent) of "being there together" in terms of volume. In fact, with enough scope for visual complexity, it would be possible to map the nature and extent of each person's mediated relationships in their entirety—and it can be imagined that all mediated relationships could be aggregated and mapped in this way—just as all face-to-face encounters and relationships could be. This would yield a complete social scientific account of mediated relations, just as we can think of all our face-to-face interactions adding up to the sum total of our micro social interaction. Such an exhaustive and complex elaboration is beyond our scope here[2]—although it will be useful to bear this thought-experiment in mind.

One further point: as mentioned in Chapter 1, the two end-states scenarios may be mixed in practice—for example, capturing the user on video but putting them into a computer-generated environment or putting a computer-generated avatar into a video-captured environment—but in their pure forms they are quite different. So again, if the technologies for immersion were fully realized, they would also be the furthest possible extensions of technologies for "being there together" because no conceivable system could go beyond providing a more fully immersive experience of being there together.[3] Mixed or augmented reality devices, where the user is partly inside a VE and partly engages with the physical world, can also be considered as approximations to the two ideal end-states. A different way to think about "being there together" is thus to think about the degree of "absence" or "removedness" from the physical world and face-to-face relationships—and in this case, with mixed and augmented reality, the user is only partially "absent."[4]

The focus on these three dimensions—and the various components of the third dimension—allow us to make some useful comparisons between the various technologies for "being there together." First, being there together in different MUVEs varies considerably on the first two dimensions. But the complexity of assessing the first two dimensions (if we think of them as occurring at a single point in time) is that they are influenced by the third; in other words, being there together is affected by the extent of experience with the medium.

Some brief examples can illustrate this point: The first is that users must learn to cope with the other person's avatar. As we have seen, sometimes it is easy to walk through another person's avatar, but at other times users will maintain an interpersonal distance to a similar extent as in face-to-face encounters. This depends on the type of MUVE system one uses—but also in immersive MUVEs on the stage of the task that people are at or how habituated to interacting with an avatar they have become.[5] In short, "being there" and "being there together" are affected by the context and by one's experience with this context (and again, as argued earlier, especially in Chapter 2, this "dependence on context" does not mean it is impossible to generalize about *how* the context affects the experience of social interaction).

Another example (from Chapter 4) is when users point out objects to the other person with an untracked arm, or they "lean" to hear the other person even when there is no spatial sound; yet at other times they use the devices appropriately. Again, this depends on the amount of time they have spent on the task and how used to the system they have become. And if these examples apply to immersive systems, we can also think of the extent to which avatars in systems like Second Life walk through each other or not, or the extent to which they use gestures for pointing—both, again, highly variable in the light of how much time has been spent in the system.

Similar phenomena can be identified for other new media. For example, as we have seen (in Chapter 9), people can treat places at the other end of a mobile phone conversation as if they were sharing the remote space—as when they gesture to the other person although the gesture cannot be seen (Ling, 2004). Or again, we saw that IM can, with routine use, create the experience of the other person's copresence in the sense that people will treat IM as a shared space in which people can step in and out of each other's awareness.

Another example can be taken from Chapter 4, whereby, in networked immersive projection technology (IPT) systems, people use their bodies as a reference point in interacting with objects when they perform spatial tasks together, using both verbal and nonverbal communication to do so. They need more verbal communication in networked desktop systems for the same task because they need to describe in words where they would otherwise have used gestures and their bodies. Again, this takes getting to used to in both cases. Notice again that people also do this in mobile phone conversations, such as when giving an indication of their location to let their partner know how they are coping with the space around them (Ling 2004). Or, to take a nonspatial example, there can be compensation for the absence of eye gaze to indicate to whom one is speaking in both telephone and MUVE situations by means of words—for example, by saying, "What's your view, Joe?" (or in MUVEs also by gestures; see Brown and Bell 2006).

Systematic comparison of different MUVE settings will be able to identify the role played by this third dimension. But we can also compare MUVEs and other new media. As we have seen (in Chapter 9), there are tradeoffs between the different factors affecting "being there" on the spatial dimension: for example, performing a (nonspatial) task and a high degree of spatial presence may be in conflict with each other, as when you might lose your sense of being in another place if you become distracted by something nonspatial, like a single-source sound in the environment that should be coming from a 3D sound source.

When it comes to "being there *together*," the factors—as we have seen—become much less well researched and much more complex. These factors include the nonverbal communication of the avatar, avatar appearance and behavior, and the extent to which people jointly exercise control over the graphical environment and its features. To give one example of this complexity: a highly immersive environment with a non-realistic avatar may afford less copresence than a nonimmersive desktop one with a realistic one, depending on whether the focus of the interaction is on the realism of the person. One point that has emerged is that the degree of control over the environment (for example, is it possible to fashion one's avatar to suit one's purposes, or improve the habitability of the environment?) is likely to be the key to the third or z dimension.

Factors Influencing "Being There Together" in MUVEs and Other Media

Before we discuss the relation between MUVEs and other media more broadly, it is worth comparing each dimension of "being there together" in MUVEs with other media. Only a few studies have compared "presence" on the first dimension in MUVEs with other media. Thus some researchers have put technologies such as IMAX screens, 3D computer games, and other technologies on the same scale as VEs (Lessiter, Freeman, Keogh, and Davidoff 2001). Comparisons can also be made with "presence" in the real world (Nisenfeld n.d.). Combining the results of Lessiter and colleagues (2001) with his own, Nisenfeld (n.d.) finds that the real world scores highest on spatial presence, with an IPT system scoring *higher* than a video game but lower than an IMAX screen. Interestingly, for engagement, which can be imagined as a strong factor in presence, a video game scores roughly the same on presence as an IPT in Lessiter et al.'s comparison. Still, as pointed out in Chapter 2, there is considerable debate about the appropriate ways to measure presence (Scheumie, van der Straaten, Krijn, and van der Mast 2001) and about comparing MUVEs with other media.

Another factor affecting presence is how much interaction is possible. On Lessiter and colleagues' (2001) measures, a passive experience like an IMAX movie provides a greater sense of (spatial) presence than IPTs (although this will depend on context and on the content), but an IPT in which objects can be manipulated provides more control over the environment. "Interactivity" and "presence" are clearly interrelated, but this relationship, as mentioned in Chapter 2, has not been subject to systematic research. Still, it is clear that (single-user) VEs of various sorts provide quite different types of interactivity and that they differ from non-VE systems.

As for the second dimension of "being there together," or copresence, the audio quality and visual appearance of the other participants are key factors for MUVEs and videoconferences. However, one factor that must be a key determinant of copresence in MUVEs as in face-to-face situations and in other media is group size, or the number of avatars in encounters or social situations: the more avatars, the more one's focus of attention is divided, and the focus on any *one* other person's copresence may therefore be diminished. Strangely, however, there is no research on this topic for MUVEs or other media. Yet this question could be asked about one's online IM contacts just as it could be about the number of avatars with whom we share the same space in MUVEs: namely, if there are more copresent participants, does their copresence become "diluted"? Interestingly, it is only recently, with the proliferation of devices for constant awareness of others' states, that the question of how many peoples' copresence one can be constantly aware of, has been raised: Think, for example, of how many people's blogs one can follow, or how many friends one can have and coordinate one's activities with on a social networking site like Facebook. Apart from the (vocal and graphical) realism of the user representation, the number of people on which one can focus attention must be a key factor on the second dimension.

On the third dimension of "being there together," many studies of mediated communication and online togetherness can be brought to bear (for example, van Dijk 1999, Chapter 8; Baym 2002). There is a plethora of issues that have been investigated in relation to the extent of mediated relationships and spaces. But as mentioned, we can distinguish between the three sub-dimensions of "being there together," the all-encompassing nature (or otherwise) of the mediation, the number of relationships that are mediated in this way, and the time spent in these mediated encounters.

If we think first about the immersiveness—or all-embracing nature—of "being there together," the variation in this case (as we saw in Chapter 2) boils down to visual representations, voice, and the environment. As we saw, Sallnas (2004) found that audio copresence "overshadows" the visual copresence of the other participant—or, as she put it, audio provides a "reality check" of the other person. This is an important finding, but we know little (apart from this work on audio) about the "weight" of different modalities in conveying the copresence of the other person in different media on a longer-term basis. Again, much research remains to be done on this topic, but with the proliferation of multimodal technologies for being there together, there will also be much more material to do research about.

Second, in terms of the number (and exclusively mediated) nature of our relationships, a key distinction is between strangers (or relations that are anonymous) against those relations that are complementary to face-to-face relations. Purely online relationships with strangers have been much discussed (see Baym 2002 for a review), but for complementary relations, too, it may be necessary to distinguish between different degrees of "complementariness" or "exclusivity" for the sake of analyzing "being there together." We could ask, for example, how far *removed* are the online relationships from face-to-face relationships? In other words, how strongly is sociability mediated, or to what extent do relationships take place in mediated form? Again, this has not been studied extensively across different forms of mediation, although some studies have tried to examine the whole ecology of mediated relationships (Licoppe and Smoreda 2006).

Finally, in terms of time spent, there are as yet not many findings for MUVEs, although some research exists for online games and nonimmersive social spaces (reviewed in Spante 2009 and, more recently, Williams, Yee, and Caplan 2008). Still, some people spend a considerable amount of time in MUVEs, at least in online games and social spaces (Yee 2002). A key finding that I have highlighted in relation to this aspect of "being there together" (in Chapter 2) is Walther's (1996) finding that even though online interaction lacks many social cues, people still get to know each other in some senses better than via face-to-face communication, but it takes them longer to do so (or what Walther calls "hyperpersonal" relationships"). One way to think of this is in terms of how people get to know each other differently in mediated relationships, and another is to consider the extent to which people exercise greater control over how they present themselves insofar as they have the possibility to do this in MUVEs and other new media.

Now the extent to which people who spend a substantial part of their day in nonimmersive (and especially immersive!) MUVEs is still limited. Yet if we think about those whose contact with others consists to a large extent in mediated relationships and who spend much of their day in this way, then this represents a sizable population and a large amount of time. How this affects their relationships has been investigated in different contexts (although not, as I have suggested, across the board). But if, in relation to our endpoints, we are interested in how these mediated relationships "add up"—an indicator of the aggregated mediatedness of our relationships—this can only be estimated. Nevertheless, our "relational economy," as Licoppe (2004) calls it, is shifting toward mediated relationships. And since the data about these relationships are digital, some are beginning to log and aggregate them (and in this way, MUVEs and other media that approximate them provide powerful tools for social science, as argued in Chapter 7).

Licoppe argues that our "entire relational economy ... is 'reworked' every time by the redistribution of the technological scene on which interpersonal sociability is played out" (2004: 142). Further, he says that there is "evidence of a gradual shift in which communication technologies, instead of being used (however unsuccessfully) to compensate for the absence of our close ones, are exploited to provide a continuous pattern of mediated interactions that combine into 'connected relationships' in which the boundaries between absence and presence get blurred" (Licoppe 2004: 135–136). This is a gradual—historical—shift, but one implication is that it could be more useful for the study of contemporary uses of communication technologies to gauge different communication technologies in relation to *each other*—to see a continuum between a fully immersed end-state of mediated relations and lesser ones as suggested in Figures 10.1 and 10.2—than to compare "being there together" with the baseline of face-to-face encounters. This would allow for a more insightful gauging of the role that different forms of mediation play in our social lives.

One question is whether the changing relational economy of "being there together" in these different modes progressively devalue face-to-face relations (Licoppe 2004: 154)? To be sure, in Figure 10.2, the largest volume (by time and number of relationships) is on the low end of "being there" and "being there together." Yet with the changing landscape of information and communication technologies, this balance will surely change. This also relates to interactivity: what kind of affordances do these mediated relations support (Hutchby 2001)? Here we are close to the point where the three dimensions of "being there together" intersect or to gauging how active or passive media are—since these "affordances," or, in the case of MUVEs, the degree of "inter-action" (manipulating the environment and engaging with the other)—are closely interrelated.

It is thus important not simply to take face-to-face encounters and physical location as the only point of departure. At the furthest extreme from face-to-face interaction are virtual places that are completely immersive and where people have created the environments that they "inhabit," and there is no reason why mediated relationships or encounters should be regarded as less authentic or less engaging than face-to-face interaction. To be sure, some of these spaces have predefined roles and activities and therefore are not interpersonal in the same sense as face-to-face encounters—like the highly realistic online computer games such as Quake or World of Warcraft. But it is important not to overlook the finding that the longer people play online games, the less they are interested in the gaming aspect and the more they are interested in the relationships they form (Axelsson and Regan, 2006). Still, apart from games, it is difficult to think of *extensive* or long-lasting day-to-day uses of online *spaces*.

Apart from online interactive spaces, in communications media it is important to consider the number of people with whom one is interacting: Many communications media support only one-to-one or one-to-several two-way relationships instead of shared spaces with many users. Broadcast communication technologies fall outside of the scope of Figure 10.1, except perhaps for interactive uses or two-way uses of media like interactive television (Craven et al. 2000). Still, the current proliferation of technologies whereby we spend time "always on" with others, tethered to them digitally and aware of each others' virtual and real locations, and sharing online spaces with them (even when these are not 3D worlds) in the case of Facebook pages or visiting each other's web page and exchanging objects on them (as with spaces such as Cyworlds (Haddon and Kim 2007)—all these are ways in which the line between VEs and other forms of interaction in mediated spaces are becoming blurred.

"Being There Together" and the Focus of Attention

This final point allows us to return to some basics of "being there together" in a new light: From the individual's point of view, if we do not take face-to-face encounters in the physical world as the baseline and instead use as a baseline the focus of attention *inside* the environment (exclusively, away from the physical world and its face-to-face encounters), then this consists of the forms of attention on the other person(s) or mutual focus on one side—and on the environment on the other (this idea was introduced in Chapter 2; now it can be taken further). In other words, the focus can be on the relationship or on the interaction with the environment—although of course the person is also part of the environment. There are bound to be environments that are rich in terms of the spatial environment and poor in terms of affording the sense of another person (or persons) being there—and vice versa. Since the spatial component—being *there* and being *there* together, which includes being able to navigate through and manipulate the environment (the presence or y dimension)—is arguably the most essential feature of MUVE technology, a critical area for future research will be to identify when this spatial component outweighs the communicative or interpersonal relationship part of MUVEs (the copresence or x dimension), which centers on avatar appearance, eye gaze, and the like—*or the other way around*. In view of the model presented here, this is perhaps the most fundamental balance that MUVEs need to achieve in order to provide "being there together" successfully. So far, there is little research that directly addresses the topic of how the two dimensions are related, although many insights could be drawn out from existing research in addition to those that have been discussed here.

In other words, the affordance of MUVEs lies in what you can *do* in the environment and *do* there together—how people can interact with each other and with the environment. This notion of interaction, however, is still too passive for gauging "being there together." What is needed is a more active notion of how relations can be maintained—or how they are enabled and constrained—in different media. So we could ask, apart from the control over the immediate activity or what holds ones' attention, about the extent to which people have control over the environment in different media or mediated environments—how much they can be modified, what control over their appearance users have, what level of interactivity the displays and tools provide, and the like (all of these have already been discussed in passing). And we should add the "depth" of the relationships—which encompasses the extent in time and the immediacy or exclusivity—that these media afford for "being there together" and for making the environment one's own (combining all three subcomponents of the z dimension mentioned earlier).

The debates about our mediated relationships with others that have arisen with "new" media are quite revealing in respect to the three dimensions. Recently, for example, the debate has been about whether the Internet contributes to fewer offline relationships and the like (Baym, 2002). Most findings, however, suggest that spending time in mediated relationships, including recently in relation to online games, for example, does not detract from spending time together or decrease the level of engagement in relationships "offline" (see, for example, Williams 2006). If we think in terms of "being there together," these debates can be put into a different perspective: It is not that purely mediated interpersonal relations should be seen as causing loneliness or being inferior to face-to-face relations and the like; rather, different media provide different possibilities for being there together in the changing landscape of interpersonal copresence. Face-to-face relationships and mediated relationships or time spent in mediated spaces should thus not be seen as a zero-sum game, despite the obvious fact that the amount of time spent in mediated relations and spaces has increased if seen in a longer-term historical perspective (Schroeder 2007b: 74–120; 2010).

Relationships are thus shaped not only by the "medium" but also by its "affordances." And these affordances apply not just to the relationship with people, but also to relationships to the environment and our control over it. Even if, as mentioned earlier, our relations in these media technologies should be described in terms of areas rather than as points on the three axes in the two figures, certain technologies and their uses nevertheless remain clustered in particular areas in relation to each other if we think, for example, about the difference between a cluster around voice-mediated relations as against a cluster of time spent together in shared spaces like games. This is an obvious point, but one that is not often made (Hutchby [2001] is an exception): different technologies provide different constraints and possibilities for "being there together," and if we put these on our three axes, we can begin to see what the futures of different media might look like.

This leads to what is perhaps the most comprehensive question that can be raised in relation to the intersection between the three dimensions of presence: Given that our relationship to the world is mediated by information and communication technology, what affordances, physical and social, do the various technologies for "being there together" provide? This is the question to which the end-states presented here can provide some suggestive answers (or perhaps raise further interesting questions). The end-state of MUVEs points to a particular form of the mediation of our physical and social worlds and particular forms of living in immersive virtual worlds. If, however, we do not take face-to-face relationships as a baseline but rather the approximations to this end-state, then we can ask: what do MUVEs, in contrast with other less immersive relations, "afford"? How do the levels of immersiveness and togetherness compare—with each other, rather than compared with face-to-face relations in the physical world? How do the computer-generated environments in which there is much control differ in this respect from the video-captured environments, which provide less control but more realism that is closer to face-to-face relations and to the physical environment with which we are familiar?

Many MUVEs provide a rich modality for "being there together" compared to other media, as well as offering more control. Yet, as we have seen, other media also provide a strong sense of mutual awareness and availability on an everyday basis, with different affordances and types of control. With the changing landscape of mediated relationships and new media technologies, the line between MUVEs and other new media technologies (which often include images and sounds of the other person and of the environment) that are shared over interpersonal networks are becoming increasingly blurred. Hence, a research program will be required that takes MUVEs beyond the laboratory and early uses, and beyond online gaming and social spaces, and puts "being there together" into the context of our multiple modes of "being there together" in everyday settings.

Figures 10.1 and 10.2 allow us to do this—to see individuals connected to others via various communication and interaction modalities, with face-to-face communication as only one among other possibilities. People are either immersed in the physical world or in the virtual world, stepping into and out of these constantly, and sometimes participating in several such worlds, yet limited by the fact that sensory attention needs to be focused on a limited set of people and features of the environment, which makes multiple simultaneous channels (communicative or relational or spatial multitasking) difficult. Increasing communication means that we are ever more continuously connected to others who are aware of our presence and copresence to a greater or lesser extent. If we think of the multiple devices for "being there together" that we use constantly throughout the day, it is possible to see that we need to manage our accessibility, mutual awareness, and focus of attention continuously with different affordances (or constraints and possibilities) in different technologies for mediated interaction. The design of MUVEs should therefore be informed by how best to combine different levels of "being there together" in our everyday lives. Further, MUVEs offer a laboratory both for researching and experimenting with a variety of VE types for finding these optimal configurations (as we saw in Chapter 7)—since the end-states are known.

The Future of Two End-States

To think about the future of "being there together," we can return to the two end-states (fully immersive VEs and fully immersive videoconferences) described in Chapter 1. Recall that the two have quite different affordances: In VEs, people's avatar representation and the environment can be programmed and designed in such a way that people can pass through each other, manipulate objects, fly around, and the like. In distributed videoconferences, the captured scene and the people in it must also be "assembled" at the other site(s) (which makes some of the possibilities of computer-generated VEs possible again), but insofar as the environment is captured realistically, the videoconferencing end-state has greater fidelity and cannot be manipulated as can a VE. These are two quite different end-states. It is of course possible to think of all sorts of variations that mix them or blur the lines between them (for example, a video-capture system in which a person can nevertheless "steer" his or her facial expression, or a system in which video-captured bodies are inserted into a virtual room or space, and the like). Still, it is useful to think of these as two extremes on a scale of "being there together."

This makes it straightforward to foresee the end-points of technological development. With other technologies, it is difficult to predict the future because there is a complex interplay between many parts: Here we can think, for example, of technologies relating to climate change or of the future developments of cars. MUVE and video-capture technology is not like this because, as already discussed, the technology has already been developed to a high standard in some forms, even if there is room for improvement. These improvements are partly to do with cost and partly to do with a number of technologies for display and interaction. A key factor, however, as should be clear from the findings presented, is that the gaps in our knowledge are mainly about how people interact with each other and with the environment—not about the technological possibilities and constraints.

Apart from this, it will be useful to compile the main reasons why technologies for being there together will and will not be widely adopted. We can start with why not:

- Videoconferencing has not been adopted widely although the technology has been available for decades. On the one hand, people do not feel the need to see each other to communicate; on the other, there is what can in shorthand terms be called the "I'm having a bad hair day" problem, which is that we do not like to be seen in certain circumstances. (Put in sociological terminology, audio-only or text-only communication means that we do not need our visual "frontstage" self-presentation.[6]

- Online worlds and MUVEs have proved to have a limited appeal in terms of the range of things that people want to do in "being there together."
- Economic activity in online worlds has so far mostly been "self-referential"—designing bodies and objects and buildings for online worlds. Except where there is an offline payoff (such as training in MUVEs for doing something better in the real world), it is difficult to see how it could be otherwise.
- It is difficult or impossible to arrange many in-world or in-space activities, such as large and small meetings, complex training, and many forms of co-visualization and co-manipulation, mainly for the social reasons that have been discussed (such as difficulties due to absent cues, limited focus of attention, size of groups).
- There is a limit to how multimodally copresent we want to be in view of the increasing volume of how we are already connected with others.

There are, however, many reasons why MUVEs will become more common:

- Time, money, and environmental reasons dictate less travel.
- Co-visualization and co-manipulation of spaces work well and there are important needs for it.
- It is possible to do many things together in online worlds and spaces that cannot be done in the real world.
- The technology for large and cheap 3D displays, intuitive devices for interaction, and bandwidth will all become cheaper and more widespread and diverse.
- People are sociable and like to see and manipulate things together, and as we have seen, interaction and sociability in MUVEs have advantages over real world sociability, and virtual shared spaces can be more imaginative, interesting, and useful than real ones.

In the future, our lives will increasingly involve "being there together" with others by means of a range of devices and modalities. MUVEs will be one option among others, and they will entail stepping into and out of room-size environments and devoting part of our attention to these environments on screens or displayed in glasses. Again, these scenarios will involve spending time or living in spaces populated by avatars or video-representations of people and jointly manipulating things and navigating together and communicating. Whatever the shape of "being there together" will be, it is useful to begin to think systematically about its mechanics and implications for our lives. One reason to think about these mechanisms and implications is that MUVEs are more malleable, in terms of the way the technology can be used on the way toward the two end-states, than others. To make MUVEs more enjoyable and useful places to interact, however, extending the reach of our knowledge about their uses, rather than technological development, will be the most important task.

NOTES

1. In fact, the Steed, Spante, Heldal, Axelsson, and Schroeder (2003) study with just over three hours and two persons in networked IPTs is the most long-term study in immersive MUVEs—in other words, the highest values for x and y, which also extends into z—that I am aware of.

2. I have mapped mediation via the old media of television and telephones in Chapters 5 and 6 of Schroeder (2007a). This is an historical mapping. It is interesting to reflect that with the advent of digital technologies that allow us to record and analyze people's mediated interactions much more powerfully, these kinds of data collection are currently mushrooming. Note that they will all fit within the schema for mediated forms of "being there together" insofar as they fit the definition of VEs, or approximate this definition.

3. Perhaps, again, some kind of brain–computer interface will make the brain think it is somewhere else, but this falls outside the definition of *displays* for the senses.

4. Boellstorff (2008: 112) also proposes "absence" as a good way to understand presence when he says that the use of the common abbreviation "away from keyboard" (or "afk") is one way to understand virtual worlds—in other words, a virtual world is something that you can be away from.

5. There will also be individual psychological differences in the experience on all three dimensions. Some of these have been explored in research, especially for spatial presence (for a recent discussion, see Jurnet, Carvallo-Beciu, and Madonaldo 2005). Yet apart from the experience of "presence," this research is still at a very early stage, and so we can focus on the nonpsychological factors here.

6. These are the limitations of videoconferencing as a medium; another constraint on the use of the technology is that there need to be enough other users who have access to the same technology to make it valuable.

References

Allwood, J. and Schroeder, R. (2000), Intercultural communication in virtual environments, *Intercultural Communication*, 3, April. http://www.immi.se/intercultural/nr3/allwood.htm

Anderson, J., Ashraf, N., Douther, C., and Jack, M. (2001). Presence and usability in shared space virtual conferencing, *Cyberpsychology and Behaviour*, 4(2), 287–305.

Antonijevic, S. (2008). From text to gesture online: A microethnographic analysis of nonverbal communication in the Second Life virtual environment, *Information, Communication and Society*, 11(2), 221–238.

Au, W. J. 2008. *The Making of Second Life: Notes from the New World*. New York: HarperCollins.

Axelsson, A.-S. (2002). The Digital Divide: Status differences in virtual environments, in R. Schroeder (Ed.), *The Social Life of Avatars: Presence and Interaction in Shared Virtual Environments* (pp. 188–204). London: Springer.

Axelsson, A.-S., Abelin, A., Heldal, I., Nilsson, A., Schroeder, R., and Wideström, J. (1999). Collaboration and communication in multi-user virtual environments: A comparison of desktop and immersive virtual reality systems for molecular visualization, in T. Fernando (Ed.), *Proceedings of the Sixth UKVRSIG Conference*, September 14, Salford University, pp. 107–117.

Axelsson, A.-S., Abelin, A. and Schroeder, R. (2003). 'Communication in Virtual Environments: Establishing Common Ground for a Collaborative Spatial Task?', *Proceedings of Presence* 2003, Aalborg, Denmark.

Axelsson, A.-S., and Regan, T. (2006). Playing online, in P. Vorderer and J. Bryant (Eds.), *Playing Video Games: Motives, Responses, Consequences* (pp. 291–306). Mahwah, NJ: Lawrence Erlbaum.

Bailenson, J. N. (2006). Transformed social interaction in collaborative virtual environments, in P. Messaris and L. Humphreys (Eds.), *Digital Media: Transformations in Human Communication* (pp. 255–264). New York: Peter Lang.

Bailenson, J. N., Beall, A. C., Loomis, J., Blascovich, J., and Turk, M. (2004). Transformed social interaction: decoupling representation from behavior and form in collaborative virtual environments, *Presence: Teleoperators and Virtual Environments,* 13(4), 428–441.

Bailenson, J. N., Beall., A. C., Blascovich, J., Loomis, J., and Turk, M. (2005). Transformed social interaction, augmented gaze, and social influence in immersive virtual environments, *Human Communication Research,* 31, 511–537.

Bailenson, J. N., Yee, N., Merget, D., and Schroeder, R. (2006). The effect of behavioral realism and form realism of real-time avatar faces on verbal disclosure, nonverbal disclosure, emotion recognition, and copresence in dyadic interaction, *Presence: Teleoperators and Virtual Environments,* 15(4), 359–372.

Bailenson, J. N., and Beall, A. C. (2006). Transformed social interaction: Exploring the digital plasticity of avatars, in R. Schroeder and A.-S. Axelsson (Eds.), *Avatars at Work and Play: Collaboration and Interaction in Shared Virtual Environments* (pp. 1–16), London: Springer.

Bailenson, J. N., Iyengar, S., Yee, N., and Collins, N. (2008). Facial similarity between voters and candidates causes influence, *Public Opinion Quarterly,* 72, 935–961.

Bainbridge, W. S. (2007). The scientific research potential of virtual worlds, *Science,* 317, 472–476.

Bainbridge, W. S. (2010). *Warcraft Civilization.* Cambridge, MA: MIT Press.

Bales, R. F., (1951). *Interaction Process Analysis; A Method for the Study of Small Groups.* Cambridge, MA: Addison-Wesley Press.

Bardzell, S., and Bardzell, J. (2006). Sex-interface-aesthetics: The docile avatars and embodied pixels of Second Life BDSM. *CHI 2006 World Conference on Human Factors in Computing Systems,* Montreal, Quebec.

Bardzell, S., and Bardzell, J. (2007). Docile avatars: Aesthetics, experience, and sexual interaction in Second Life. *Proceedings of the 21st British CHI Group Annual Conference on HCI 2007,* Lancaster, UK, pp. 3-12.

Bardzell, S., and Odom, W. (2008). The experience of embodied space in virtual worlds: Ethnography of a Second Life community, *Space and Culture,* 11(3), 239–259.

Baron, N. (2008). *Always On: Language in an Online and Mobile World.* New York: Oxford University Press.

Bartle, R. (1990). *Interactive multi-user computer games*. Retrieved April 10, 2009, from http://www.mud.co.uk/richard/imucgo.htm

Baym, N. (2002). Interpersonal life online, in L. Lievrouw and S. Livingstone (Eds.), *The Handbook of New Media* (pp. 62–76). London: Sage.

Baym, N. (2006). Interpersonal life online, in L. Lievrouw and S. Livingstone (Eds.), *The Handbook of New Media* (updated student edition; pp. 35–54). London: Sage.

Becker, B., and Mark, G. (2002). Social conventions in computer-mediated communication: A comparison of three online shared virtual environments, in R. Schroeder (Ed.), The Social Life of Avatars: Presence and Interaction in Shared Virtual Environments (pp. 19–39). London: Springer.

Benford, S., and Fahlen, L. (1992). Aura, focus and awareness, in L. Fahlen and K.-M. Jää-Aro (Eds.), *Proceedings of the Fifth Multi-G Workshop*. Stockholm: Royal Institute of Technology.

Benkler, Y. (2006). *The Wealth of Networks: How Social Production Transforms Markets and Freedom*. New Haven, CT: Yale University Press.

Bente, G., Rüggenberg, S., and Krämer, N. C. (2005). Virtual encounters. Creating social presence in net-based collaborations. *Proceedings of the 8th International Workshop on Presence,* London, September, pp. 21–23, 97–102.

Bente, G., Rüggenberg, S., Krämer, N., and Eschenburg, F. (2008). Avatar-mediated networking: Increasing social presence and interpersonal trust in net-based collaboration, *Human Communication Research,* 34, 287–318.

Biocca, F. (1997). The Cyborg's dilemma: Progressive embodiment in virtual environments, *Journal of Computer-Mediated Communication,* 3(2). www.ascusc.org/jcmc

Biocca, F., and Delaney, B. (1995). Immersive virtual reality technology, in F. Biocca and M. R. Levy (Eds.), *Communication in the age of virtual reality* (pp. 57–124). Hillsdale, NJ: Lawrence Erlbaum Associates.

Biocca, F., et al. (2002). Visual cues and virtual touch: Role of visual stimuli and intersensory integration in cross-modal haptic illusions and the sense of presence. *Presence 2002: Fifth International Workshop,* Porto, Portugal, October 9–11, pp. 376–394.

Biocca, F., Harms, C., and Burgoon, J. (2003). Toward a more robust theory and measure of social presence: Review and suggested criteria, *Presence: Journal of Teleoperators and Virtual Environments,* 12(5), 456–480.

Blascovich, J. (2002). Social influence within immersive virtual environments, in R. Schroeder (Ed.), *The Social Life of Avatars: Presence and Interaction in Shared Virtual Environments* (pp. 127–145). London: Springer.

Blascovich, J., Loomis, J., Beall, A., Swinth, K., Hoyt, C., and Bailenson, J. (2002). Immersive virtual environment technology as a methodological tool for social psychology, *Psychological Inquiry,* 13(2), 103–124.

Boellstorff, T. (2008). *Coming of Age in Second Life: An Anthropologist Explores the Virtually Human*. Princeton, NJ: Princeton University Press.

Börner, K., and Penumarthy, S. (2003). Social diffusion patterns in three-dimensional virtual worlds, *Information Visualization*, 2(3), 182–198.

Bowers, J., Pycock, J., and O'Brien, J. (1996). Talk and embodiment in collaborative virtual environments, *Proceedings of CHI'96*, ACM Press, pp. 58–65.

Bowman, D., Kruijff, E., LaViola, J., and Poupyrev, I. (2001). An introduction to 3-D user interface design, *Presence: Journal of Teleoperators and Virtual Environments*, 10(1), 96–108.

Bowman, D., Gabbard, J., and Hix, D., (2002). A survey of usability evaluation in virtual environments: Classification and comparison of methods, *Presence: Teleoperators and Virtual Environments*, 11(4), 404–424.

Bowman, D., Kruijff, E., LaViola, J., and Poupyrev, I. (2004). *3D User Interfaces: Theory and Practice*. Boston: Addison-Wesley.

Bridgestock, M., Burch, D., Forge, J., Laurent, J., and Lowe, I. (1998). *Science, Technology and Society: An Introduction*. Cambridge: Cambridge University Press.

Brooks, F. P. (1999). What's real about virtual reality? *IEEE Computer Graphics and Applications*, 19(6), 16–27.

Brown, B., and Bell, M. (2006). Play and sociability in there: Some lessons from online games for collaborative virtual environments, in R. Schroeder and A.-S. Axelsson (Eds.), *Avatars at Work and Play: Collaboration and Interaction in Shared Virtual Environments* (pp. 227–245). London: Springer.

Bull, P. (2002). *Communication under the Microscope: The Theory and Practice of Microanalysis*. Hove, East Sussex: Routledge.

Burgoon, J., Bonito, J., Bengtsson, B., Ramirez, A., Dunbar, N., and Miczo, N. (2000). Testing the interactivity model: Communication processes, partner assessments, and the quality of collaborative work, *Journal of Management Information Systems*, 16, 33–56.

Castronova, E. (2001). Virtual worlds: A first-hand account of market and society on the Cyberian Frontier, *The Gruter Institute Working Papers on Law, Economics, and Evolutionary Biology*, 2, article 1. http://www.bepress.com/giwp/default/vol2/iss1/art1

Castronova, E. (2005). *Synthetic Worlds: The Business and Culture of Online Games*. Chicago: University of Chicago Press.

Cawson, A., Haddon, L., and Miles, I. (1995). *The Shape of Things to Consume: Delivering Information Technology into the Home*. Aldershot, UK: Ashgate Publishing.

Cheng, L., Farnham, S., and Stone, L. (2002). Lessons learned: Building and deploying shared virtual environments, in R. Schroeder (Ed.), *The Social Life of Avatars: Presence and Interaction in Shared Virtual Environments* (pp. 90–111). London: Springer.

Cherny, L. (1999). *Conversation and Community: Chat in a Virtual World*. Cambridge: Cambridge University Press.

Churchill, E., Snowdon, D., and Munro, A. (Eds.) (2001). *Collaborative Virtual Environments: Digital Spaces and Places for Interaction*. London: Springer.

Cohen, M., and Wenzel, E. (1995). The design of multidimensional sound interfaces, in W. Barfield and T. A. Furness (Eds.), *Virtual Environments and Advanced Interface Design* (pp. 291–346). New York: Oxford University Press.

Collins, R.(1988). *Theoretical Sociology*. New York: Harcourt Brace Jovanovich.

Collins, R. (1994). Why the social sciences won't become high-consensus, rapid-discovery science, *Sociological forum* 9(2): 155-177.

Collins, R. (2004). *Interaction Ritual Chains*. Princeton, NJ: Princeton University Press.

Crabtree, A. (2003). *Designing Collaborative Systems: A Practical Guide to Ethnography*. London: Springer.

Craven, C. et al. (2000). Ages of Avatar: Community Building for Inhabited Television. In E. Churchill and M. Reddy (Eds.) *CVE2000: Proceedings of the Third International Conference on Collaborative Virtual Environments*. New York: ACM Press, pp. 189-194.

Cruz-Neira, C., Sandin, D., and DeFanti, T. (1993). Surround-screen projection-based virtual reality: The design and implementation of the CAVE, *Proceedings of SIGGRAPH 93*, pp. 135–142.

Crystal, D. (2001). *Language and the Internet*. Cambridge: Cambridge University Press.

Csikszentmihalyi, M. (1990). *Flow: The Psychology of Optimal Experience*. New York: Harper & Row.

Curtis, P. (1992). *Mudding: Social Phenomena in Text-Based Virtual Realities*. Palo Alto, CA: Xerox PARC (unpublished technical report).

Damer, B. (1998). *Avatars! Virtual Worlds*. Berkeley, CA: Peachpit Press.

Damer, B., Gold, S., de Bruin, J., and de Bruin D.-J. (2000). Conferences and trade shows in inhabited virtual worlds: A case study of Avatars 98&99, in J.-C. Hedin (Ed.), *Virtual Worlds. Lecture Notes in Computer Science* (pp. 1–11). Berlin: Springer.

Danet, B. and Herring, S. (Eds.). (2007). *The Multilingual Internet: Language, Culture and Communication Online*. Oxford: Oxford University Press.

DiMaggio, P.J., Hargittai, E., Neuman, W.R. and Robinson, J. (2001). Social Implications of the Internet. *Annual Review of Sociology*. 27, 307–336.

Dodds, T. J., and Ruddle, R. A. (2008). Mobile group dynamics in large-scale collaborative virtual environments. *Proceedings of IEEE Virtual Reality (VR'08)*, pp. 59–66.

Donath, J. (2001). Mediated faces, in M. Beynon, C. L. Nehaniv, and K. Dautenhahn (Eds.), *Cognitive Technology: Instruments of Mind, Proceedings of the 4th International Conference,* Warwick, UK, August 6–9, 2001, pp. 373–390.

Ducheneaut, N., and Moore, R. J. (2004). Gaining more than experience points: Learning social behavior in multiplayer computer games. *CHI 2004 Workshop on Social Learning Through Gaming,* April 19, Vienna.

Ducheneaut, N., Yee, E., Nickell, E., and Moore, R. J. (2006). Building an MMO with mass appeal: A look at gameplay in World of Warcraft, *Games and Culture,* 1(4), 281–317.

Ducheneaut, N., Yee, N., Nickell, E., and Moore, R. J. (2006). Alone together? Exploring the social dynamics of massively multiplayer games. *Proceedings of the SIGCHI conference on Human Factors in computing systems 2006*, Montreal, PQ, Canada, 407–416.

Durlach, N. and Slater, M. (2000). Presence in Shared Virtual Environments and Virtual Togetherness, *Presence: Teleoperators and Virtual Environments* 9(2), 214–217.

Ellis, S. (1995). Origins and elements of virtual environments, in W. Barfield and T. Furness (Eds.), *Virtual Environments and Advanced Interface Design* (pp. 14–57). New York: Oxford University Press.

Ess, C., and the Association of Internet Researchers (AoIR) Ethics Working Group. (2002). *Ethical Decision-Making and Internet Research: Recommendations from the AoIR Ethics Working Committee*. www.aoir.org/reports/ethics.pdf

Ess, C. (2006). Ethics and the use of the Internet in social science research, in Joinson, A., McKenna, K., Postmes, T., and Reips, U.-D. (Eds.) *Oxford Handbook of Internet Psychology*. Oxford and New York: Oxford University Press, pp. 487–503.

Eynon, R., Fry, J., and Schroeder, R. (2008) The ethics of Internet research, in G. Blank, R. Lee, and N. Fielding (Eds.) *Handbook of Online Research Methods* (pp. 23–42). London: Sage.

Fielding, N., and Macintyre, M. (2006). Access Grid nodes in field research, *Sociological Research Online*, 11(2). www.socresonline.org.uk/11/2/fielding.html

Finn, K. (1997), Introduction: An overview of video-mediated communication literature, in K. Finn, A. Sellen, and S. Wilbur (Eds.), *Video-Mediated Communication* (pp. 3–21). Mahwah, NJ: Lawrence Erlbaum.

Finn, K., Sellen, A., and Wilbur, S. (Eds.) (1997). *Video-Mediated Communication*. Mahwah, NJ: Lawrence Erlbaum.

Fischer, C. (1992). *America Calling: A Social History of the Telephone to 1940*. Berkeley: University of California Press.

Fox, J., Arena, D., and Bailenson, J. (2009). Virtual reality: A survival guide for the social scientist. *Journal of Media Psychology*, 21(3), 95–113.

Fraser, M. (2000). *Working with Objects in Collaborative Virtual Environments*. Ph.D. dissertation, Computer Science Department, University of Nottingham.

Frécon, E., and Stenius, M., (1999). DIVE: A scaleable network architecture for distributed virtual environments, *Distributed Systems Engineering Journal: Special Issue on Distributed Virtual Environments*.

Frécon, E., Smith, G., Steed, A., Stenius, M., and Stahl, O. (2001). An overview of the COVEN platform, *Presence: Teleoperators and Virtual Environments*, 10(1), 109–127.

Friedman, D., Steed, A., and Slater, M. (2007). Spatial behaviour in Second Life, in C. Pelachaud (Ed.), *Intelligent Virtual Agents* (pp. 252–263). New York: Springer.

Fry, J. (2006). Google's privacy responsibilities at home and abroad [editorial], *Journal of Librarianship and Information Science*, 38(3), 135–139.

Gabbard, J. L., and Hix, D. (1997). *A Taxonomy of Usability Characteristics in Virtual Environments*. Blacksburg:Virginia Polytechnic Institute and State University.

Garau, M. 2003. *The Impact of Avatar Fidelity on Social Interaction in Virtual Environments*. Ph.D. thesis, Department of Computer Science, University College London.

Garau, M. (2006). Selective fidelity: Investigating priorities for the creation of expressive avatars, in R. Schroeder and A.-S. Axelsson (Eds.). *Avatars at Work and Play: Collaboration and Interaction in Shared Virtual Environments* (pp. 17–38). London: Springer.

Goffman, E. (1959). *The Presentation of Self in Everyday Life*. New York: Doubleday.

Greenhalgh, C. M., Bullock, A. N., Tromp, J. G., and Benford, S. D., (1997). Evaluating the network and usability characteristics of virtual reality conferencing, *The British Telecom Technology Journal (BTTJ), Special Issue on Shared Spaces*, 15(4).

Gross, M., Wurmlin, S., Naef, E., Lamboray, C., et al. (2003). blue-C: A spatially immersive display and 3D video portal for telepresence, *Proceedings of ACM SIGGRAPH, July,* pp. 819–827.

Haddon, L., and Kim, S.-D. (2007), Mobile phones and Web-based social networking: Emerging practices in Korea with Cyworld, *Journal of the Communications Network* 6(1), January–March.

Harris, H., Bailenson, J., Nielsen, A., and Yee, N. (2009). The evolution of social behaviour over time in Second Life. *Presence: Journal of Teleoperators and Virtual Environments,* 18(6) 294–303.

Harrison, S. (Ed.). (2009). *Media Space: 20+ Years of Mediated Life*. London: Springer.

Heldal, I. (2004). *The Usability of Collaborative Virtual Environments: Towards an Evaluation Framework*. Ph.D. dissertation, Chalmers University, Gothenburg.

Heldal, I., Schroeder, R., Steed, A., Axelsson, A.-S., Spante, M., and Wideström, J. (2005a). Immersiveness and Symmetry in Copresent Scenarios. *Proceedings of IEEE VR 2005*, Bonn, Germany, pp. 171-178.

Heldal, I., Steed, A., and Schroeder, R. (2005). Evaluating collaboration in distributed virtual environments for a puzzle-solving task. *HCI International 2005, the 11th International Conference on Human Computer Interaction,* 22–27 July 2005, Las Vegas

Heldal, I., Steed, S., Spante, M. Schroeder, R., Bengtsson, S., and Partanen, M. (2005b). Successes and failures in co-present situations, *Presence: Journal of Teleoperators and Virtual Environments,* 14(5), 563–579.

Heldal, I., Spante, M., and Connell, M. (2006a). Are two heads better than one? Object-focused work in physical and virtual environments, in *Proceedings of VRST'06,* Limmasol, Cyprus, November 1–3, pp. 287–296.

Heldal, I., Brathe, L., Steed, A. and Schroeder, R. (2006 b). Interaction Fragments influencing Collaboration in Distributed Virtual Environments, in R. Schroeder and A.-S. Axelsson (Eds.), *Avatars at Work and Play: Collaboration and Interaction in Shared Virtual Environments*. London: Springer, pp. 97–130.

Hindmarsh, J., Fraser, M., Heath, C., Benford, S., and Greenhalgh, C. (1998). Fragmented Interaction: Establishing mutual orientation in virtual environments, *Proceedings of the ACM Conference on Computer Supported Cooperative Work (CSCW'98)*, pp. 217–226.

Hindmarsh, J., Fraser, M., Heath, C., and Benford, S. (2002). Virtually missing the point: Configuring CVEs for object-focused interaction, in E. Churchill, D. Snowdon, and A. Munro (Eds.), *Collaborative Virtual Environments: Digital Places and Spaces for Interaction* (pp. 115–139). London: Springer.

Hinds, P., and Kiesler, S. (Eds.) (2002). *Distributed Work*. Cambridge, MA: MIT Press.

Hirose, M., Ogi, T., and Yamada, T. (1999). Integrating Live Video for Immersive Environments, *IEEE MultiMedia*, 6(3): 14-22.

Hirsh, S., Sellen, A., and Brokopp, N. (2005). Why HP people do and don't use videoconferencing systems. *Technical Report HPL-2004-140R1*, Hewlett-Packard Laboratories, Bristol, UK. http://www.hpl.hp.com/research/mmsl/publications/bristol.html

Holmes, J. G., and Rempel, J. K. (1989). Trust in close relationships, in C. Hendrick (Ed.), *Close Relationships*. Newbury Park: Sage.

Hudson-Smith, A. (2002) 30 Days in ActiveWorlds Community, design and terrorism in a virtual world, in R. Schroeder (Ed.), *The Social Life of Avatars: Presence and Interaction in Shared Virtual Environments* (pp. 77–89). London: Springer.

Hughes, T. (1998). *Rescuing Prometheus*. New York: Pantheon Books.

Hutchby, I. (2001). *Conversation and Technology: From the Telephone to the Internet*. Cambridge: Polity.

Ijsselsteijn, W. (2003). Presence in the past: What can we learn from media history? in G. Riva, F. Davide, W. A. IJsselsteijn (Eds.), *Being There: Concepts, Effects and Measurement of User Presence in Synthetic Environments* (pp. 17–39). Amsterdam: IOS Press.

Ito, M., and Okabe, D. (2005). Technosocial situations: Emergent structuring of mobile e-mail use, in M. Ito, D. Okabe, and M. Matsuda (Eds.), *Personal, Portable, Pedestrian: Mobile Phones in Everyday Life* (pp. 257–273). Cambridge: MIT Press.

Jacobsen, J. (2003). Using "Cave UT" to build immersive displays with the unreal tournament engine and a PC cluster. *ACM SIGGRAPH* 2003 *Symposium on Interactive 3D Graphics*, pp. 221–222.

Jakobsson, M. (2002). Rest in peace, Bill the Bot: Death and life in virtual worlds, in R. Schroeder (Ed.), *The Social Life of Avatars: Presence and Interaction in Shared Virtual Environments* (pp. 63–76). London: Springer.

Jää-Aro, K.-M. (2004). *Reconsidering the Avatar: From User Mirror to Interaction Locus.* Ph.D. thesis, Royal Institute of Technology, Stockholm.

Kalawsky, R. (1993). *The Science of Virtual Reality and Virtual Environments.* Boston: Addison Wesley.

Kaur, K. (1998). *Designing virtual environments for usability,* Center for Human-Computer Interface Design. Unpublished Ph.D. thesis. London: City University.

Kiesler, S., and Cummings, J. (2002). What do we know about proximity and distance in work groups? A legacy of research, in S. Kiesler and P. Hinds (Eds.), *Distributed Work* (pp. 57–80). Cambridge, MA: MIT Press.

Kirk, D., Sellen, A., and Cao, X. (2010). Wish you were Here: Home video communication: Mediating closeness. *Proceedings of CSCW 2010,* Savannah, Georgia, pp. 135–144.

Klimmt, C., and Vorderer, P. (2003), Media psychology "is not yet there": Introducing theories on media entertainment to the presence debate, *Presence: Journal of Teleoperators and Virtual Environments,* 12(4), 346–359.

Kraut, R., Gergle, D., and Fussell, S. (2002). The use of visual information in shared visual spaces: Informing the development of virtual co-presence, in *Proceedings of CSCW 2002,* November 16–20, New Orleans, LA, pp. 31–40.

Lastowka, F. G. (2008). Virtual law. *Presented at the Cultures of Virtual Worlds conference,* University of California-Irvine (April 2008).

Lastowka, F. G, and Hunter, D. (2003). The laws of the virtual worlds. *University of Pennsylvania Law School Working Paper,* available online from Social Science Research Electronic Paper Collection, www.ssrn.com.

Lea, M., and Spears, R. (1995). Love at first byte? Building personal relationships over computer networks, in J. T. Wood and S. Duck (Eds.), *Understudied Relationships: Off the Beaten Track.* Thousand Oaks, CA: Sage Publications.

Lee, K. M., and Peng, W. (2006). What do we know about social and psychological effects of computer games? A comprehensive review of the current literature, in P. Vorderer and J. Bryant (Eds.), *Playing Video Games: Motives, Responses, and Consequences* (pp. 327–345). Mahwah, NJ: Lawrence Erlbaum.

Lee, R. (1993) *Doing Research on Sensitive Topics.* London: Sage.

Lenhart, A., and Madden. M. (2007). Social networking and teens: An overview. *Pew Internet and American Life Project.* http://www.pewinternet.org/PPF/r/198/report_display.asp

Lenoir, T. (1999). Virtual reality comes of age, in *Funding a Revolution: Government Support for Computing Research* (pp. 226–249). Washington, DC: National Research Council.

Lessiter, J., Freeman, J., Keogh, E., and Davidoff, J. (2001). A cross-media presence questionnaire: The ITC-Sense of Presence Inventory, *Presence: Journal of Teleoperators and Virtual Environment,* 10(3), 282–297.

Lewis, K., Kaufman, J., Gonzalez, M., Wimmer, A., and Christakis, N. (2008). Taste, ties and time: A new social network dataset using Facebook.com, *Social Networks*, 30(4), 330–342.

Licoppe, C. (2004). "Connected" presence: The emergence of a new repertoire for managing social relationships in a changing communication technoscape, *Environment and Planning D: Society and Space*, 22, 135–156.

Licoppe, C., and Inada, Y. (2006). Emergent uses of a multiplayer location-aware mobile game: The interactional consequences of mediated encounters, *Mobilities*, 1(1), 39–61.

Licoppe, C. and Smoreda, Z. (2006). Rythms and Ties: Toward a Pragmatics of Technologically Mediated Sociability, in R. Kraut, M. Brynin and S. Kiesler (Eds.). *Computers, Phones and the Internet: Domesticating Information Technology*. New York: Oxford University Press, pp. 296–313.

Ling, R. (2004). *The Mobile Connection: The Cell Phone's Impact on Society*. Amsterdam: Morgan Kaufmann.

Ling, R. (2008). New Tech, *New Ties: How Mobile Communication is Reshaping Social Cohesion*. Cambridge, MA: MIT Press.

Löber, A., Schwabe, G., and Grimm, S. (2007). Audio vs. chat: The effects of group size on media choice. *Proceedings of the 40th HICCS Hawaii International Conference on System Sciences*, pp.41b.

Löber, A., Grimm, S., and Schwabe, G. (2006). Audio vs. chat: Can media speed explain the differences in productivity? *Proceedings of the European Conference on Information Systems*, available at http://is2.lse.ac.uk/asp/aspecis/

Lok, B., Naik, S., Whitton, M., and Brooks, F. (2003). Effects of Interaction modality and avatar fidelity on task performance and sense of presence in virtual environments, *Presence: Journal of Teleoperators and Virtual Environments*, 12(6), 615–628.

Lombard, M., and Ditton, T. (1997). At the heart of it all: The concept of presence. *Journal of Computer-Mediated Communication*, 3(2). www.ascusc.org/jcmc

Meehan, M., Insko, B., Whitton, M., and Brooks, F. (2002). Physiological measures of presence in stressful virtual environments, *ACM Transactions of Graphics, Proceedings of ACM SIGGRAPH 2002*, 21(3), pp. 645–653.

Meyrowitz, J. (1985). *No Sense of Place: The Impact of Electronic Media on Social Behaviour*. Oxford: Oxford University Press.

Misztal, B. (1996). *Trust in Modern Societies*. Cambridge: Polity Press.

Mori, M. (1970). Bukimi no tani (The uncanny valley). *Energy*, 7(4), 33–35.

Morningstar, C., and Farmer, R. (1991) The lessons of Lucasfilm's habitat, in M. Benedikt (Ed.), *Cyberspace: First Steps* (pp. 273–301). Cambridge, MA: MIT Press.

Munro, Höök, K., and Benyon, D. (1999). (Eds). *Social Navigation of Information Space*. London: Springer.

Nardi, B. (2010). *My Life as a Night Elf Priest: An Anthropological Account of World of Warcraft*. Ann Arbor: University of Michigan Press.

Nardi, B., Whitaker, S., and Bradner. E. (2000). Interaction and Outeraction: Instant Messaging in Action. *Proceedings of CSCW'00*, December 2–6, Philadelphia, PA, ACM, pp. 79–88.

Nardi, B., and Whitaker, S. (2002). The place of face-to-face communication in distributed work, in P. Hinds and S. Kiesler (Eds.), *Distributed Work* (pp. 83–110). Cambridge, MA: MIT Press.

Nardi, B., and Harris, J. (2006). Strangers and friends: Collaborative play in World of Warcraft, in *Proceedings of CSCW'06*, Banff, Canada, November 4–8, pp. 149–158.

Nesson, R., and Nesson, C. (2008). The case for education in virtual worlds, *Space and Culture*, 11(3), 273–284.

Nilsson, A., Heldal, I., Schroeder, R., and Axelsson. (2002). The long-term uses of shared virtual environments: An exploratory study, in R. Schroeder (Ed.), *The Social Life of Avatars: Presence and Interaction in Shared Virtual Environments* (pp. 112–126). London: Springer.

Nisenfeld, S. (n.d.). *Using Reality to Evaluate the ITC Presence Questionnaire* (unpublished paper, Brown University).

Nissenbaum, H. (1998). Protecting privacy in an information age: The problem of privacy in public, *Law and Philosophy*, 17, 559–596.

Norberg, A., and O'Neill, J. (1996). *Transforming Computer Technology: Information Processing at the Pentagon, 1962–1986*. Baltimore, MD: Johns Hopkins University Press.

Oldenburg, R. (1989). *The Great Good Place*. New York: Marlowe and Company.

Olson, G., and Olson, J. (2000). Distance matters, *Human-Computer Interaction*, 15, 139–179.

Osterhammel, J. (1994). Raumerfassung und Universalgeschichte im 20. Jahrhundert, in G. Huebinger, J. Osterhammel, and E. Pelzer (Eds.), *Universalgeschichte und Nationalgeschichten* (pp. 51–74), Freiburg: Rombach.

Pan, X. (2009). *Experimental studies of the interaction between people and virtual humans with a focus on social anxiety*. Ph.D. thesis, Department of Computer Science, University College London.

Pargman, D. (2000). *Code begets community: On social and technical aspects of managing a virtual community*. Ph.D. thesis, Department of Communication Studies, The Tema Institute, Linkoping University, Sweden.

Pausch, R., Proffitt, D., and Williams, G. (1997). Quantifying immersion in virtual reality. *Proceedings of the 24th annual conference on Computer Graphics and Interactive Techniques*, August 1997, pp. 13–18.

Penumarthy, S., and Boerner, K. (2006). Analysis and visualization of social diffusion patterns in three-dimensional virtual worlds, in R. Schroeder and

A.-S. Axelsson (Eds.), *Avatars at Work and Play: Collaboration and Interaction in Shared Virtual Environments* (pp. 39–61), London: Springer.

Persky, S., and Blascovich, J. (2006). Consequences of playing violent video games in immersive virtual environments, R. Schroeder and A.-S. Axelsson (Eds.), *Avatars at Work and Play: Collaboration and Interaction in Shared Virtual Environments* (pp. 167–186), London: Springer.

Raskar, R., Welch', G., Cutts, M., Lake, A., Stesin, L., and Fuchs, H. (1998). The office of the future: a unified approach to image-based modeling and spatially immersive displays, in *Proceedings of the 25th Annual Conference on Computer Graphics and interactive Techniques SIGGRAPH'98* (pp. 179–188). New York: ACM Press.

Reeves, B., and Nass, C. (1996). *The Media Equation: How People Treat Computers, Television and New Media Like Real People and Places.* Cambridge: Cambridge University Press.

Rheingold, H. (1991). *Virtual Reality.* London: Secker and Warburg.

Riegelsberger, J., Sasse, A., and McCarthy, J. (2007). Trust in mediated interactions, in K. McKenna, T. Postmes, U. Reips, and A. N. Joinson (Eds.), *Oxford Handbook of Internet Psychology* (pp. 53–69). Oxford: Oxford University Press.

Rittenbruch, M., and McEwan, G. (2007). *Awareness Survey: A historical reflection of awareness in collaboration, HxI Technical Report*, March 21. Retrieved Februrary 16, 2009, from http://www.hxi.org.au/index.php?option=com_contentandtask=blogsectionandid=12andItemid=55

Roberts, D., Wolff, R., Otto, S., and Steed, A. (2003). Constructing a gazebo: Supporting team work in a tightly coupled, distributed task in virtual reality, *Presence: Journal of Teleoperators and Virtual Environments,* 12(6), 644–668.

Sadagic, A., Towles, H., Holden, L., Daniilidis, K., and Zeleznik. B. (2001). Tele-immersion portal: Towards an ultimate synthesis of computer graphics and computer vision systems. *Fourth Annual International Workshop on Presence,* Philadelphia, PA, May 21–23, 2001.

Sallnas, E.-L. (2002). Collaboration in multi-modal virtual worlds: Comparing touch and text and voice and video, in R. Schroeder (Ed.), *The Social Life of Avatars: Presence and Interaction in Shared Virtual Environments* (pp. 172–187). London: Springer.

Sallnas, E.-L. (2004). *The effect of modality on social presence, presence and performance in collaborative virtual environments.* Ph.D. thesis, Royal Institute of Technology, Stockholm.

Scheumie, M.J., van der Straaten, P. Krijn, M., and van der Mast, C. (2001). Research on presence in virtual reality: A survey, *Cyberpsychology and Behaviour,* 4(2), 183–201.

Schiano, D. (1999). Lessons from LambdaMOO: A social, text-based virtual environment, *Presence: Journal of Teleoperators and Virtual Environments,* 8(2), 127–139.

Schiano, D., and White, S. (1998). The first noble truth of cyberspace: People are people (even when they MOO), in *Proceedings of CHI 1998*, pp. 352–359.

Schroeder, R. (1996). *Possible Worlds: The Social Dynamic of Virtual Reality Technology*. Boulder, CO: Westview.

Schroeder, R. (1997). Networked worlds: Social aspects of networked multi-user virtual reality technology, *Sociological Research Online*, 2(4). http://www. socresonline.org.uk/socresonline/2/4/5.html

Schroeder, R. (Ed.) (2002). *The Social Life of Avatars: Presence and Interaction in Shared Virtual Environments*. London: Springer.

Schroeder, R. (2002). Copresence and interaction in virtual environments: An overview of the range of issues, *Presence 2002: Fifth International Workshop*, Porto, Portugal, October 9–11, pp. 274–295.

Schroeder, R. (2006). Being there and the future of connected presence, *Presence: Journal of Teleoperators and Virtual Environments*, 15(4), 438–454.

Schroeder, R. (2007). *Rethinking Science, Technology and Social Change*. Stanford: Stanford University Press.

Schroeder, R. (2010). Mobile phones and the inexorable advance of multimodal connectedness, *New Media and Society*, 12(1), 1–16.

Schroeder, R., Heather, N., and Lee, R. (1998). The sacred and the virtual: Religion in multi-user virtual reality, *Journal of Computer-Mediated Communication*, 2(14). http://www.ascusc.org/jcmc/vol4/issue2/schroeder.html

Schroeder, R., and Axelsson, A.-S. (2001). Trust in the core: A study of long-term users of Activeworlds. *Digital Borderlands, a Cybercultural Symposium*, Norrköping, Sweden, May 12–13.

Schroeder, R., Huxor, A., and Smith, A. (2001). Activeworlds: Geography and social interaction in virtual reality, *Futures: A Journal of Forecasting, Planning and Policy*. 33: 569–87.

Schroeder, R., Steed, A.-S. Axelsson, A.S., Heldal, I., Abelin, A., Wideström, J., Nilsson, A., and Slater, M. (2001). Collaborating in networked immersive spaces: As good as being there together? *Computers and Graphics*, 25(5), 781–788.

Schroeder, R. and Axelsson, A.-S. (Eds.). (2006). *Avatars at Work and Play: Collaboration and Interaction in Shared Virtual Environments*. London: Springer.

Schroeder. R., Heldal, I., and Tromp, J. (2006). The usability of collaborative virtual environments and methods for the analysis of interaction, *Presence: Journal of Teleoperators and Virtual Environments*, 15(6), 655–667.

Schroeder, R., and Bailenson, J. (2008). Research uses of multi-user virtual environments, in G. Blank, R. Lee and N. Fielding (Eds.), *Handbook of Online Research Methods* (pp. 327–342). London: Sage.

Schubert, T., Friedmann, F., and Regenbrecht, H. (2002). The experience of presence; Factor analytic insights. *Presence: Journal of Teleoperators and Virtual Environments*, 10(3), 266–232.

Scott, C. R. (1999). Communication technology and group communication, in L. R. Frey (Ed.), *The Handbook of Group Communication Theory and Research* (pp. 432–472). Thousand Oaks, CA: Sage.

Sellen, A. (1997). Assessing video-mediated communication: A comparison of different analytic approaches, in K. Finn, A. Sellen, and S. Wilbur (Eds.), *Video-Mediated Communication* (pp. 95–106). Mahwah, NJ: Lawrence Erlbaum.

Shanahan, J., and Morgan, M. (1999). *Television and Its Viewers: Cultivation Theory and Research.* Cambridge: Cambridge University Press.

Short, J., Williams, E., and Christie, B. (1976). *The social psychology of telecommunications.* London: John Wiley.

Shotton, M. (1989). *Computer Addiction? A Study of Computer Dependency.* London: Taylor and Francis.

Singhal, S. and Zyda, M., (1999). *Networked Virtual Environments: Design and Implementation.* Reading, MA: Addison Wesley.

Slater, M. (2004). How colorful was your day? Why questionnaires cannot assess presence in virtual environments, *Presence: Journal of Teleoperators and Virtual Environments,* 13(4), 484–493.

Slater, M. (2009). Place illusion and plausibility can lead to realistic behaviour in immersive virtual environments. *Philosophical Transactions of the Royal Society B,* 364: 3549–3557.

Slater, M., and Steed, A. (2000). A virtual presence counter. *Presence: Journal of Teleoperators and Virtual Environments,* 9(5), 413–434.

Slater, M., Sadagic, A., Usoh, M. and Schroeder, R. (2000). Small group behaviour in a virtual and real environment: A comparative study, *Presence: Journal of Teleoperators and Virtual Environments,* 9(1), 37–51.

Slater, M., Steed, A., and Chrysanthou, Y. (2001). *Computer Graphics and Virtual Environments: From Realism to Real-Time.* Reading, MA: Addison Wesley.

Slater, M., and Steed, A. (2002). Meeting people virtually: Experiments in shared virtual environments, in R. Schroeder (Ed.), *The Social Life of Avatars: Presence and Interaction in Shared Virtual Environments* (pp. 146–171). London: Springer.

Slater, M., Antley, A., Davison A., Swapp, D., Guger, C., Barker, C., Pistrang, N., Sanchez-Vives, M. (2006). A virtual reprise of the Stanley Milgram obedience experiments, *PLoS ONE,* 1(1): e39.

Smith, M., Farnham, S., and Drucker, S. (2002). The social life of small graphical chat spaces, in R. Schroeder (Ed.), *The Social Life of Avatars: Presence and Interaction in Shared Virtual Environments* (pp. 205–220). London: Springer.

Sonnenwald, D. (2003). Collaboration in the large: Using video conferencing to facilitate large group interaction, in *Collaboration in the Large* (pp. 115–136). Hershey, PA: Idea Group Publishing.

Sonnenwald, D., Whitton, M., and Maglaughlin, K. (2003). Evaluating a scientific collaboratory: Results of a controlled experiment, *ACM Transactions on Human-Computer Interaction,* 10(2), 150–176.

Sonnenwald, D. (2006). Collaborative Virtual Environments for Scientific Collaboration: Technical and Organizational Design Frameworks. In R. Schroeder and A.-S. Axelsson (Eds.), *Avatars at Work and Play: Interaction and Collaboration in Shared Virtual Environments*. (pp.63–96) London: Springer.

Spante, M. (2009). *Connected Practice: The Dynamics of Social Interaction in Shared Virtual Environments* Ph.D. Dissertation. Chalmers University of Technology.

Spence, J. (2008a). Demographics of virtual worlds, *Journal of Virtual Worlds Research*, 1(2). http://www.jvwresearch.org/v1n2.html.

Spence, J. (2008b). Virtual worlds research: Consumer behaviour in virtual worlds, *Journal of Virtual Worlds Research*, 1(2). http://jvwresearch.org/index.php?_cms=1248913220

Stanney, K. M., Mourant, R. R., and Kennedy, R. (1998). Human factors issues in virtual reality: A review of the literature, *Presence: Teleoperators and Virtual Environments,* 7(4), 327–351.

Steed, A., Benford, S., Dalton, N., Greenhalgh, C., MacColl, I. Randell, C. and Schnadelbach, H. (2002). Mixed reality interfaces to immersive projection systems. *Immersive Projection Technology Workshop*, March 2002, Orlando, FL.

Steed, A., Spante, M., Heldal, I., Axelsson, A.-S., and Schroeder, R. (2003). Strangers and friends in caves: An exploratory study of collaboration in networked IPT systems. *ACM SIGGRAPH 2003 Proceedings on Interactive 3D Graphics* (pp. 51–54). New York: ACM Press.

Steed, A., and Parker, C. (2004). 3D Selection Strategies for Head Tracked and Non-Head Tracked Operation of Spatially Immersive Displays. *8th International Immersive Projection Technology Workshop*. Available at http://www.cs.ucl.ac.uk/staff/a.steed/papers.html (last accessed June 10, 2010).

Steed, A., Roberts, D., Schroeder, R., and Heldal, I. (2005). Personal interaction between users of immersion projection technology systems. *HCI International 2005, the 11th International Conference on Human Computer Interaction, 22–27 July 2005*, Las Vegas, NV.

Steed, A., and Oliveira, M. F. (2010). *Networked Graphics: Building Networked Games and Virtual Environments*. San Francisco: Morgan Kaufman.

Steen, F., Davies, M. S., Tynes, B., and Greenfield, P. (2006). Digital dystopia: Player control and strategic innovation in the Sims Online, in R. Schroeder and A.-S. Axelsson (Eds.), *Avatars at Work and Play: Collaboration and Interaction in Shared Virtual Environments* (pp. 247–273). London: Springer.

Stephenson, N. (1992). *Snow Crash*. New York: Bantam.

Steptoe, W., Wolff, R., Murgia, A. Guimaraes, E., Rae, J., Sharkey, P., Roberts, D., and Steed, A. (Forthcoming). Eye-tracking for avatar eye-gaze and interactional analysis in immersive collaborative virtual environments. *ACM Conference on Computer Supported Cooperative Work*.

Steptoe, W., Steed, A., Rovira, A., and Rae, J. (2010). Lie tracking: Social presence, truth and deception in avatar-mediated telecommunication. *Proceedings of CHI 2010*. Atlanta, GA, April.

Steinkuehler, C., and Williams, D. (2006). Where everybody knows your (screen) name: Online games as "third places," *Journal of Computer-Mediated Communication,* 11(4). http://jcmc.indiana.edu/vol111/issue4/steinkuehler. html

Steuer, J. (1995). Defining virtual reality: Dimensions determining telepresence, in F. Biocca and M. R. Levy (Eds.), *Communication in the age of virtual reality* (pp. 33–56). Hillsdale, NJ: Lawrence Erlbaum Associates.

Tan, D., Gergle, D., Scuppelli, P., and Pausch, R. (2003). With similar visual angles, larger displays improve spatial performance. *Proceedings of CHI* 2003, Fort Lauderdale, FL, April 5–10, pp. 217–224.

Taylor, T. L. (2002). Living digitally: Embodiment in virtual worlds, in R. Schroeder (Ed.), *The Social Life of Avatars: Presence and Interaction in Shared Virtual Environments* (pp. 40–62). London: Springer.

Taylor, T. L. (2003), Intentional bodies: Virtual environments and the designers who shape them, *International Journal of Engineering Education,* 19(1), 25–34.

Taylor, T. L. (2006). *Between Worlds: Exploring Online Game Culture.* Cambridge, MA: MIT Press.

Toennies, F. (1957). *Community and Society.* East Lansing: Michigan State University Press.

Tomita, H. (2005). Keitai and the intimate stranger, in M. Ito, D. Okabe, and M. Matsuda (Eds.), *Personal, Portable, Pedestrian: Mobile Phones in Everyday Life* (pp. 183–201). Cambridge, MA: MIT Press.

Towles, H., Chen, W.-C., Yang, R., Kum, S.-U., Fuchs, H., et al. (2002). 3D Tele-collaboration over Internet2. *International Workshop on Immersive Telepresence (ITP2002)* Juan Les Pins, France, December 2002. Available at http://www. cs.unc.edu/Research/ootf/publications/Sadagic_Presence01.pdf

Tromp, J. (2001). *Systematic usability evaluation and design for collaborative virtual environments.* Unpublished Ph.D. dissertation, University of Nottingham, Nottingham, UK.

Tromp, J., Steed, A., Frecon, E., Bullock, A., Sadagic, A., and Slater, M. (1998). Small group behaviour in the COVEN Project, *IEEE Computer Graphics and Applications,* 18(6), 53–63.

Tromp, J., Steed, A., and Wilson, J. (2003). Systematic usability evaluation and design issues for collaborative virtual environments, *Presence: Journal of Teleoperators and Virtual Environments,* 12(3), 241–267.

Turkle, S. (1995). *Life on the Screen.* New York: Simon and Schuster.

Turner, F. (2006). *From Counterculture to Cyberculture.* Chicago: University of Chicago Press.

Turner, J. (2002). *Face to Face: Toward a Sociological Theory of Interpersonal Behaviour.* Stanford: Stanford University Press.

Usoh, M., Catena, E., Arman, S., and Slater, M. (2000). Using presence question-naires in reality, *Presence: Journal of Teleoperators and Virtual Environments,* 9(5), 497–503.

van Dijk, J. (1999). *The Network Society*. London: Sage Publications.

van der Kleij, R., Paashuis, R. M., and Schraagen, J. M. C. (2005). On the passage of time: Temporal differences in video-mediated and face-to-face interaction, *International Journal of Human-Computer Studies, 62*, 521–542.

Vasalou, A., Joinson, A., Bänziger, T., Goldie, P., and Pitt, J. (2008). Avatars in social media: balancing accuracy, playfulness and embodied messages, *International Journal of Human-Computer Studies, 66*(11), 801–811.

Venkatesh, A., Kruse, E., and Shih, E. C.-F. (2001). *The networked home: An analysis of current developments and future trends*. CRITO Working Paper. www.crito. uci.edu

Vertegaal, R. (1998). *Look who's talking to whom: Mediating joint attention in multiparty communication and collaboration*. Ph.D. thesis, Cognitive Ergonomics Department, University of Twente, Netherlands.

Vinayagamoorthy, V. (2006). *User responses to virtual humans in immersive virtual environments*. Ph.D. thesis, Department of Computer Science, University College London.

Vorderer, P., and Bryant, J. (Eds.) (2006). *Playing Video Games: Motives, Responses, and Consequences*. Mahwah, NJ: Lawrence Erlbaum.

Wadley, G., Gibbs, M., and Benda, P. (2007). Speaking in character: using voice-over-IP to communicate in MMORPGs. Presented at the *Australasian Conference on Interactive Entertainment*, Melbourne.

Wadley, G., Gibbs, M., and Ducheneaut, N. (2009). You *can* be too rich: Mediated communication in a virtual world. Presented at the *Proceedings of OzChi 2009*.

Wadley, G., and Ducheneaut, N. (Forthcoming). The "out-of-avatar" experience: object-focused collaboration in Second Life.

Walther, J. (1996). Computer-mediated communication: Impersonal, interpersonal, and hypersonal interaction. *Communication Research, 23*, 3–43.

Walther, J. (2002). Research ethics in Internet-enabled research: Human subjects issues and methodological myopia, *Ethics and Information Technology, 4*(3), 205–216.

Walther, J. B., Gay, G., and Hancock, J. T. (2005). How do communication and technology researchers study the Internet? *Journal of Communication, 55*, 632–657.

Waterworth, J., Waterworth, E., and Westling, J. (2002). Presence as performance: The mystique of digital participation. *Proceedings of Presence 2002*, Porto, Portugal, October 9–11.

Whittaker, S., and O'Conaill, B. (1997). The role of vision in face-to-face and mediated communication, in K. Finn, A. Sellen, and S. Wilbur (Eds.), *Video-Mediated Communication* (pp. 23–49). Mahwah, NJ: Lawrence Erlbaum.

Whyte, W. H. 1971. *The Social Life of Small Urban Spaces*. New York: Anchor Books.

Willer, D., and Walker, H. (2007). *Building Experiments: Testing Social Theory*. Stanford: Stanford University Press.

Williams, D. (2006). Virtual cultivation: Online worlds, offline perceptions, *Journal of Communication*, 56(1), 69–87.

Williams, D., Ducheneaut, N., Li, X., Zhang, Y., Yee, N., and Nickell, E. (2006). From tree house to barracks: The social life of guilds in World of Warcraft, *Games and Culture*, 1, 338–361.

Williams, D., Caplan, S., and Xiong, L. (2007). Can you hear me now? The impact of voice in an online gaming community, *Human Communication Research*, 33, 427–449.

Williams, D., Yee, N., and Caplan, S. (2008). Who plays, how much, and why? Debunking the stereotypical gamer profile, *Journal of Computer Mediated Communication*, 13, 993–1018.

Wuchty, S., Jones, B. F., and Uzzi, B. (2007). The increasing dominance of teams in production of knowledge, *Science*, 316, 1036.

Yee, N. (2006a). The psychology of massively multi-user online role-playing games: Motivations, emotional investment, relationships and problematic usage, in R. Schroeder and A.-S. Axelsson (Eds.), *Avatars at Work and Play: Collaboration and Interaction in Shared Virtual Environments* (pp. 187–207). London: Springer.

Yee, N. (2006b). The labor of fun: How video games blur the boundaries of work and play, *Games and Culture*, 1, 68–71.

Yee, N. (2007). Motivations for play in online games, *Cyberpsychology and Behavior*, 9, 772–775.

Yee, N., Bailenson, J. N., Urbanek, M., Chang, F., and Merget, D. (2007). The unbearable likeness of being digital: The persistence of nonverbal social norms in online virtual environments, *Cyberpsychology and Behavior*, 10, 115–21.

Yee, N., Bailenson, J., and Rickertsen, K. (2007). A meta-analysis of the impact of the inclusion and realism of human-like faces on user-experiences in interfaces. *Proceedings of CHI 2007*, April 28–May 3, San Jose, CA, pp. 1-10.

Zyda, M., Mayberry, A., Wardynski, C., Shilling, R., and Davis, M., (2003). The MOVES Institute's America's Army Operations Game (pp. 219–220). *ACM SIGGRAPH 2003 Symposium on Interactive 3D Graphics*.

Index

Note: Page numbers followed by *f* and *t* denote figures and tables, respectively. References to notes are indicated by *n*.